A METAPHYSICS FOR THE FUTURE

'Professor Allinson's work is impressive. I do not remember when in recent years I have read a more exciting systematic study. With a new phenomenology, a distinctive method and unique modes of validation for philosophy, and an extraordinary command of both Eastern and Western philosophy, Professor Allinson develops his own bold, imaginative, and challenging system of philosophy.'

Professor Lewis Hahn, Editor of Library of Living Philosophers, including Quine, Gadamer and Davidson.

A Metaphysics for the Future is a work of original philosophy but at the same time is a humanistic commentary on the moral malaise of our time. It reviews the intellectual events that have brought us to our present point of relativism in ethics and skepticism in knowledge and presents a new viewpoint which offers a way out of our intellectual impasse.

Philosophers discussed include Plato, Aristotle, Augustine, Descartes, Leibniz, Kant, Hegel, Husserl, Wittgenstein, Searle and Rorty. The thoughts of the physicists Penrose and Hawking are examined. Topics covered include the philosopher as diagnostician, the mind-body problem, the foundation of truth in mathematics, preconceptual and postconceptual knowledge, representationalism, the picture theory of truth, Wittgenstein's Ladder, the concept of metaphysical truth, the concepts of Yin and Yang and post-Modernism. A sophisticated text for courses in metaphysics and epistemology.

Professor Robert E. Allinson is the author of many books including the forthcoming Ashgate title, *Space, Time and the Ethical Foundations*, and *Understanding the Chinese Mind: The Philosophical Roots*, New York: Oxford University Press, 2000 (Tenth Impression). He serves on eight editorial boards including *The Journal of Chinese Philosophy and Asian Philosophy*. His work has been translated into Chinese, Japanese, French, German and Italian. Professor Allinson has been a Senior Associate Member of St. Antony's College, Oxford University, an Associate Member of Balliol College of Oxford University and Visiting Fellow at the Graduate School of the Department of Philosophy at Yale University. He is now a professor in the Department of Philosophy at The Chinese University of Hong Kong.

For Irèné, who makes me feel alive

A Metaphysics for the Future

ROBERT ELLIOTT ALLINSON
Department of Philosophy
The Chinese University of Hong Kong

Routledge
Taylor & Francis Group

LONDON AND NEW YORK

First published 2001 by Ashgate Publishing

Reissued 2018 by Routledge
2 Park Square, Milton Park, Abingdon, Oxon OX14 4RN
711 Third Avenue, New York, NY 10017, USA

Routledge is an imprint of the Taylor & Francis Group, an informa business

Publisher's Note
The publisher has gone to great lengths to ensure the quality of this reprint but points out that some imperfections in the original copies may be apparent.

Disclaimer
The publisher has made every effort to trace copyright holders and welcomes correspondence from those they have been unable to contact.

A Library of Congress record exists under LC control number: 00044195

ISBN 13: 978-1-138-73277-3 (hbk)
ISBN 13: 978-1-138-73276-6 (pbk)
ISBN 13: 978-1-315-18808-9 (ebk)

In grateful acknowledgement of the receipt of The Vice-Chancellor's Special Fund for Excellence granted by The Vice-Chancellor of The Chinese University of Hong Kong which was a key source of encouragement and support of the writing of this book, for the graciousness of the very distinguished professors, John E. Smith, Clark Emeritus Professor of Philosophy at Yale University and Lewis Hahn, Editor of that illustrious series, The Library of Living Philosophers, who were both kind enough to read earlier versions of this work and in appreciation for my wife, Irène, whose faith in me has been the mainstay of this project from its beginning to its completion.

'Never Reject anything. Nothing has been proved. If you reject anything, that is the beginning of the end as an intellectual.'
William James (quoted in *Charmed Circle, Gertrude Stein & Company*), James R. Mellow, New York: Avon Books, 1974, p. 50).

'*Raffiniert ist der Herr Gott, aber boshaft ist er nicht.*' ('G-d is subtle, but he is not malicious.')
Albert Einstein (over the fireplace in the professors' lounge of Fine Hall, Department of Mathematics, Princeton University).

Contents

Tempo di Giga. Vivacissimo e leggero
With great animation and a skipping touch

Preface

A Legitimization of Philosophy

This work is intended to serve not only as an expression of a new idea of a philosophy, but as an *apologia* for philosophy as a legitimate and independent discipline in its own right. It became fashionable, in the waning of the twentieth century, to speak of the end of philosophy. In 1986, an entire issue of the *Proceedings* of the American Philosophical Association was actually devoted to raising the question whether philosophy was viable as a discipline any more. In 1994, an entire issue of a literary periodical, *Thesis Eleven*, No. 37, published by the Massachusetts Institute of Technology, was paradoxically entitled, 'Philosophy after Philosophy', thus raising the morbid spectre of the resumption of philosophy after its death. One review, by Richard Rorty, was of a [philosophical] work written in 1991 entitled *The Grandeur and Twilight of Radical Universalism*.

Philosophy is carrying out an undue amount of navel staring, and philosophers are going around with slumped shoulders as if ashamed that they may be caught representing a discipline that has no legitimate calling. The project of philosophy is questioned in the critical assessments found in the works of fellow philosophers such as Richard Rorty. In his later phases Rorty disclaims the need for evidence altogether and turns instead to literature and poetry for intellectual nourishment and enlightenment. As the distinguished German philosopher Karl-Otto Apel has remarked in a private conversation with the present author, Rorty preaches that philosophers should be writing novels like Proust. But Rorty is not practicing what he preaches. He has not shown any overt evidence of writing novels like Proust. He is going about exhorting others to do so. As Apel astutely observed, Proust himself did no such preaching.

The second half of the twentieth century of philosophy represented a stage of philosophy in which the best received works were dialogues with or discussions of other philosophies (such as Bernstein's and Rorty's near journalistic commentaries and conversations about philosophers), rather than individual works of a constructive nature themselves. *This differed from the output at the early part of the twentieth century, and such a difference should be noted.*[1]

The conversationalists, among whom Rorty and Bernstein reign supreme, flit from philosopher to philosopher, sampling their truth fare and finding it wanting, but providing none of their own dishes for the philosophical audience to sample. They, too, are as much influenced by positivism as the others. They have elevated the art of conversation to a new level of truth finding. Philosophers have become at best divine eavesdroppers of and intellectual gossips about the past, with no new truths of their own to offer. Today's philosophers (how much longer will they tolerate the label?) have become the hosts and hostesses of the intelligentsia, serving up the cold dishes of the past, impressively laid out on their metaphysically-dishwasher safe dinner service.

Even in the philosophically rich writings of Gadamer, there is a movement away from the certification of truth and a bowing to history, rather than science, as a limitation upon the methodology of philosophy. One can take this much further, if one moves in the direction of post-Modernism, where the role of philosophy is not merely circumscribed, questioned or humbled, but is actively deconstructed. Here, one is not merely satisfied with delimiting the role of philosophy, but one is inveighed to do away with it altogether as a constructive discipline which constructs a system of truth in accordance with its own internal criteria of verification. With post-Modernism one passes the crisis of philosophy and moves onto its post-mortem.

The reason for philosophy's low self-esteem is well known. It commenced with Kant who for many successfully put paid to the pure science of metaphysics for time immemorial. From then on, if one had any interest in metaphysics at all, it was only after one had thoroughly washed one's hands with the soap of epistemology. The result of this was that an epidemic of two centuries of compulsive hand washing came about. The positivists of the nineteenth century, such as Mach, set the stage for the logical positivism of the twentieth century which has dominated Anglo-American philosophy ever since. The residues of logical positivism are still evident. In its unsolicited service to science, philosophy was still confined to taking in the washings of other disciplines, or borrowing the detergents of other disciplines for doing its own laundry.

To put all of this rather simply, the concept of scientific objectivity, by which one generally has reference to some form of empirical justification, whether in common sense experience, or in the form of scientific tests, has dominated the stage of truth. There is scarcely a concept anymore that there can be a different or competing source of truth. Philosophy, as a result, has been confined to a role of supernal commentator on the works that are being produced in various scientific disciplines, or upon its own pitiful products, in the manner of a grand radio newscaster who broadcasts interpretations upon scientific documentaries that are produced, presented and viewed in more up-to-date media.

A short historical explanation for the plight of philosophy today has appeared above. Because of the dominance of the scientific model of explanation and truth, philosophy has been seen as a relic of another age. After all, if science has the corner on truth, then what place is there for philosophy? Basically, there are four options that can be discussed in short compass. First of all, philosophy represents a quest for the same truth as that which is pursued by and offered up by science. In this case, philosophy becomes a poor cousin of science. If philosophy were attempting to explicate and deliver the same truth as that which is offered up by science, then it would appear to be a very clumsy intellectual choice. The competition between philosophy and science would be a race between a model T Ford and a Concorde. There would simply be no contest.

The second option is that philosophy pursues a different kind of truth, one that is not available to or reachable by the methods of science. This alternative is anathema to most scientifically trained minds, as it puts philosophy back in the role of some form of medieval transcendentalism, pursuing and perhaps even reaching a kind of truth which lacks any semblance of scientific verification. This is metaphysics at its worst. Surely, there cannot be two kinds of truth. It is precisely against this kind of thinking that science arose in the first place. Philosophy can no longer claim to be a kind of discipline in its own right, which pursues its own kind of truth.

At best, perhaps, as some have claimed, philosophy can be an activity which takes place within every scientific discipline, but lacks any subject matter of its own. This is the third alternative. Philosophy, perhaps, can be an activity of thinking that is relevant at a certain level within a scientific discipline, but there are no longer any separate philosophical truths, nor is there any body of philosophical ideas that form the content of the discipline of philosophy. This third alternative was a frequently traveled road in the twentieth century.

If in the Middle Ages, philosophy served as a handmaiden to Theology, by the twentieth century, it had become the chambermaid of Science. Philosophy would step in after the work of science was over. It polished the language of the truth claims of science (was philosophy not most elegant in its high chambermaid role?); it organized the various kinds of truth claims made in the process of scientific discovery and verification, and set the house of truth of science in order. For much of the twentieth century, this variation of the third alternative was the last word in Anglo-American analytic philosophy. There was a flurry of activity in philosophy that borrowed the maid's uniform.

The fourth alternative, represented by post-Modernist trends, is no real alternative at all within philosophy, as it is to leave philosophy altogether, and to ironically turn philosophy into a kind of intellectual piranha which devours everything which falls into its intellectual waters, including, presumably itself. Post-Modernism represents a new height of intellectual cannibalism that devours itself along with all other intellectual products.

Before this turns into a funeral oration on the death of philosophy, a few more final comments are in order. The problem, as set out above, has been the success of Kant and the triumph of science. Either one gives up philosophy altogether, or one sets about the humbler role of cleaning out the house of science. What of metaphysical system building? There are, after all, a few examples, however few, which seem notable attempts of philosophy attempting to construct its own house of truth. What of Husserl and Whitehead and Hartshorne ? Are these all to be passed over in the current assessments of the status of philosophy?

The problem with these philosophies - and that of Husserl is a special case and must be treated separately - is that by and large they are pre-Critical. They do not benefit at all from Kant's epistemological handwashing, but directly engage in the work of metaphysics. For all their new claims, they are rationalisms of the pre-Kantian variety. To test the truth of their individual truth claims, one must decide whether their entire systems, taken as a whole, represent a coherent explanation of reality. But this, to a large extent is based upon which ultimate presupposition or set of presuppositions, one accepts. If one starts out with the concept of the process Divinity of Hartshorne, one may be led inextricably to a certain set of conclusions. Is this not rationalism all over again even if the contents are very different? New wine in old bottles as the saying goes.

What of the philosophic genius and spiritually rich inheritance of American pragmatism? Why has the influence of such figures as Peirce, James and Dewey not been considered? While figures of such immense stature of Pierce and James would require a separate discussion that would take one beyond the limits of this inquiry, it may be said that in the case of some of the work of Dewey, that philosophy was envisioned as undertaking a role of chambermaid, if not to science, then to a concept of experimental method that was borrowed from the sciences.[2] Philosophy, while not confined to taking in the washings of other disciplines, was still borrowing the detergents of other disciplines for doing its own laundry.

One may raise the question at this point, what of Hegel's famous objection to the primacy of epistemology? Why should one insist upon taking an epistemological bath before entering metaphysical waters? This is, in his famous phrase – 'the error of refusing to enter the water until you have learnt to swim'[3] But, in the case of metaphysical starting points that are adopted as assumptions or put forth as assertions, there is no verifiable evidence of the truth of the metaphysical assumptions or assertions. In contrast, in the case of appropriate epistemological claims to knowledge, in the understanding of what is true, one is provided with a certification of truth in the very knowing of their content. In the case of epistemological starting points of the right sort, one *is* already in the water at the moment that one learns how to swim and *one cannot be in the water without knowing how to swim.* Thus, Hegel's complaint about the privileged starting point of epistemology does not take into account appropriate epistemological starting points in which one knows the truth of what one knows *as* one knows. This is a bit surprising given that, for Hegel, one is already thinking when one alleges that thought requires scrutiny: '... the forms of thought should be subjected to a scrutiny before they are used: yet what is this scrutiny but *ipso facto* a cognition'[4] On the other hand, Hegel recommends that thought be criticized not in its particular claims of truth (as in this present work), but in its overall schematic development: 'The forms of thought must be studied in their essential nature and complete development ...'[5] The truth, for Hegel, after all, is the whole. For those Hegelians who came after Hegel, perhaps it could be said that truth became a product of the coherence and comprehensiveness of the system as a whole, rather than a property of particular discoveries which are known to be true in and of themselves apart from their relationship to any other truths or sets of truth.

The present approach, in this context, bears a greater resemblance to Bonaventura, than it does to Hegel or to his followers. For Bonaventura, 'The intellect is said to comprehend truly the meaning of propositions when it knows with certitude that they are true. For it knows that such truth cannot be otherwise than it is'.[6] Appropriate epistemological truths are known to be true in the very knowing of them which is otherwise than is the case with metaphysical assumptions *simpliciter*. When one commences with the right sort of epistemological truths, then, one starts with what one already knows as opposed to starting with an assumption of one kind or another. Thus, to begin with proper epistemological truths is to begin in the water, already knowing how to swim. Augustine ventures further arguing that in the case of epistemological acts, even when one does *not* know, one knows: '... if he doubts, he understands he doubts; if he doubts, he wishes to be certain; if he doubts, he thinks; if he doubts, he knows what he does not know, if he doubts, he judges he ought not to assent rashly.'[7]

The work of the philosopher, Husserl, represents a considerable philosophical advance. For the first time since Kant's argument from transcendental conditions, a new source of verification is proposed, a concept of phenomenological inspection. However, as with all philosophies, perhaps even with that of the present author, Husserl's practise is not consonant with his theory. It seems that he lodges claims concerning the constitution of the world, which lack valid forms of phenomenological verification. In addition, there is another sense in which he is not sufficiently phenomenological. Although, he claims not to be interested in the natural standpoint, he, like Descartes, endeavors to prove the natural standpoint after all. Phenomenology, while it begins, with Husserl, as an enterprise of great promise to set philosophy on its own feet again, soon declines into the role of an imitator of science, wherein philosophy once more renders the truths of science, this time with the promise that its version of objectivity will be a finer one than that which science delivers. The *epoché*, which begins as a new road of philosophical methodology, still attempts to make contact with the world of perception. In this respect, Husserl is in the same camp as his famous forerunner, Descartes. While he does not rely upon strictly a rationalistic approach, as does Descartes to a greater extent, he still quests for and attempts to establish what Descartes attempted, to make contact with and thus in some weak sense, to establish a link with or a proof of an external world.

Anglo-American philosophy of the twentieth century, with the exceptions that proved the rule of Whitehead and Hartshorne, proved to be a flight from truth. Philosophy was turned on its head. That of which Marx claimed Hegel was guilty was turned into an accomplished fact by the twilight of the twentieth century, the twilight of reason. If Western philosophy commenced as a search for truth with the ancient Greeks, in twenty-five centuries it found itself in full retreat. Why had philosophers become so frightened by truth?

It will be argued that the foregoing is cant and hyperbole. Truth has not been abandoned, but merely modified. Instead of the language of truth, it is simply more modern (post-Modern?) to speak of hermeneutics and dialogue. Truth has been sequestered inside the safe walls of historical situationalism. Or, it has been relegated to the consensus of (scientific?) observers whose terminology of choice is justification rather than truth. Philosophers are freed from the restraints of truth. They may talk freely within their historical and linguistic (and non-translatable) confines. Justified (?) beliefs rather than truths have won the day.

Perhaps so. But, if this is the case, relativism cannot be denied. What right is there for any philosopher to defend her or his position, which has only a unique historical applicability and a particularistic linguistic and cultural limitation to its validity? Carried through to its logical limits, the scope of a philosopher's claims is limited to a particular claim designed for a particular audience comprised of those who share the same assumptions and criteria of justification. Truth within these confines has become incestuous.

This present, respective work is proposed as a return to truth. Representationalism, while providing clues to the nature of truth, is not complete as a model of truth. There is no need to envision every form of truth as a literal attempt to picture something else referred to as 'reality' Some forms of truth provide their truth value directly, independently of whether or not they mirror reality. While there is an important sense in which the philosopher does hold a mirror up to the world, this image is too simplified. The philosopher first holds up a mirror to her or his own consciousness. It is only after apprehending the truths of consciousness that the philosopher's mirror may become a kaleidoscope through which reality may be contemplated. First order truth lies in the realm of discovery, and discovery takes place only within the moment of subjective reenactment. What Collingwood says about the understanding of historical thought in his *The Idea of History* possesses viability for philosophy as well. What truth claims are lodged must be reenacted by the subject reader. There are no truths that are not discovered to be true by the knowing subject. Just as the great works of art are not the paintings on the walls of museums, but the subjective experiences of them in their re-creations in the minds of the audience, so the truths of philosophy live only in their reenactments and rediscoveries by the students of philosophy. The objection to this way of putting things will doubtless be that different observers or philosophical readers will not agree with the truth claims that are lodged in this present, respective work. But, this must be tested in philosophical experience, and not laid down as a caveat which is treated as an unchallenged and unchallengeable truth.

The idea of empirical truth is by no means denied in this present, respective work. It is interesting to reflect upon the fact that within the contemporary intellectual climate, empirical truths that are stated as universal truths are not questioned. For example, if it were to be said that all human beings have two eyes, this statement would not be questioned. Of course, there are monstrous births and accidents, but these, it would be said, form exceptions to the rule. However, if anyone were to make a statement such as, 'awareness can be aware of itself', it would be greeted with a stunned silence. Why? Either this "philosophical utterance" is treated as trivial, or it is treated as a statement that has no means of verification, and hence is speculative conjecture and not philosophy. The method of testing truth claims via the subjective reenactment of truth claims is not credited. Or, if it were, then such a claim as, 'awareness can be aware of itself' is treated as a trivial truth.

In order to discover that awareness can be aware of itself, no recommendation is made here to conduct an empirical survey. The sort of truth claim as this one lodged by a philosopher is not an empirical truth claim. It may be in fact corroborated, or, as it is more precise to say, illustrated by empirical experience, but it is not discovered and known by outer confirmation. Human beings possess the capacity to know that which is universal within their particular cognitive acts. *This* is the domain of philosophy.

Not every truth claim that may be lodged in this present, respective work may be a universal truth. A claim may be lodged as true which is in fact false. But, it does not follow from this that every claim that is lodged within as true is false, or that it is thereby impossible to lodge truth claims at all. On the contrary, the discovery that a truth claim is false is also made via the same test of subjective thought experiment.

The fear that besets the philosophically wary reader of this present, respective work is that if one adopts a methodology as that which is proposed herein, a veritable Pandora's claim box will be opened. Who is to gainsay the subjective claim made by one who argues that he has talked with G-d, for example; or, the subjective claim of another, who argues that twice two makes five. It is safer to return to the safety of scientific testing and replication of tests. Otherwise, one runs the risk of returning to the Middle Ages. A witch will be proven guilty if she does not drown when her limbs are shackled and she is thrown into the river. Then, she can be burned at the stake for her trouble. If she drowns, she will have been proved innocent. While there is no magical answer to such a worry, there is one safeguard. All necessary truth claims that are philosophical in nature are confined to the realm of phenomenological experience. No necessary truth claims are being made concerning the empirical world. No philosopher can make a claim to possess special knowledge about the world. Let the Caesars of science take care of the world.

It must be remembered that the above strictures are meant only in a provisional sense. If it were ever to be alleged that the truths of philosophy would and in fact must have application to the truths of empirical science, it would only be the case that this kind of convergence would be possible after philosophical truths have gained their own stature from their own form of verification. Applications to the empirical world can only come afterwards. It is necessary, on a preliminary basis, to confine philosophical inquiries to the pure data of phenomenological experience. While such a sequestering of philosophical truth is only a provisional quarantine, it remains the case that phenomenological purity is an essential precondition to philosophical truth proper. Nevertheless, in order to make it plain that empirical issues will be discussed in the sequel, it is important to note that while the domain of philosophy is the domain of pure phenomenological experience, and the philosopher is not interested in the empirical world, one must bear in mind that this is also only true in a qualified sense. It is only if the philosopher is not interested in the empirical world that it becomes possible to arrive at philosophical truths concerning the empirical world. There may be an analogy here with the brilliant discoveries made by Bolgai Lobatchevski, Georg Friedrich Bernhard Riemann and Karl Friedrich Gauss in non-Euclidian geometries which were made only after these mathematicians freed themselves from attempting to make their geometries conform to the physical world. Ironically, it was not until the next century that

Einstein's general theory of relativity was to prove that the non-Euclidian geometries did possess application to the physical world. Thus, it was only when the geometries were freed from the concerns of application that they were found to possess application to the empirical world. While there is also a significant disanalogy with non-Euclidian geometries in that the philosophical truths referred to here are phenomenological, nonetheless there is also an analogical resemblance. Though the philosopher is not initially interested in obtaining knowledge of analogically derived truths, and whereas they might not by themselves constitute philosophical knowledge proper, in so far as such truths are part of the knowledge of the whole, they also come under the general sphere of philosophical knowledge. By pursuing the pure path of philosophical truth, the philosopher will eventually discuss applications to reality, but the road to the proper understanding of such issues must and will have first been paved by grounding philosophical truths in phenomenological experience. In this way, it may be said that, contrary to Hegel's claim, *there is a Royal Road to Knowledge*, and such a road will wend its way through the entire kingdom of knowledge, the foundation of which will be constituted by the truths which are first discovered within the palace of phenomenological experience.

What is the domain of philosophy proper is the domain of pure phenomenological experience. However, even within this realm, it will be argued, differences will crop up between different phenomenological witnesses. How is it possible to adjudicate between the claims of a Heidegger and those of a Sartre? About these figures, while something could be said, it is more to the point that one should address one's critiques to the truth claims that are made in this present, respective work. Whether Heidegger or Sartre were correct, or if either one were correct, is not the point at issue here. What is important to remember here is that one philosopher's project and/or her or his products cannot be the standard by which one measures the projects and products of another. It is for this reason that the label 'phenomenology' is employed here with great trepidation. No sooner than one applies a label to a philosopher than she or he is regarded as a finished product, one who fits into an already predetermined scheme of things which already has been attempted, carried out and evaluated.

It is proposed that the truth claims that are lodged herein are to be appraised on their own merits and by the methodologies that are advanced herein, and not as representing any school or schools of thought. It will be obvious, for example, that the present work owes a great debt to Kant and to Husserl, but that the present, respective work nonetheless differs from theirs. One could label this present work neo-phenomenological, and if it pleases the reader to affix a label, then this label may be adopted. It is, however, only to be adopted with caution. Labels are only tools of convenience, and possess the danger of lumping together philosophers who are only broadly similar to each other and may differ radically in crucial respects.

It will also be obvious that the present, respective work cannot help but have been influenced by the analytic propensities and methodologies of the twentieth century. The number of sweeping claims that are advanced seems to be kept to a minimum. They are elaborated in detail and subjected to qualifications. But for all that, they still retain a universality of reference and a claim to necessary truth that place them within the grand philosophical tradition to which this work calls the reader to attend.

This is not the place to set out particular claims, but attention could be directed to one example so as to set the stage for the work that will follow. This example will also prove to illustrate the kind of argument that is intrinsic and unique to the philosophical method of truth discovery and validation that is advanced in this work. Earlier, the simple claim was advanced that awareness can be aware of itself. Consider the nature of this claim. It is made only via the fact that self-awareness is introspected to belong to the claimant. That others possess self-awareness is a self-discovery that they must make for themselves. That awareness can be aware of itself is not true because everyone can reflect upon this and find it to be true. That everyone can make the discovery of consciousness is a universal illustration of the claim, but does not constitute or contribute toward its verification. The truth bearing nature of the claim is discovered in and only in each subjective act of inner awareness: that is the only source of its validation. The fact that human beings share a common nature means that the truth (that awareness can be aware of itself) will be necessarily true *for* every human being.

Necessary truths of consciousness are those truths which could not be otherwise. The truth that all human beings, under normal circumstances, are equipped with two arms is an empirical truth.[8] This latter truth is strictly empirical because it is a truth that is discovered through observation and comparison. It is not a truth that is discovered to be necessarily true in the act of discovering it as true. A necessary condition for the identification of a first order philosophical truth is not the fact it is true, but that its truth status is a function of its being discovered as true.

In other words, once a philosophical truth is discovered as true, it cannot be otherwise, because it could not have been discovered as a philosophical truth, unless it were necessarily true. The discovery of a first order philosophical truth is a function of its truth, such that, once it is discovered, it cannot not be true. (It will be understood that when the philosopher refers to first order philosophical truths, truths of philosophy or truths of consciousness, that pure phenomenological truths are indicated here.) Empirical truths are not discovered *as* necessarily true. Truths of philosophy or of consciousness are such that the truths of consciousness cannot be known at all without their being known to be true. An empirical truth can be known without its being known to be true. One can infer from a limited sample that all (normal) human beings have two legs without (or before) knowing that this is true as an empirical generalization. One cannot know with certainty that consciousness knows itself directly without knowing that it is necessarily and thus *a priori* true that every consciousness knows itself directly. What is discovered to be true in consciousness is discovered as necessarily true. What is a philosophical truth of one consciousness is a philosophical truth of every consciousness.

This discussion is not about the structure of consciousness. No claim is being made that all knowledge must be of an object. It may not in fact be true that all knowledge must be of an object. It is a danger to think that when one refers to the realm of consciousness that one must subscribe to the shibboleths of phenomenologists who have followed Husserl's claim that all consciousness is of an object. Husserl's claim that all consciousness is of an object or that the structure of consciousness is intentional, is false. While this is not the place to prove it to be false, in fact, not to be sufficiently phenomenologically rigorous, all that can be stressed at this present point is that the work of the respective author is concerned solely with describing the data and not the structure of consciousness. The structure of consciousness is a theoretical construction, not a phenomenological datum. To discuss the structure of consciousness is to import speculative metaphysics into phenomenology and theorize about that which can only be known through direct awareness.

But, in any event, a claim appears to have been made which has implications for human nature. This is metaphysics. But, it is a metaphysics which follows only as a conclusion from the inspection of the data of pure consciousness. Pure descriptions of consciousness remain a checkpoint on rampant metaphysical claims at the same time that they serve as indicators of true metaphysical claims.

Why, one may very well ask, is the language of 'pure consciousness' or 'pure experience' being utilized? Is this a kind of subscription to a mysterious, presuppositionless consciousness? Is it being said here that the subject knower is free from the limitations of language and culture?

Provisionally speaking, such a phrase as 'pure consciousness' is only an ideal. However, it is a very useful ideal. And, in so far as the claims with which the pure phenomenologist is concerned are ones which fall within the inspection parameters of 'pure consciousness', cultural presuppositions are irrelevant to such claims. Otherwise, philosophy disappears altogether into the abyss of cultural anthropology.

Within pure consciousness the subject knower may come upon knowledge claims that are preconceptual. Preconceptual claims have to do with knowing quantities or quantitative pluralities such as that there is more than one. Conceptual claims are those with which the philosophical reader is very familiar such as the definition of empirical knowledge as that kind of knowledge which can only be verified in specifiable and specified ways. Postconceptual claims have to do with knowing that which transcends the application of concepts. For example, when the claim is made that there are two sources of knowledge (as Kant made), a postconceptual claim (which may be the product of a third, albeit unacknowledged source of knowledge) is being made. Something is known (which will be explicated in the sequel) that exceeds the competence of conceptualization. It is not something that is known preconceptually (without concepts) such as one and one make two; it is something which is known only by surpassing the limits of conceptual knowledge. It may include conceptual knowledge within it; e.g., one of its domains of knowledge may be conceptual, but it itself is not limited by the knowledge restraints of conceptual knowledge. It is this area that is of greatest interest to the philosopher, and it is this area that most clearly demarcates the province of the philosopher. For this, the label meta-conceptual could be affixed, but this might lead the reader in the direction of thinking that the primary interest of this work is in discourse about concepts, which is far from being the true area of interest of this work.

A primary area of interest in this work is in directing the reader's attention to the domain in which that which is known cannot be known by the use of concepts. The debate can be recalled in which it is argued that one cannot know anything that one cannot put into words.

The spheres of the preconceptual and the postconceptual, which clearly define realms of pure consciousness in and with which this work is strongly concerned, are comprised of those knowledge claims which can be put into words, but which are not known to be true by knowing the definitions of the words that are employed. This is, to be sure, a most difficult area to enter. It is the area of pure consciousness, or, pure experience, or, pure phenomenology. It is the area, which Plato referred to in *Republic VI* as the area of pure ideation and in the *Seventh Epistle* as the Fourth.

One can make use of words to adumbrate what one knows, but what is known does not originate from nor can it be wholly contained in those words. Knowledge always transcends the ciphers with which it must perforce express itself. This is most clearly evident in the cases of preconceptual and postconceptual knowledge but is true of all knowledge including so-called conceptual knowledge. As this fact is not so easily discerned in the case of conceptual knowledge, it is initially pedagogically advantageous to utilize examples from the preconceptual and the postconceptual domains. Pure consciousness does not leave language behind altogether, but its knowledge claims cannot be reduced to or explained by the linguistic forms of its descriptions.

A word concerning the much maligned concepts of human nature and human emotions. While it is not uncommon for co-temporary philosophers to tend to avoid such topics as human nature or human emotions as the plague, philosophers such as Plato, Aristotle, Descartes, Hobbes, Hsün-Tzu, and Spinoza did not shirk from examining human nature or human emotions. What these philosophers may have discovered about human nature or the human emotions may not have been true.[9] But in no way does this invalidate their quest for knowledge, the areas they sought to possess knowledge about, or their methodologies of discovery. Some of their methodologies for truth discovery may not have been what are now considered to be the methodologies of choice. Or, in some instances, their methodologies may have been valid, but they may have made mistakes despite the soundness of their methodologies of truth discovery. Centuries from now, or even this very morning, someone may discover some mistakes in the present analysis. But, this discovery can only be made by applying the same methodology of truth finding which is elaborated herein.

If there were no universal human nature, there would be no method of discovery of any truths or falsities about that human nature. The philosopher would have to be satisfied with silence. The universality of human nature is the condition of the truth or falsity of discoveries about that human nature. In that which follows, no claim is being made that everything that is asserted is true. But, attention is being drawn to that realm in which truth can be discovered, and in the spirit of this age, one may take this to be, if nothing else, an essay in the legitimization of philosophy.

Notes

1. Excellent examples of the type of works in question are provided by Richard Rorty, *Philosophy and the Mirror of Nature*, Oxford: Basil Blackwell, 1983 and Richard J. Bernstein, *Philosophical Profiles*, Cambridge: Polity Press, 1986 (the latter book includes comments on the former, thus providing an example of a commentary on a commentary). Robert Neville remarks that, 'The situation of our own time is not a competing plurality of well developed systems but a dearth.' *Cf.*, Robert C. Neville, (ed.), *New Essays in Metaphysics*, Albany: State University of New York Press, 1987, p. 254. A general discussion of the issue of whether or not philosophy is coming to an end can be found in Kenneth Baynes, James Bohman, and Thomas McCarthy, (eds.), *After Philosophy, End or Transformation*, Cambridge, Massachusetts and London, England: The MIT Press, 1987. In future years, it is to be suspected, such debates may be perceived to be taking place on the same plane of absurdity as the perennial debates concerning the end of the world. Is it a mere coincidence that the concept of the end of philosophy has come into prominence with the end of the world prognostications that seem to attend the end of millennia? The importance of the traditional version of philosophy as that discipline which takes as one of its concerns the knowledge of reality can be seen in the Hawking-Penrose. debates in which Platonism is ascribed by Hawking to Penrose (who prefers to describe his position as realism [which is true Platonism]) as constituting one of the chief differences between their positions. *Cf.*, Stephen Hawking and Roger Penrose, *The Nature of Space and Time*, Princeton: Princeton University Press, 1996. *Cf.*, also, 'The Nature of Space and Time', *Scientific American*, July 1996, p. 49. It should be noted that the description of the plight of philosophy that characterizes this work is of necessity an edited one both in order to avoid undue prolixity and to create the proper atmosphere for a needed polemic. Thus, the discussions of available metaphysical viewpoints are by no means exhaustive; e.g., there is no discussion of Thomism or Marxism. This is in part because Thomism and Marxism do not have their origins in the twentieth century and in part because their influence is not, at the moment, powerfully affecting current trends. Whitehead is also not discussed but a fairly substantial discussion of his student and process philosopher

Hartshorne in a later chapter does to a certain extent make up for this omission. Discussions of mentioned viewpoints are abbreviated and simplified in order to suit the purposes of the argument as in the case of pragmatism, discussed in the following note.

2. The reference to Dewey is correct only if one takes the Dewey of *Reconstruction in Philosophy* rather than the Dewey of *Art as Experience*. According to Lewis Hahn, a celebrated authority on Dewey among his other accomplishments, in the earlier work, *Reconstruction in Philosophy*, Dewey emphasized instrumental, scientific knowledge over against contemplative knowledge. *Cf.*, Lewis Hahn, *Enhancing Cultural Interflow Between East and West*, Taipei: Promotion of China Modernization Foundation, forthcoming, p. 88. In this regard it is also instructive to refer to Hahn's discussion in the same volume of the reluctance of the pragmatists to accept the label. Dewey preferred instrumentalism or experimentalism; Pepper and Hahn elected contextualism; James decided it was too late to switch even though he considered pragmatism, in his famous phrase, as a new name for some old ways of thinking, and Peirce decided upon "pragmaticism" because it was a name ugly enough to protect his views from unwanted associations with pragmatism. *Cf.*, *Ibid.*, p. 100.

3. Hegel, *Encyclopaedia*, 41, *Zusatz* 1.

4. *Ibid.*

5. *Ibid.*

6. Bonaventura, *Itinerarium Mentis in Deum*, III, 3.

7. Augustine, *De Trinitate*, X, x, 14.

8. This truth, of course, may one day cease to be a truth. In his chapter, 'The Relevance of Philosophy to Physics,' T. Settle attributes to Maimonides the point that 'Experience cannot tell us that what we take to be the laws of nature will not alter in the future (say, tonight)'. *Cf.*, Mario Bunge, (ed.), *Problems in the Foundations of Physics*, Berlin: Springer-Verlag, 1971, p. 152.

9. More recently, philosophers have taken up the discussion of emotions again. *Cf.*, Martha C. Nussbaum, *The Therapy of Desire*, Princeton: Princeton University Press, 1994.

Allegro vivace e brioso
With great animation and sweep

Prologue

On Finding a Suitable Label

The nagging question, to which philosophical school the work by this respective author belongs, will in greatest likelihood be impossible to dismiss. This is a terrible question as any genuine philosopher, even one who professes to do so, does not strictly adhere to any one method, style, or set of concerns. For example, if one were to have put this question to Plato, what would he have answered? Would he have said, 'I am a Platonist'? This, of course, would have been totally absurd.

Many disparate Western traditions, perhaps all of them, if Whitehead is to be taken seriously, can claim to have found their origins, or at least anticipations in Plato. Exponents of language analysis can point to the *Cratylus* as an example of what they are interested in doing; existentialists can look to the early Socratic dialogues for the vision of the philosopher who is willing to die so that her or his life would not have been lived in vain; those cosmologically oriented can look to *Timaeus*; epistemologists can satisfy themselves with *Theatetus*; Hegelians can point to *Parmenides*. Will the real Plato please stand up?

The real Plato, presumably, would have answered, 'all of the above'. The true philosopher cannot be perfectly circumscribed inside any one methodology, set of concerns or set of presuppositions about the world. Nonetheless, one may argue, things are far more specialized today. At the beginning of philosophy, it may be argued, it was possible for a philosopher to be more broadly based. However, even then, Plato was not a Sophist (although he may have been contaminated by their methods to some extent). Thus, it is not fair to hide beneath the skirts of Plato. Come on out then, and proclaim yourself as to what you are! There is no further point in dillying and dallying around!

It is fair to satisfy this interest by delimiting to a certain extent the philosophical approach that is being followed. After all, the reader who has been willing to read this far does deserve some consideration. And, her or his indulgence is begged in not having fully satisfied this curiosity at the very beginning. For, had that been done, it is feared that the reader may have labelled this work in accordance with the preconceived associations that always accompany any such classification as is offered, and, most probably, proceeded to misunderstand it. For the truth is, the work by this respective author does not belong to any school. However, having said that, it is only fair to say something which will place this work in relationship to some tradition.

As what some might say was Aristotle's favourite pastime, it is always easier to say what something is not. It could be argued that the method elaborated within is not that of the Ancients in the simplistic and popularly misunderstood sense, since it is obvious that the present work is influenced by the Cartesian approach of beginning with experience rather than with questions about the objective world. On the other hand, when the Ancients are more closely examined, as in the present author's work, *Space, Time and the Ethical Foundations*, the starting point of the respective work of this author is shown to bear some resemblance to that of the Ancients. It could be argued that this respective work is not exactly Modern, since, unlike Descartes, the respective work, although foundationalist in the sense that a foundation for truth is sought, or, to speak more accurately, truth is considered to be a foundation, does not appear to intentionally seek such a foundation as a foundation primarily for the sake of giving support to other less foundational truths. In addition, the respective work does not appear to be primarily interested either in finding a single absolutely certain foundation on which to rest any further beliefs, nor is it interested in proving the existence of the external world, or other minds. There is, however, a clear interest in the element of certainty, which is traceable to a Platonic/Cartesian/Kantian influence that clearly separates such an approach from that of, and here comes that dreadful and dreaded label, post-Modernism.

It is more or less obvious that the method of this present work is something other than pure language analysis, so that the concept of the proper object of philosophical work is something other than the study of the medium of communication. It should be equally obvious that this work is not Whiteheadian, since no special assumption is made that the ultimate physiology of the world is process rather than substance. This work is not Thomist, since it does not attempt to provide a further justification of this great contribution to Christian philosophy. This work is plainly not Marxist, since no beliefs are set out that all change follows a necessary social dialectic; this work is not Hegelian, since no beliefs are set out that the ultimate concern of the philosopher is with the dialectical logic of concepts.

This work is also not primarily a work of hermeneutics, since it is not ultimately concerned with how one should interpret philosophical texts, and also for the reason that current hermeneutics also seems to abandon the need to discover some source of certainty in philosophical discoveries. This work is not phenomenological in Husserl's sense, since this work is in no way committed to a view of realism in perception, nor is it committed to the existence of, or in describing the alleged intentional structure of consciousness. This work is not existentialist since it appears to take the stance that rational inquiry can possess some sort of satisfactory outcome, and moreover, it does not seem to take as its primary interest, the place of man in the world. This work should also not be confused with a transcendental philosophy in the Kantian sense, since nowhere in this work is the view put forward that the proper or major concern of philosophy should lie in finding the conditions without which empirical experience would not be possible. Thus, for the foregoing reasons, none of the above labels are suitable.

How can one go about the task of self-labelling? Perhaps, it is better to practise this lesser vice than to submit oneself to the greater peril of being mislabelled by others. Two major criteria suggest themselves as means by which one may consider the appropriateness of some sort of label or affiliation with some kind of philosophical orientation: first of all, the subject matter with which the philosopher seems to be primarily concerned; secondly, the methodological procedure and the presuppositions by which she or he is guided in establishing the conclusions which she or he seeks to establish in relation to those concerns.

As to the first, one could argue that despite the titling of this work, it might appear at this point that the subject matter with which this work will be primarily concerned is that which is traditionally associated with the sub-heading of epistemology. However, such a characterization would only be valid in a provisional sense. This work is undoubtedly interested in special epistemological questions for their own sake, but ultimately such an interest also exists for the sake of understanding more about the nature of reality. However, the interest in knowing more about the nature of reality must not be instantly gratified. It must await the outcome of knowing more about the nature of truth. And the desire to know more about how one knows and what one knows must be the subject of a pure inquiry. It is only when such an inquiry is a pure inquiry that its results may be investigated for their possible clues to the nature of reality as such. If one's inquiry is not pure, but is motivated by ulterior concerns, there is no assurance that the results that are obtained are not influenced by the hopes of obtaining one's ulterior objectives.

With respect to the second criterion, that of method and presupposition, it is if anything, even more difficult, to classify the stance taken here. The methodology is decidedly not scientific any more than the proper object of the inquiry is an empirical object. Thus, the method of the natural sciences is certainly not being appropriated. On the other hand, it would also not be accurate to describe the method of this present work as pure rationalism, as there is no straightforward reliance upon the pure logic of concepts for the deduction of the conclusions to be reached.

Perhaps, the closest philosophical school with which the present, respective work could be affiliated would be the method of phenomenology as outlined by Husserl in his *Ideas, General Introduction to Pure Phenomenology*.[1] The present work does not share with Husserl his interest in the intentional structure of consciousness, his perceptual realism, his method of variations, his belief in the Transcendental Ego (with which at one point it is reported that he identified himself), or his interest in the Life World. However, to some extent, this work finds some affinity with Husserl's preoccupation with the field (not the structure) of consciousness to be the correct focus for the starting point of philosophical investigation, and his presupposition that some certain knowledge can be reached through insight or intuition concerning the nature of this field. This latter point, however, requires further qualification.

One aspect of the work which is to be carried out in the sequel would be to take the concerns of Kant (both those that he addressed and those that he raised but did not address) and address them as phenomenological questions. Space and time, for example, are treated in the course of this work. But, these topics (space and time) are not treated so as to discover their necessary condition for empirical experience, as Kant did, but rather as constituting a different type of truth. This present treatment is phenomenological only in the sense that space and time are not considered as objects of the natural standpoint (in Husserl's sense), but as pure phenomenological objects. This may, in fact, have been how Kant was treating space and time (although he may not have been fully aware of this), despite the equal fact that he has been accused of being overly influenced by Newtonian science, a confusion to which he himself was partially both contributor and victim.

The concept of the phenomenological object as the true object of philosophical inquiry is one which is borrowed with due respect from Husserl. However, this work is not at all interested in describing its intentional structure. This work is in a preliminary sense primarily interested in sketching the relationships that obtain among different phenomenological objects, in particular the different types of truth that obtain among the objects (in the special sense to be detailed in the sequel) of space and time on the one hand, and concepts on the other. This is what is meant by understanding the present approach as that of taking the concerns of Kant in his Transcendental Aesthetic in particular and treating them as phenomenological questions. It is only after a thoroughgoing grounding in this approach that one is entitled to seek either for metaphysical correlates in the universe outside of the phenomenological standpoint or for ontological grounds for the phenomenological truths that are discovered.

As a preliminary classification, bearing in mind that the technical terms introduced are not intended to be taken in Husserl's sense, the present, respective work may be said to belong to *noetic* phenomenology, so long as one qualifies this by realizing that there is no especial concern with the structure of the intentional object, but rather only with the differences that obtain between different types of intentional objects. In addition, the method of variations is not employed, and there is no commitment to perceptual realism. On the other hand, the present work could be said to belong to *noematic* phenomenology if one considers mental objects to be objective in the sense of being discovered rather than being invented. Since, however, in certain cases the different mental objects are known by different types of knowledge, the inquiry could be said to be a *noetic* one. In the sequel to this work, *Space, Time and the Ethical Foundations*, the reader will be advised that since analogical knowledge of metaphysical correlates is posited, one should most properly consider this approach to be primarily a *noematic* phenomenology. However, for fear of associating *noema* with objects of perception, it is best, at least at the outset, to consider the present work as a work of *noetic* phenomenology. If the reader would benefit by finding another philosopher who practiced *noetic* phenomenology, one could turn to the writings on imagination by Jean-Paul Sartre.[2] In the end, however, it may well be that the distinction between *noesis* and *noema* is blurred and hence neither label, taken by itself, is satisfactory. One must be careful, moreover, not to confuse the present work with phenomenological ontology, as the necessary point of departure for the development of this present work is one which must initially completely divorce itself from the question of what in an ultimate sense really is. In one sense, the label of phenomenological ontology already betrays a contradiction in terms since the phenomenological standpoint is one that suspends judgement about any ontology. In another sense, the simple conjunction of terms, 'phenomenological ontology' implies that reality is directly experienced and this view is to be more associated with traditional metaphysics than the present work. The label phenomenological reason could have a valid employment if one considers that ultimately an ontology is generated which derives from and at the same time makes phenomenological truths possible. Such a label, however, is exempt from the important qualification that the initial phenomenological discoveries are not based on a process of ratiocination.

Can this work be labelled post-Modern?[3] If post-Modernism is associated with anti-foundationalism, this work would appear to be unashamedly foundationalist and therefore Modern rather than post-Modern.[4] However, this work also reveals some influences absorbed from classical Eastern and notably ancient Chinese philosophy which would make the label 'Modern' seem inappropriate. On the other hand, if the reader takes her or his clue from the structuring or the style of the chapters of this work, it appears as if there are chapters which are strung together in a sequence of developmental argument building, chapters which feature Kantian like distinction making, and an intrusion of some chapters such as the present one which do not appear to strictly follow upon or lead to others and borrow more from Nietzsche in style than from Kant. In this sense it is neither totally sequential and linear in its development, and thus is not purely Modern, nor is it composed of seemingly non-sequential chapters, and therefore is not totally deconstructionist in the sense of not having any structure to it at all. Certain ideas, and certain truths (such as the truths of arithmetic or the axioms of geometry) are returned to again and again in the style of Confucius.[5] In the manner of Plato, the truths of mathematics are accorded a high degree of respect and it may be said of this work no less than that of the philosophy of Plato, that the "school prohibition" that was written over the door to the entrance to his Academy applies, 'Let No One Enter Here Who Does Not Know Geometry'. In this present, respective work, the point of this injunction should become intelligible. It is not that one must know the content of geometry before one can properly learn the content of philosophy. But if one knows how one knows the truths of geometry to be true, this can be an invaluable propadeutic to knowing how one knows the truths of philosophy to be true. Knowing geometry, according to this interpretation of this famous injunction, is not a matter of simply knowing the various axioms of geometry or knowing how to construct geometrical proofs. To know geometry is to know the nature of the truths in geometry and how one knows those truths to be true.

The present, respective work appears to be a hybrid, borrowing both some of the element of structural development and relatedness of chapters building up to and creating a kind of sequential conclusion, and also containing chapters and arguments which do not totally fit into a linear structure. In this sense, if the definition of post-Modernism is hybridization (as it appears to be in architecture) rather than anti-foundationalism, then this work could be considered post-Modern.[6] For, this present, respective work is not a deductive system in the spirit of rationalist metaphysics, and it contains chapters and arguments which do not seemingly follow a sequential direction.

However, since the label of post-Modernism carries with it so many other unpleasant associations and implications, not the least of which is nihilism; it is better not to employ it. In addition, since Plato's writings also reflect both deductive argumentation and digressive musings, and no one would consider calling Plato post-Modern, this justification is insufficient. This work is offered up as a work, which is interested in discovering foundations, but also is not totally tied to that quest, and as is the case with Plato's dialogues, is equally fascinated by digressions. The philosophical value of digressions has long since been lost. While lip service is paid to how digressions play an important role for Plato, after this obligatory service has been performed, the value, nay even the existence of digressions, similar to the passing of gas in distinguished company, is politely ignored. Digressions may be "tolerated" as if constituting a necessary part of the Platonic heritage such as an illegitimate, mentally retarded child, but not constituting a part of the heritage that represents any significant legacy. If it is possible to restore some of the time honoured value of digressions, it may be said that, in this respect, this present work reaches back to the Ancients as well as the Moderns.

What is, after all, the value of digressions? While Plato made much use of digressions, did he explain their value? To digress, it must be said that the value of digressions lies precisely in the fact that they are digressions. It is essential that one depart and depart significantly from the direction that one has initially taken. For it is only in such a significant departure that the area of true discovery lies.

If post-Modernism is understood as a mixture of Ancient, Modern and Eastern philosophy, then this work may be called post-Modern in this sense of the term. The confusion, however, that such a labelling would bring in its wake would be so immense as to be counterproductive and therefore inadvisable. It would, on the other hand, possess the merit of clearing an otherwise neutral label of an unsavoury and undeserved reputation. If clearing or rectifying a name is sufficient justification for the choice of a label, then one could call this work an exercise in true post-Modernism.[7] But, when one considers the added burden of explanation such a name would bring with it, it is best to leave up to future journalists the task of labelling and take this altogether out of the hands of philosophers.

Notes

1. Edmund Husserl, *Ideas, General Introduction to Pure Phenomenology*, W. R. Boyce Gibson, (trans.), New York: Macmillan Publishing Co. Inc., 1962. *Cf.*, Part One, Chapter One, Sections 7 and 8.

2. A good example of Sartre's focus on *noetic* phenomenology can be found in his *Sketch for a Theory of the Emotions*, London: Methuen and Co., 1962. Sartre's focus is on the structure of consciousness in *Being and Nothingness, A Phenomenological Essay on Ontology*, Hazel E. Barnes, (trans.) New York: Washington Square Press, 1966. *Cf.*, Part Two, Chapter Two, pp. 159-211, Part Four, Chapters One and Two, pp. 559-707. For these references the present author is grateful to Lester Embree who drew attention to them in his presentation during a conference on phenomenology held at The Chinese University of Hong Kong in December, 1996.

3. Literature is now replete with descriptions of and references to post-Modernism. Hans Bertens remarks that according to Wolfgang Welsh, author of *Unsere postmoderne Moderne,* Weinheim: Acta Humaniora, 1987, the term 'postmodern' was used as early as the 1870s. *Cf.*, Hans Bertens, *The Idea of the Postmodern, A History*, London: Routledge, 1995, p. 12. Bertens considers that the term came into more continuous use from the 1950s onwards in literary criticism especially with the Black Mountain poet, Charles Olson (p. 20). He also cites Irving Howe's article, 'Mass society and post-modern fiction' of 1959 (p. 22). The present author was astonished to discover that some of the idols of his youth such as J.D.

Salinger, Saul Bellow and incredibly enough even Bernard Malamud were one and all marked with the brush of post-Modernism. This astonishment was perhaps similar to that which Monsieur Jourdain experienced when he discovered in Molière's *Le Bourgeois Gentilhomme* that all of his life he had been speaking prose. [Molière himself played the role of Monsieur Jourdain in the first performance of the play]. But here, the language of the present, respective author is ironic since both Malamud and Bellow must be deleted from this list on the grounds that their work is a search for meaning and too clearly and too resonantly resounds of the past and Salinger on the grounds that his work all too plaintively searches for meaning which post-Modernism banishes as an illusion. According to Lawrence Cahoone, the term gradually came into expanded use in the 1970s. *Cf.*, Lawrence Cahoone, *from Modernism to Post modernism*, Oxford: Blackwell Publishers, 1996, p. 9. What is interesting is to read definitions of *Modernism* just before the phenomenon of post-Modernism came into prominence. An insightful work which appears just at the dawn of post-Modernism when the label had just emerged as a recognizable term, but had not yet reached wide currency of usage is Peter Gay, *Freud, Jews and Other Germans, Masters and Victims in Modernist Culture*, New York: Oxford University Press, 1978. While Gay distances himself from the conception of Modernism as nihilism, the reading of Modernism, which Gay accepts, bears a significant similarity to the intentions of the present work. Post-Modernists today would benefit from attending to late pre-post-Modern (in this work Gay shows no awareness of the existence of the label or the phenomenon of post-Modernism) definitions of Modernism such as Gay's in order to more precisely differentiate that sort of thinking from that which they consider themselves to be emerging or to be surpassing in order to better and more precisely define themselves. *Cf.*, Gay, pp. 22-26. One aspect of Gay's definition of Modernism (new forms of expression in search of truer foundations) actually resembles in some respects ancient Greek scepticism (scepticism in search of truth) whereas current notions of post-Modernism (word play which avows no truth) resemble more Hume's scepticism (with the same irony of reliance upon the validity of sensory perception which the more rigorous Greek sceptical doubt and Cartesian doubt called into question). In his famous Section of the *Treatise* on 'Of Scepticism with regard to the senses', Hume was more concerned with the absence of any proof of a continuous object than with distrusting the reliability of the sense impressions themselves. In this respect, in its naïve acceptance of the data of the senses as valid, post-Modernism is actually more Humian or modern than ancient. It accepts the validity of sense impressions, e.g., that the words on the paper are really there; it simply doubts that they possess univocal meanings. Its doubt of meaningfulness is not in search of truth; it is an aimless, petulant doubt, which seems to exist simply as a form of defiance. In another sense, however, if one equates Medievalism with superstitious thinking (the type of thinking which existed prior to the arising of scientific thought that would differentiate between truth and superstition), then post-Modernism bears more similarities with Medieval thinking than Modern thinking. If one equates Modernism with the rise of science, scientific method and scientific truth, then in this respect so-called post-Modernism is Medievalism and hence pre-Modern rather than post-Modern. All definitions and classifications are of course subject to a certain degree of bias. While in philosophy, Descartes is considered the father of Modern philosophy, in certain significant ways, particularly in his belief in a good Deity, Descartes is still very medieval in his thinking. On the other hand, if one considers that Descartes' vision of the world is that it may be inherently absurd since G-d for Descartes (unlike Leibniz) is not obliged to follow the laws of rationality, in this respect, Decartes is decidely post-Modern since a G-d not bound by the laws of rationality would be similar to a post-Modern thinker. Harry Frankfurt argues that since for Descartes, Galileo is not more right than revelation, that, for Frankfurt frees Descartes from scholasticism, but this argument is difficult to follow. *Cf.*, Harry Frankfurt, 'Descartes on Eternal Truths', in Willis Doney, (ed.), *The Philosophy of DESCARTES*, New York & London: Garland Publishing Co., 1987, p. 243. On the other hand, if one is to credit Frankfurt's argument, if for Descartes, Galileo is not more right than revelation, then Descartes is the most post-Modern of all thinkers, a conclusion that surely displays the absurdity of all temporal labels. It might be far more accurate to take Ockham, despite his appearance three centuries before Descartes as a more fitting augurer of modernity in his penchant for nominalism, his emphasis on precision in language and in his Spartan attitude toward unnecessary beliefs. Ockham in fact might even be more post-Modern than modern since he was no foundationalist. One could venture even further and argue that the entire concept of the Middle Ages in the West is a myth, as does the medievalist historian, Warren Hollister. Descartes, with his rigorous doubt in search of foundations and his distrust of the senses, is more akin to an ancient Greek sceptic, albeit one who has found his foundation. One is reminded of Democritus and Empedocles (Sextus, *Against the Logicians* II, 125, fragment 117, 139, 1-4). In this sense, Descartes is more appropriately classified with the Ancients.

4.   To cite Lawrence Cahoone's concise depiction of the late Lyotard, '... postmodern culture no longer needs any form of legitimacy beyond expediency ...' *Cf., from Modernism to Postmodernism*, Oxford: Blackwell Publishers, 1996, p. 481. For Cahoone, 'In the late 1970s, three books galvanized postmodernism as a movement: Jenck's *The Language of Post-Modern Architecture* (1977); Jean-Francois Lyotard's *La Condition postmoderne: rapport sur la savoir* (1979); ... and [interesting enough] Richard Rorty's *Philosophy and the Mirror of Nature* (1979)' (p. 481).

5.   In Book II of the *Analects*, Confucius states that 'A man is worthy of being a teacher who gets to know what is new by keeping fresh in mind what he is already familiar with'. Confucius also speaks of going more

deeply into what one has learned in Book VII of the *Analects*. This might be taken as an archetype of the philosophical method practiced in this present, respective work.

6. In architecture, according to Hans Bertens, *The Idea of the Postmodern, A History*, the term post-Modern makes its first appearance in an article by Charles Jencks, 'The rise of post-Modern architecture', Architecture Association Quarterly, 7, 4: 3-14, 1975. *Cf.*, Hans Bertens, *The Idea of the Postmodern, A History*, London: Routledge, 1995, p. 22.

7. An interesting trend which has emerged is that a sense is being given to reconstructive or constructive post-Modernism in a volume entitled *Foundations of Constructive Postmodern Philosophy*, David Ray Griffin, John B. Cobb Jr., Marcus P. Ford, Pete A.Y. Gunter and Peter Ochs, (eds.), Albany: State University of New York Press, 1993. In this volume, Hartshorne (discussed in the sequel) is included as one of the constructive post-Modernists. With such a usage the term comes full circle. However, in a strict sense, this usage appears more legitimate since it implies that certain philosophies are the heirs of modernism such as Hartshorne whose philosophy resembles that of Leibniz with the difference of an emphasis on process as a foundation. The label post-Modernism is in a sense misleading when it is used to categorize works and approaches which are in reality attempting to reverse or go against modernism rather than completing it or continuing in a similar vein. In another sense, the label post-Modernism is uninformative as it only indicates that which comes afterwards without indicating in what sense it comes afterwards, is a reaction to, or is in some sense different from modernism in particular.

Moderato ma con spirito
Easily, yet with spontaneous movement

Introduction

Freeing Wittgenstein's Prisoner

No one apparently has been able to come up with a satisfactory explanation as to why the dinosaurs died out after reigning as the triumphant life form on earth for so many millions of years. In the current climate of opinion, it seems that intellectual dinosaurism is dying. In future years, if intellectual dinosaurism becomes extinct, will it be possible to understand how or why this happened? Or, will anyone even possess an interest in answering this question? No one who is up to date seriously upholds the quest for certainty, which was presumably put to rest by John Dewey, in his *Quest for Certainty* in 1929. No one who is *au courant* speaks in terms of absolute values, apodeictic truth, human nature, and of all things, metaphysics. And, no one who wishes to be in intellectual vogue can or should resist the strictures of the post-Modernists who consider that all words are capable of an infinite variety of interpretations, or that knowledge at best represents a form of power rather than truth.

By what right can the present exposition exist in light of these co-temporary currents which would argue that absolute truth and foundationalism are not only unfashionable, but are impossible? It seems that such words as absolutism and foundationalism are so abominable that as soon as one hears them that one must immediately refuse to have anything to do with them. Foundationalism has become an 'F' word. Either it is unutterable in intellectually polite (respectable) company, or it functions as a bogeyword such that when one is accused of it, one must immediately as an intellectual dog, roll over and play dead.[1] But, in this case, words function as negative shibboleths, and as intellectuals, there is no more reason to follow a negative shibboleth than a positive one. And, what if the present work does imply a qualified absolutism in certain respects, and does entail qualified universalism and qualified foundationalism in certain very finely delineated forms? It may very well be that earlier foundationalists were not wrong about pursuing foundations: they may simply have had the wrong foundations in mind. That the previous foundations sought and found, such as rationalist assumptions or enlightenment beliefs, (just to utter this latter phrase is to commit anyone who subscribes to an enlightenment belief to absolute naïveté if not outright idiocy), may not in the end have been the proper foundations, is no argument against foundationalism as such.

Consider the alternative. First of all, it is boring. If all accounts are historicistic and relativistic, then why follow any one of them with any particular interest? If each person is circumscribed by her or his personal history and culture, then why attempt to move out of them or learn about other cultures or discourse with other persons? As Spinoza once said, the consistent sceptic must remain dumb. And, this seems to be true in both senses of the term.

Secondly, although one does not need a second reason, as the first seems sufficient onto the day, the reasons and arguments put forth to attest to the unobtainability of certainty and the unrealizability of universalism are weak. If certainty is not obtainable, then let the opponent of certainty come to grips with the particular arguments set forth in this book for which certainty is claimed. It is not enough to simply assert that certainty is an impossible goal and leave it at that. The general assertion must be tested against particular certainty claims. If Kant's arguments that truth x is certain can be faulted, that does not prove that the claim to certainty in all arguments of any form is to be rejected. Each argument must be assessed on its own merits.

Relativism or nominalism exists in many forms, and in sophisticated versions as in Rorty's formulations, it appears very seductive. On the one hand, Rorty certainly does claim to be a nominalist. On the other, he also takes up the cause of what he calls the "liberal ironist", one who is always willing to question his ultimate terms of discourse, and yet one who is committed to the liberal causes of easing the suffering in the world, promoting human rights and condemning invasions of human dignity. What could be wrong with an approach such as this? And, why burden it with the unnecessary ballast of universal claims and the retrograde quest for certainty?

It is indeed difficult to find fault with a position as elegantly posed as that which Rorty embraces. It has all the advantages of being liberal on the one hand, and none of the disadvantages of being encumbered with unfashionable and presumably culturally blind notions of universal truth and universal human nature on the other. It possesses all the advantages as Bertrand Russell once put it, of theft over honest labour. How can it possibly be faulted?

The problem with Rorty's position is that because of the lack of any universal truth that is supposed to belong to the standpoint of the "liberal ironist", the motivation to join the ranks of liberal ironists is lacking. (This is not to mention that the label 'liberal ironist' is not very inviting as well as not being self-evidently coherent. Is the word 'liberal' being employed as an adjective to modify the noun, 'ironist'? Is a 'liberal ironist' one who is ironic in liberal quantitites? Is a liberal ironist one who is unimpeded in one's quest to parody and ironize? Is a liberal ironist one who is democratic in one's rhetorical innuendos? What would a conservative ironist be? Or a conservative rhapsodist? The solution to these mysteries is to be found in the second endnote to this introduction). Truth, certainty and universality are clarion calls for human beings. If the standpoint to which one is called lacks any truth-value, then why should anyone feel strongly impelled to adopt that standpoint? If it were the case that the sensibility of the "liberal ironist" appealed to our sympathetic imagination, that would surely not be enough, for Hitler also was successful in engaging millions of sympathetic imaginations. Otherwise, there is no reason, according to Rorty, to prefer *Contingency, Irony, and Solidarity* to *Mein Kampf*.[2]

Another way of indicating this problem is the following. If liberalism is to be presented as a valued perspective, then what is the difficulty with providing it with a solid foundation on which to rest? Is liberalism better off without a foundation than with one? If reasons could be offered as justifications for liberalism, would this not strengthen the position of the proponent of liberalism? The liberalism that possessed a foundation would seem to be preferable to a liberalism that lacked a foundation.

It may be argued that liberalism has its roots in a natural expression of human nature, just as eating has its roots in a natural expression of human nature. If one's standpoint can be shown to flow naturally from one's own nature, then that is a further reason for embracing and adhering to one's standpoint. How can liberalism be shown to be related to human nature? It may be shown in the following way. If one considers that every human being naturally feels compassion for other human beings, then compassion may be taken as a defining feature of human beings. Liberalism may be taken as a means of showing that compassion toward others. Liberalism may be construed as having its roots in a feeling of compassion and concern towards others. It need not be construed as a standpoint that exists on its own, which simply possesses theoretical interest as an alternate to the otherwise humdrum choice of totalitarianism. It may be construed as coming into existence and finding favour with sensitive and informed thinkers because it answers a need of human nature: the need to be compassionate toward others. Liberalism as a political theory is ultimately an expression of an ethical concern, and ethics is an outgrowth of natural compassion. While this is only the briefest of arguments, the reader may be directed towards the present author's, *Space, Time and the Ethical Foundations* for further discussions of ethics. It need hardly be stated that such a liberalism as described above is anything but ironic.

If one aspires to and claims to be a liberal, is it not better to be a liberal with foundations than a liberal without foundations? What is wrong with foundationalism? Is it an intellectual disease or an intellectual embarrassment because it is associated with retrograde eighteenth century thinking? Are human beings to be accused of being enlightened? Can there be any worse intellectual *faux pas* than to appear to argue that liberalism has a justification? Are those who argue that human beings do possess innate compassion, intellectual dinosaurs who are fated inevitably to die out and be replaced by those intellectuals who are devoted to the cause of better and better word play?

What misunderstandings and confusions lie in the way of following the way of foundationalism? The main impediments are negative shibboleths. One is afraid of being accused of being old fashioned, of being out of step with the times, of being of all things "modern" in one's thinking. One is afraid of being accused of falling prey to the Rortian argument that one has believed in truth, because it is forced upon one, a vestigial influence from theology, deriving from those educated in the West, who thought that they needed to be compelled to believe in truth, because of a past tradition of feeling compelled to prove the existence of G-d. While this argument is parochial – there are examples of Eastern thought which display reliance upon the idea of truth without a parallel presence of the Western Medieval tradition of arguments to prove the existence of G-d - the notion of truth as compulsive is only an attribute or a side-effect of truth and not its essence. The essence of truth is that it is self-certifying, not that it is overpowering or compulsive. The essence of truth lies in its discoverability and the *manner* of its discoverability as will be detailed in the sequel.

In ethics, one needs to bear in mind Aristotle's notion that the relationship of man to living well is analogous to the relationship of playing the lyre to playing the lyre well.[3] The notion of doing something with excellence must be incorporated into the defining feature of what is the good for man. If this is true, definitions of ethics must always include a value added element: an element to do what one has to do with excellence. In arguments employed on behalf of liberalism, it is no different. If one's strong commitment to a position is to assume any importance, and one, like Rorty, professes to be a liberal, then why not marshal all the best arguments possible on behalf of liberalism? Why characterize one's choice to be a liberal as a subjective judgement of a culturally bound individual, when, even in terms of rhetorical persuasiveness, this is the weakest possible rhetoric that can be deployed on behalf of liberalism? Even on the Rortian grounds that all that one can ever do is to employ the best rhetoric one can on behalf of one's own positions, (a position that may be shared by Hitlerism), is to leave liberalism at the mercy of a subjective, culture bound prejudice and to leave it as rhetorically ill defended. Is this the attitude to take toward an end to which one presumably is passionately committed? What then is passion? Passion becomes an effete and supercilious defense of liberalism. Passion becomes equated with the passionless. One is doomed to accept Sartre's definition of man as the useless passion. Passion dirempt from its roots in value becomes indistinguishable from bestiality.

Truth and excellence are passions. Man is a metaphysical animal. Truth is no less a need of the nature of man than food or sex. To deny truth or to degrade it to a position of cultural relativism is no different than adopting the position that sex is an arbitrary cultural prejudice, and has no demands that are universal in nature. Why should philosophy be degraded to the position of a cultural prejudice? If philosophy is relegated to the status of a cultural quirk, it, like the dinosaurs, will also become extinct.

There is a veritable cacophony of post-Modernist voices today who in one form or another argue that words can mean anything at all and/or values are relativistic and are founded on language, culture or power.[4] These are the co-temporary counterparts of the ancient Greek Sophists. Rorty's case seems to be a unique one, one in which he uses the style of argument of the Sophists, but on the side of "good" values, while at the same time attempting to refrain from calling them or considering them to be good. In contrast, the self-appointed task of this work appears to be to rail against these Titans, and to direct the attention of philosophers back to the quest for Beauty, Truth, Goodness and Unity.

One way of distinguishing the discipline of philosophy from other disciplines which seek truth, is that in philosophy one seeks to establish truths which are known with certainty. While many have debated the appropriateness of such a quest and others have considered it to be a futile pastime, in the tradition of Plato and Kant, this work is also devoted to the pursuit and establishment of apodeictic and universal truths.

It is the character of 'can never be otherwiseness' that provides the certainty of philosophical truth. The certainty that accompanies the discovery of philosophical truth arises from the side of the objectivity and the universality of the truth; it is not psychological certainty. When something is known with certainty in the sense in which the concept of certainty is used in this work, the certainty arises from the inescapability of the truth in question - not from a psychological conviction. When one considers psychological aspects, one concerns oneself with the emotive aspect or emotive charge of the *cognoscendum*. The certainty that is discussed here is a felt certainty, but the feeling of certainty is only an epiphenomenon. What is of relevance to the philosophical dimension of the certainty is the *fact* of the certainty and the *origin* of the certainty. Strictly speaking, the certainty of which is spoken is one which may be logically abstracted from but is epistemically inseparable from the content of the truth in question. This certainty is not to be identified with the psychological conviction that one is certain that one's viewpoint is correct.

In the case of philosophical certainty, certainty arises from the universality and the objectivity of the truth in question. *The truth is what makes it certain; the certainty is not what makes it true.* If this distinction is grasped, much headway can be made.

Does it mean that what is being discussed here is a version of rationalistic, metaphysical truth? Or, is it the case that what is being discussed is "only" a truth about the limits of the human imagination or, human psychology. While it is premature to offer a full answer to this intriguing question at this point, it is worthwhile to consider that even if it could be said that the truths that are discovered only reflect that the subject knower would know something about the limits of human imagination, it is of profound importance that one could even know something about the limits of human imagination with certainty and universality. No other discipline yields truths about contents which are not known beforehand (with the exception of mathematics), that are known with certainty, other than philosophy. This by itself would be enough to characterize philosophy as a unique discipline, the methods and goals of inquiry of which differ from all other disciplines.

However, what of the above charge? What if conclusions that were reached were "only" true of the current limits of human imagination and thus limited in this sense? Could it not be said that the limits of imagination could change and what was once thought to be a truth invested with the attribute of 'can never be otherwiseness' was not really a case of 'can never be otherwiseness' after all? The point is that the 'can never be otherwiseness' is a part of the very act or event of cognizing when philosophical truths are being known. To say that a philosophical truth may not be true in the future is possible to say in language, but it carries no more weight than the grammatical and semantic possibility that the moon could be made of Danish Havarti cheese. Yes, the limits of imagination could change - but in this case the philosophy of Plato, Berkeley and this philosophy would no longer be a philosophy of human knowledge, and a new philosophy will be required to fit this new human (or what could essentially be a non-human or extraterrestrial) sensibility.

That what is spoken about here is limited to the present limits of human sensibility is not a serious defect of philosophy; it is only a statement of fact and carries no implication that what is advanced within these limits is thereby without value. What is being advanced is advanced with the possibility of certification; the claim that human limits may change is an assertion which is lodged without any accompanying certification, and thus may be disregarded until or unless conditions change to make its merely assertoric and putative claim relevant. Until that time arises, the hypothetical assertion that the limits of human sensibility may change carries no more weight than any other assertion that can be made outside of a certifying consciousness. All such statements are simply outside of the phenomenological and certifying consciousness, and for this reason possess no particular significance. They are mere speculations or conjectures and should not be given the power to stifle philosophical inquiry.

Whether or not the object of knowledge is "only" a form of representation, what remains true is that this object is known with necessity and universality. The fact is that necessary and universal knowledge is possible within the limits of experience - such will be shown in the course of this work. Wherein such knowledge arises is another question. Whereinsoever or whatsoever is the origin of such knowledge, the certainty and universality of its truth is a matter of cognition.

There is a further feature of necessity and universality in philosophical truth cognition that should be noted. Truths which possess the characteristic of 'can never be otherwiseness' can be utilized to make accurate predictions concerning the physical world as it is known. This in itself is a highly remarkable fact and carries with it profound implications as well. That a truth which is universal and necessary and is about the limits of human imagination, and at the same time can be applied to, or has analogues in the truths discovered by physicists, suggests that the status of philosophical truth is *not only* a function of the limits of human imagination. Or, even if the truth of philosophical truths were to prove itself to be a function of the cognitive limits of human imagination, and an analogue of those limits were to be provided by the experimental data of the physicist in terms of the limits of the universe, then the limits of the human imagination could provide clues to what is true about physical reality and hence are not to be lightly regarded.

Of course, it is still possible that the world of the physicist may change and the laws of physics that obtain at the moment may not obtain in the future. If the laws of physics can change, are the truths of the philosopher more sacrosanct? While such a possibility cannot be gainsaid, it must be noted that while the claims advanced herein in this work could conceivably no longer be valid, what is being suggested is that there could be new necessary and universal philosophical truths which would be applicable and analogically true of that new co-temporary world of physics.

If philosophy is to be possible in the future, there must be a difference between truths which are empirical truths, and truths which are necessary and universal truths, even if the contents of each kind of truth were completely different from their present-day contents. It could be further countered that even this possibility takes for granted the existence of future contingent truths. What if it were to be the case that in the future, either the world constantly altered such that there were no empirical truths at all, or that the world stayed exactly the same, so that the distinction between a philosophical truth and an empirical truth were to vanish? All this could conceivably come to pass. It cannot be denied any more than it is logically possible (though empirically absurd) that the moon could be made of Brie cheese in the future. But, it would still remain true that within the limits of phenomenological consciousness set out in this work that there could be necessary and universal philosophical truths, and that it might be possible to point to an analogical relationship between these truths and whatever physical world and whatever reality might exist. Beyond this nothing can really be asserted.

Could all of this change? Could the world be totally different than it is? Could time go backwards and even the truths that are true today become not only false, but not even possess the characteristic of having once been true? In contrast to the Cartesian viewpoint that what once was true will always carry the property of having once been true, it may be that the birth of a new cosmos or new technology might even possess the characteristics of time reversal, such that what is being written at this present moment might not yet even have been written.[5] But, what remains true in and through all of this is that within the phenomenological consciousness adopted in this present work, there are truths which are known with certainty and universality, and which apply to the laws of physics as they are known, and these truths, while themselves possibly not unalterable, remain philosophical truths so long as one is willing to adopt the phenomenological standpoint proposed in this present work. Once one adopts this phenomenological standpoint, the future prospect of the changing of truth remains only and always a part of a standpoint outside of the phenomenological consciousness, and as such, a philosophical position that is of no material significance. One may well ask what would be the meaning of 'cannot be otherwise' if 'cannot be otherwise' could be otherwise. One can only answer that the meaning of 'cannot be otherwise' has reference only to the capacities of phenomenological consciousness that exists in the form that it exists at the present moment as there is no other court of appeal.

One day human beings may not need brains to think and may not need to eat to live. Should they still be called human beings? Perhaps so and perhaps not. But, all that is required for the present work to possess validity is that the phenomenological standpoint, once adopted, reveals a certain set of truths and a relationship between those and other types of truths. There is nothing more strange or untrue about this assertion than the assertion that it is always possible to step inside a historical framework. Does this mean that, in the end, all claims made within that framework are relative? Claims within a framework are relative to that framework, but again the wider and deeper notion being advanced in this work is a notion which points to a relationship between phenomenology and metaphysics such that there are certain and universal truths, and there are distinctions between different kinds of certain and universal truths. This knowledge is knowledge that remains untouched and untouchable by the claims of time in a timeless, philosophical sanctuary of truth. It is with these claims that a philosopher is most properly concerned. If the contents of these claims are no longer the same in future years, then it is with the contents of the future claims that the philosopher of the future should occupy herself or himself. Until such future claims to truth reveal themselves, the truths of the present are sufficient onto the day.

The Cult of Linguisticism

Wittgenstein thought that philosophical problems were pseudo-problems due to the distorting influence of language, such that, as one became aware of the misleading properties of language, the "philosophical problems" would disappear. This thesis (together with the influence of the Vienna Circle and the late A. J. Ayer's Verification Principle) was one of the most important influences of early twentieth century philosophy on subsequent twentieth century Anglo-American analytic philosophy.

While the question of the relationship between language and the world was on the mind of the Wittgenstein of the *Tractatus*, for earlier philosophers, such as Hume, the question was, what was the relationship between thought and the world. In Rorty's preface to the 1992 edition of *The Linguistic Turn*, he states that the linguistic turn's distinctive contribution to philosophy was to help shift from talk about experience as a medium of representation to talk of language as such a medium - a shift which, as it turned out, made it easier for linguistic philosophers to set aside the notion of representation itself.

From the point of view of this present work, this changing of the question of philosophy was due perhaps to the consideration that since it was thought that one could not know anything directly, without going through language, then it was idle to query the relationship between thought and reality. While the putative falseness or at least the incompleteness or the oversimplification of the belief that one cannot know reality directly without the device of language will be discussed at length in the sequel, it is important to note that this belief has played a large role in preventing philosophers from engaging in an inquiry such as this present one.

From the point of view of Rorty, contemporary analytic philosophers have attempted to move away from representationalism in general. Taking their cue from Wittgenstein's movement away from his notion of picturing facts, their attitude toward language has been that it is behavioristic: language is not an attempt to picture reality. Their argument seems to assume the following form. If there are no more representations, (language is not representational), then there is no problem of representationalism, or of whether or how language represents reality. Wittgenstein's slogan, 'Don't ask for the meaning, ask for the use' appears to be the driving force behind the critique and consequent abandonment of representationalism as a quest or concern of philosophy. Language simply becomes a species of behavior - a tool to satisfy desires. Language is not a representational system.

If there are contemporary analytic philosophers who argue that there is no such thing as knowledge and all that can be said to exist are organisms using sentences and holding the best justified sentences to be true, what follows from this?[6] Such a view amounts to a kind of behaviorism but a behaviorism which implies that someone is aware of or possesses knowledge of this behavior.[7] It may be alleged that the attempt to claim that behavior must be known can also be reduced to another form of behavior but surely at some point behavior must be witnessed. One cannot totally dispense with the cognitive dimension of experience. If there are philosophers who consider that one only thinks that there are beliefs and emotions, because otherwise behavior will appear to be unintelligible, then such philosophers must consider that they possess no direct access to the experiencing of beliefs and emotions. Recent empirical research concerning animal behavior suggests that certain animals, such as higher primates, do possess higher consciousness including beliefs and emotions.[8] Based on the observation of the behavior of animals, the possession of emotions are attributed to them. Philosophers who consider that beliefs and emotions are only attributed to human beings because they make sense out of observed behavior are treating the knowledge of human beings on the same level as the knowledge of non-human animals. This is, so it seems, to make a monkey out of oneself (which is the opposite of the evolutionary process).

From the point of view of the present, respective author, if there were no such thing as knowledge, then there no longer would be a subject matter for philosophy. With no subject matter, philosophy ceases to exist. From the point of view of the present author, whatever relationship one assumes that language has to the world, it would be interesting as a point of departure to assume that it has *some* relationship to the world.[9] After all, at the very least, it is a part of the world, if one were to consider the world to be the totality of everything that there is, or, everything that is the case. If it were acceptable, then, to consider that language is a part of what there is, then if one were to wish to consider the possibility of there being a metaphysical reality in addition to the physical world, one could entertain the notion that whatever relationship language has to the physical world, it bears some analogy to the relationship that thought possesses to this putative higher reality.

Ironically, it must be said that in a certain sense yet to be defined, Wittgenstein's picture theory of meaning was correct. His early theory of how language functioned, as a picture of reality, only reflected one use of language, the descriptive use. On the other hand, his early picture theory was not completely inaccurate in that any symbolic system must bear some resemblance to that which it symbolizes. The implication that the early Wittgenstein drew from this, that meaningfulness required pictorial representation, was not justified. As noted below, the resemblance, as Wittgenstein's own examples demonstrated, need not be a visual resemblance.

But, it was unfortunate that Wittgenstein abandoned or largely amended the picture theory in order to take up the position that language was not representational (in his famous dictum, 'Don't ask for the meaning, ask for the use').[10] His earlier picture theory of meaning, even if not totally true, possessed rich implications. The starting point that in one of its uses, language does in some sense mimic reality, is an important starting point, for, according to the view of the present author, it is revelatory of an analogous relationship that exists between representational knowledge and its object. If this point were to be generalized, then it could be said that, in some contexts, meaningfulness involves a relationship between a symbol and what is symbolized. Language symbolizes its descriptive object in that it is composed of signs which are symbolic images, (in ancient Chinese the image may be a pictograph in addition to being an ideograph), which are representations of things or objects which are known. In some cases the ideographic and the pictographic functions of language coalesce such as in the case in which an ideograph such as the Arabic numeral 1 in its vertical representation or the Chinese numeral one in its horizontal representation represents its object, a singular object or number. Any act of representational knowledge will be composed of a relationship between a sign and a known such that the sign bears some resemblance to the known. *All representational knowledge is composed of analogous relationships.* This is the importance of Wittgenstein's discovery though it is doubtful if he were aware of the nature or the importance of his discovery as conceived by the present author. In fact, his use of this discovery was counterproductive for, at an influential point in his philosophical development, he thought that all knowledge should stop at the analogy that existed between language and its physical object of description, which he described as pictorial.

In a broad sense, the correspondence theory of truth is correct in that there is a correspondence between the way of knowledge and reality, and there must be if knowledge is to be of anything at all. The way in which something is known *corresponds on some level* with the structure of reality. Just as language can picture objects in the sense defined above, higher knowledge can picture higher reality, and the phenomenon of picturedness, (or analogy more properly speaking), is both the key to knowing reality, and is somehow also descriptively true of the structure of reality itself.

If analogy were not part of the structuredness of reality, how could it be employed to know reality at all? If there were no proportional relationship between signs and objects, however indirect or historically removed from co-temporary usage such a relationship might be, then language could not have been used to designate or describe a physical object in the first place. If a built-in analogous relationship between language and its objects on this level of representational knowledge were to exist, then it could be said that such a built-in analogous relationship must exist on every level of representational knowledge. Reality, in short, must possess the characteristic of being known via analogy. After all that has been said in the foregoing, one need no longer feel afraid of, or intimidated from attempting to know something about reality.

The leap from a pictorial representation to a non-pictorial representation might require a quantum leap of the philosophical imagination. When one says in English, 'the monkey is in the tree', one can conjure up a picture of a monkey perched in a tree. If there were a monkey in the tree, then the previous sentence could be said to have been an indicator or a sign or a linguistic "picture" which stood for reality. This point would be clearer if one actually drew a picture of a monkey in a tree and showed it to someone, and then pointed to the real monkey in the tree. The spoken sentence possesses the same function as a picture. In the sequel to this work, *Space, Time and the Ethical Foundations*, it will be suggested that there is a further analogical equation which possesses the following form: the relation of the image (or linguistic sign) to the empirical object is analogous to the relation of the empirical object to metaphysical reality.

This does not mean, of course, that if a word exists, then an object must exist to correspond to that word. It only means that if language can be used to describe physical objects, then at some point in time, a proportional relationship between descriptive language and its object must have existed. If there were a built-in analogous relationship between language and its object on this level of knowledge, then it could be analogically (not deductively) inferred that such a built-in analogous relationship might characterize every level of representational knowledge.

If it could be so argued that intelligibility is a reality feature, could it not also be argued that one could thereby justify meaninglessness or unintelligibility as a reality feature? This argument cannot be made. Meaningfulness is a condition that is required for the construction of and in the understanding of all subsets that fall within the matrix of 'meaningfulness', and therefore 'meaningfulness' is a feature of reality. Meaninglessness cannot be understood without meaningfulness, but the reverse is not true. Meaninglessness is a derivative and a parasitic concept, and is not part of reality as such, but is a privation or absence of reality. In any case, there is no absolute meaninglessness; meaninglessness is always a lack of some particular meaning of one kind or another.

Whenever an attempt is made to understand some particular that is a part of the meaningful matrix of reality proper, that particular must be a genuine microcosm of the macrocosm that is reality as a whole. If it is the case that the question raised is so general that it transcends all subsets of the matrix and at the same time must be employed in the construction and the understanding of any subset, the question that is being raised must form a part or be dependent upon a portion of the matrix proper. For example, 'meaningfulness' is a condition that is required for the construction of and in the understanding of any and all matrix subsets and therefore must be an inherent feature of the general matrix. 'Meaningfulness', therefore, is an inherent feature of reality. (If a concept is not a matrix concept, it does not follow that it is not revelatory of the matrix. It only follows that it is not known if the matrix is mirrored by the concept. For example, it appears that the concept of G-d is not a matrix concept.)

The whole must already exist in some sense in the part. There may be more in the whole than there is in the part, but what is in the part must be in the whole. The following conclusions can be drawn from the foregoing argument: (i) higher levels of reality can be known, albeit imperfectly, by lower levels; (ii) higher levels of reality must possess characteristics which are analogous to lower levels of knowledge; (iii) there can be metaphysical knowledge, or, metaphysics is possible as a discipline; (iv) there is a metaphysical reality.

It is possible to venture even further. Since knowledge (as will be shown in the course of this work) is possible, then it must be the case that the nature of metaphysical reality is such that: (i) it is analogically structured or textured; (ii) its structure is comprised of both epistemological and ontological levels; (iii) it forms a whole. It must be borne in mind that the characteristics of and the conditions for the possibility of knowing metaphysical reality cannot be perfectly illustrated on the lower levels of knowledge and reality even though the higher levels of both knowledge and reality are the conditions both for the existence, the operation and the understanding of the lower levels.

Wittgenstein was also mistaken about the use of his ladder. It is not to be discarded after one has employed it to ascend. It is both a useful tool for ascension, descension and for the examination of its features which bridge what is below with what is above. That the ascension to what is above requires the use of a linguistic ladder reveals that the ladder itself contains *clues* both to the nature of higher reality, and the nature of how that higher reality is known.

If there were a whole, as the foregoing argument suggests, and human knowledge and human existence form a part of that whole, then what can be known about human knowledge can be utilized as a clue to conjecture about the reality that contains human knowledge within it, but which itself transcends both human knowledge and human existence. To diverge from Wittgenstein, that of which we can speak, albeit indirectly, imperfectly and darkly, we can, and indeed we must babble. And the baubles that are thereby produced, like dark jewels, if held carefully to the light, and contemplated with diligence, can be a source of knowledge and insight for the future.

Why does philosophical talk frequently resemble babbling? This stems from the fact that one is attempting in philosophy to say what cannot be said. It may well be that the mark of a philosophical question is that it is inherently frustrating, and while it can be posed in ordinary language, it requires extraordinary language to forage an attempt at an answer. As every beginning student of philosophy learns, when Augustine asked himself what time was, even though he thought that he knew, he could not say what time was. (Augustine's inability to say what time was may be related to the fact that time is nothing in itself but requires space for its explanation - a point to be elaborated in the sequel). For Wittgenstein, the asking of philosophical questions always produced what he referred to as mental cramps. Contrary to Wittgenstein, the purpose of philosophizing is not to rid oneself of the mental cramps.[11] The purpose of philosophizing is first of all to become aware that it is possible to raise questions which do not appear to have immediate answers, and that such questions may be philosophical questions. That Socrates could raise questions about the immortality of the soul is a remarkable feature in itself, whether or not his conjectures at solutions to the problem were correct. If a question brings with it a certain degree of discomfort, this may be a sign that it is the right sort of question to ask. When one experiences physical pain, the correct response is not simply to remove the physical pain. The physical pain may be a signal that something deeper in the organism requires attention, and the removal of the symptom of pain may prove to be a disservice to the organism in that it may allow for the progression of the disease.

When one is willing to contemplate what is space and what is time, one has arrived at the willingness to pursue philosophical questions. Such questions cannot simply be passed over because either no immediate answers to them seem to be available, or because they appear trite or hackneyed, or because they appear to be better answered by empirical investigations. Such questions as what is time and what is space are meant to be contemplated, to exist and to *linger* as questions in one's mind. It is important to resist Wittgenstein's directives to dissolve such questions. It is vital for the future of philosophy that such questions remain as questions and do not get removed or dissolved. The willingness not merely to tolerate, but to actively and persistently engage in the contemplation of such questions requires philosophical courage. That such questions linger carries with it the consequence that they will be continually addressed and not forgotten.

Augustine's asking of the question, 'what is time?', achieves importance, because he thought it was a legitimate question to ask despite the appearance of the awkwardness or the naïveté of the question. If the pressure to resist the raising of such questions as improper or naïve is not resisted, then such an inquiry as the present one into the nature of space and time would not be possible. Such timeless questions as, 'what is time?', possess a meaning all of their own such that even in the form of unanswered questions they possess the potential to produce meaning in the lives of humanity. The very existence of such questions *as meaningful* is a condition of creating meaning in the life of humanity. That an answer to such questions can be found is an additional level to the philosophical answer that may be humanity's birthright. Human beings are *metaphysical* animals - not only can such questions not be avoided, the very existence of such questions is an indication that eventually an answer may be discovered just as the existence of hunger is an indication that food may be discovered. That human beings cannot help but raise such metaphysical questions means that human beings must raise such questions and should raise such questions, and that it is the nature of human beings to ask them. Such a metaphysical nature should not be denied or repressed at the risk of producing emotional and mental illness in individuals and/or holocausts in societies.

The existence of metaphysical questions suggests that such questions can be answered, or at least leads one to such inquiries or contemplative insights that provide meaning in life. In a sense, such questions function in an analogous vein to Kant's Regulative Ideas: they are necessary to lead human beings in directions which are necessary to take in order that human existence be complete. Such questions are required in order to afford the recognition that human beings possess an intrinsic value or right to exist, a value which does not exist for the sake of accomplishing any utilitarian aim outside of the recognition and affirmation of the value of human existence. Such an affirmation of the value of human existence is the essential feature of self-respect that forms the foundation of the respect each human being should feel and show towards others. The recognition of the intrinsic value of human beings is the foundation of all ethics. Thus, the asking of metaphysical questions is of fundamental importance to the provision of a foundation of ethical values. That there is an intrinsic value in the asking of metaphysical questions is an essential reminder that there is an intrinsic value in human life, and in the human condition, and in the human intellect in and of itself - that it is intrinsically valuable and precious for no other purpose outside of its own existence. Indeed, such an ethical attitude may be extended beyond the intrinsic value of human beings to all sentient beings, but such an extension would require significant qualifications.

If all truth were ultimately practical or utilitarian, then acts of exterminating certain groups of human beings could always be justified on the grounds that some utilitarian value would thereby be served. The legitimacy of raising metaphysical questions is a way of preserving intrinsic value in and for human life and also for restoring dignity, that element that makes life worth living, worth preserving, and worth continuing and extending to others. If it were not for this, if life were merely for physical enjoyment or for material gain, then life would truly be a meaningless, useless passion, and there would be no purpose to its preservation.

Such is the importance of keeping these ancient questions alive and well, honoured, and what is most important, *asked afresh*. The asking of these questions must be encouraged as a practise. One can consider the belief that if there were a word 'meaning', that might lead one to the thought that there exists something such as 'meaning'. Then it is important to take philosophical courage and proceed in the reverse direction of Wittgenstein to the exploration and celebration of the problem of meaning.

Those philosophers who come in time after Wittgenstein can be grateful that he called attention to the phenomenon that he described as the bewitchment of language. To take the road less traveled by, one must embark upon a different path from that which Wittgenstein and his followers took. The "bewitchment" should be taken not as a "bewitchment" from which either to escape or to focus upon as a pseudo-problem to dissolve, but as a valuable and important clue to follow up upon to discover truth about the nature of reality. That such a word as 'meaning' exists in one's vocabulary is one of the most important and valuable possessions to which humanity can lay claim. Rather than concentrating upon freeing humans from linguistic traps that mislead them into thinking that philosophy possesses a subject matter, in the initial phases of philosophical inquiry, one should praise language and return to language as a valuable deposit and repository for intriguing guidance in answering the questions that one cannot help but asking and that one should never stop asking.

To attempt a description of reality based on the starting point suggested above, those more literally minded readers might be tempted by the following. The question, 'what does a word look like?', can be answered in the following way. A word looks like an abstract drawing: it is made up of marks which are: (a) artistic; (b) structured; (c) composed of systematic, reappearing elements; (d) form a whole. Given the resemblance theory stated above, these four elements may be taken as features of higher reality. While higher reality cannot be seen by itself, an approximate description of it can be given through its exemplar, language. From this standpoint, it can be projected that reality possesses the features of beauty, form, order and unity. While this description is only true by analogy, it does not follow that analogical truth is totally without knowledge value. While such comments as these can only be considered hints, and are by no means candidates for necessary and universal knowledge, they are suggestions for how, with proper phenomenological grounding, one may be able to lay claim to what might be called metaphysical glimpses of reality.

No doubt such a statement as the previous one will raise all sorts of fears that one is thereby exceeding the limits of language and violating the basic adage that all knowledge is linguistic. It must be borne in mind that, to the contrary, on the highest level of understanding, no knowledge is linguistic. The fear that lies behind the insistence that all knowledge is linguistic is the fear that if one were able to transcend the limits of language, one would fly off into all of the dreaded vagaries and speculations afforded by sightseeing on the magic carpet of "intuitionism".

Does it follow that if one's knowledge were not limited to precise and literal descriptions that one could circumscribe with language that one would thereby be committed to "intuitionism"? One answer to this would be to say that since no truth can be known which is limited to language, "intuitionism" may be a feature of all knowledge. Even the simple truth of $1 + 1 = 2$, when known, is not known simply about the set of symbols of which one is currently aware. It is a truth that transcends and applies to all such symbols, and it is the awareness of this fact that grants the particular truth a universal and necessary status. In this kind of case, language cannot demarcate the limits of knowledge. Language is, as it were, inadequate or insufficient to account for the knowledge that it seemingly conveys.

Even when language attempts to be specific, it cannot. One recalls Hegel's famous examples of 'Here' and 'Now' that he discusses in his *Phenomenology*. These examples make the point that knowledge is not and cannot be contained by or limited to language. Whenever the word, 'Now', is employed, one cannot make this word refer to the particular, because language is by itself universal and exceeds the intention of the moment. In these cases, it is not that language is not sufficient onto the day for knowledge: it is too much. Such cases should be enough to illustrate that language is at best a clumsy instrument that attempts to focus knowledge, but can neither totally contain nor demarcate it. And yet, one can make and does make use of this clumsy instrument to successfully communicate precisely what is meant in certain instances despite language's powerlessness to do so on its own. The issue is not confined to the problem of whether knowledge is possible without language; the issue is also whether linguistic knowledge is by itself adequate to, or precise enough, to account for knowledge.

It may be that language is, as will be discussed in the chapter, 'The Forgotten Fourth', a necessary phase in every act of representational knowledge. It does not follow that language alone is enough to account for any act of knowledge whether representational or non representational knowledge is the the object of reference. While at different stages of the development of the argument of this present work different positions may appear to be advanced regarding the nature of the relationship between language and knowledge, it must be understood that the argument is developmental and its fullest articulation cannot be discovered in its intitial expositions. It must also be understood that philosophical argument is context driven and variations are adapted in order to address specific problems. When certain problems are solved some variations of the argument are no longer necessary. An anwer to a problem at one level is not the same answer to a problem at another level. A developmental argument is also not necessarily sequential for certain problems may appear at late levels that were not present at earlier levels.

Does "intuitionism" follow in the wake of coming out from under mother's skirt of language? Such a fear is due to the fallacy of misplaced concreteness. The fallacy of misplaced concreteness is to hypostatize an individual occurrence as an abstract form of existence, and to hypostatize that generalized existence into a real existence. One takes an individualized activity, such as being able to discern the truth of a proposition, which in a particular case may be on one level due to the truth value of the proposition, (to be discussed in the sequel), and attributes the truth discernment to a magic faculty which is labeled, 'intuition'. Anyone who claims to be able to discern truth in such a fashion is then labeled an 'intuitionist'. From this point onwards, all examples of truth discernment of a seemingly like kind are attributed to the power of 'intuitionism'.

The process is to infer from the existence of a concrete result (such as knowledge) that such knowledge must be the result of a mental faculty. One then confers onto this faculty a label, which then appears to give it abstract or general existence, and then proceeds to criticize the existence or powers of the fictionalized existential power. In a sense, one could also label this fallacy the fallacy of misplaced abstractness in that that which has no existence in the abstract save as a general name which is given to situations which appear to have similar traits is treated outside of its actual context where it exists only as an abstract shell. However, if one pays more attention to the genesis of the fallacy, it is the fallacy of misplaced concreteness for the reason that one exports that which exists only in a concrete situation to a realm of abstract entities, and thereafter treats its export as an abstract existence. If one pays more attention to the common applications of the fallacy, it is the fallacy of misplaced abstractness. In any case, there is no need to call in the powers of a special faculty known as 'intuition' as to do so diverts attention from the proper repository of truth-value, the *cognoscendum*.

The brandishing or bandying of such labels should by now lose their power to intimidate philosophical thinking. Whether or not one is labeled an 'intuitionist', this by no means validates everyone's intuition any more than the label of 'rationalist' validates everyone's reasoning or the label 'analyst' validates everyone's analysis. To raise the question of whether or not "intuition" is a valid source of knowledge is to commit the fallacy, at this level, of misplaced abstractness. Intuition can no more be assessed as possible or not, any more than reasoning can be assessed as possible or not, in the absence of an example of reasoning.

The worry that one will not have a way of distinguishing between the intuition of a sage and a fool is a pseudo-worry, since the person in question must always offer up her or his example of intuitive reasoning for a public inspection.[12] One can always return to the examples taken from arithmetic or geometry as foundation examples. There is no need and indeed no value in attempting to make a case for "intuition" in the abstract. This, as is argued above, is the fallacy of misplaced concreteness, abstracting what is always and only an element of experience and hypostatizing it to be an independent, abstract reality. Such is the value of Plato's Fourth, and the unfortunate emphasis upon and misunderstanding created by the hypostatizing of Plato's Forms, which, from the point of view of knowledge of the present work constitutes the most famous example in the history of Western philosophy of both misplaced concreteness and misplaced abstractness.

If 'intuition' or 'phenomenological knowledge' are removed from the Analysts' Index of forbidden words, one need not fear that everyone's intuitions will therefore be uncriticizable, or that an appeal to intuition will be circular or self-justifying. The procedure that is to be followed is that any particular candidate for knowledge must be offered up for a phenomenological vetting. It is only after each candidate has been thoroughly vetted that a knowledge claim can subsequently be set forth. The knowledge claim must contain its own truth content. But, the claim of the truth content arises from the side of the content; it does not arise from the intuitive power or special faculty of knowledge of the subject knower.

Despite Rorty's argument to the contrary, there is no logical connection between the idea that language mirrors reality and the idea that philosophy must be conceived of as an attempt to contact reality. (This is a separate issue from the fact that any putative connection that exists between language and reality may possess implications concerning the nature of reality). The stunning example of Plato stands as a refutation that a concern with knowing reality is necessarily related to the concept that language mirrors reality. The project of knowing reality was for Plato by no means tied to a picture theory of meaning or a concept that language mirrored reality. For Plato, unlike Rorty, the incapacity of language to mirror reality was not a disincentive to the attempt to discover the nature of reality. On the contrary, the inability of language to mirror reality was an indicator that the highest truths of philosophy could not be reached by or depicted in language.

On the other hand, if Rorty is mistaken, and language does in some sense provide a mirror to nature, then his argument that philosophers will turn away from reality as soon as they discover that language is no mirror to reality is flawed because they will make no such discovery. One can attempt to know reality from either standpoint. Either one can go it alone, without language, or, one can enlist the service of language to provide some clues as to what reality might be like. The knowledge that results from the inspection of what clues language provides as to the nature of reality is not itself linguistic.

One must not, of course, mistake language for reality. Language is a means to attempt to classify and describe attempts to understand reality, in the same fashion that a library is an attempt to house books, but in no way is a library a collection of knowledge: it is a collection of books with written marks. Language can be thought of as Wittgenstein's proverbial ladder: a helpful tool to attempt to bring one a bit closer to reality, but by no means a literal or a comprehensive photograph of it any more than a directional sign which points one in the right direction is a mirror image of that to which it points.

Rorty considers that philosophy must once and for all give up its quest for representationalism on the grounds that the inadequacy of language to the task of truth discovery is a sufficient justification to give up the attempt to discover reality. Rorty thinks that if it were beyond the competence of language to picture truth, then one should not attempt to reach truth, because if reaching truth exceeds the competence of language, then one would have to contact reality without the use of language which would represent an even more arduous task, in fact, a task that Rorty would consider an impossible one.

But, it need not be a case of either/or. Even if it were true that language could not picture truth, it would not follow that language would of no help at all in assisting one to grasp reality or truth because language possesses other uses which are also aids in the discovery of or approach to truth. Evocative and exhortative language may be useful in raising a state of consciousness such that one becomes more capable of understanding truth - Plato saw this with regard to justice in both *Republic* and the *Seventh Letter* in which he commented that without becoming just, (thus employing the language of exhortation to persuade the subject reader to become just), the subject knower had no hope of understanding justice. If and only if one became just, according to Plato, could one understand justice. Thus, exhortative language could be employed as an aid in the quest for truth discovery, in this case the understanding of the true nature of justice.

It is also the case that if one understands the picture theory of language in a metaphorical rather than a literal sense, that one can employ analogical language to discover possible truths between the language of science and the language of phenomenology, (as in the case of space and time to be discussed in the sequel), which can serve as clues to the nature of reality. It is important to consider that just because language could not in every instance of its usage literally picture reality, it would not follow that it would be of absolutely no assistance at all in encountering reality.[13]

Furthermore, if it were possible to know truth without the employment of language, or to know truth which transcended the boundaries of language, then whether or not language could represent truth would be irrelevant to one's project of the pursuit of truth. This discussion must await further development, in Part II, Chapter 1, *et passim*. For the moment it may be remembered that Augustine compellingly argued in *De Magistro* that nothing can be learned through language. Augustine did think that truth could be known. Therefore, he held that truth could be known which was not learned through language.

Paradoxically, while Wittgenstein thought that language had been responsible for the creation of philosophical pseudo-problems, his drawing attention to language created more pseudo-problems for philosophers to sort out than language had been accused of creating in the first place. Indeed, because of the obsession with linguistic forms which was to follow in Wittgenstein's wake, the very solution which Wittgenstein presented itself became the source of an untoward proportion of the analytic philosophers' twentieth century's "philosophical" problems. One hesitates to think of how many doctoral dissertations in philosophy have been the result of just such a preoccupation.

It was to be the ironic fate of Wittgenstein who fathered the thought that philosophical problems were pseudo-problems created by the bewitchment of language, that his solution of language analysis was to become an even more powerful bewitchment. The twentieth century became Wittgenstein's century. Philosophy was to become increasingly insular, petty and parochial, because it could not expand beyond its self-appointed linguistic boundaries. What was presented as a solution to rid mankind of philosophical problems became the pseudo-source of philosophical problems. Only this time, since the real philosophical problems had never been addressed in the first place, not only were the original problems left unsolved, but the attempts to distract philosophers from problem solving added to the philosophical problematic.

By attempting to replace "pseudo"-philosophical problems by attending to the notion of language games, Wittgenstein had created a philosophical Hydra of pseudo-philosophical problems. In the place of a finite number of linguistic puzzles, Hydra's heads were to multiply geometrically, generating linguistic and hermeneutic schools all claiming to possess the answer of how to dissolve philosophy's linguistic puzzles. Wittgenstein's solution was to create far more problems than it had imagined it would solve.

The irony of Wittgenstein's fate was that he had thought that philosophy had been working with false credentials on bogus problems. Now, philosophy buttressed with borrowed credentials, (the new science of linguistic forms), found that its counterfeit problems had multiplied many times over. Philosophy was now required to attempt to sort out a variety of solutions to its genuine "pseudo"-problems and was thereby even more caught up in a false pastime than ever before. For, if *bewitchment by language* was responsible for its previous false pastime, now *an obsession with language* had spawned a dizzying array of false pastimes masquerading as philosophical problems. In addition, philosophy's real problems, the pseudo pseudo-problems, would resurface, demanding a solution. Before one could address them, however, one would first be required to dissolve the solutions of the multifarious pseudo-schools, which had arisen to solve the genuine pseudo-problems.

Other tendencies in philosophy such as scientism, (reducing philosophy's role to being the handmaiden of the sciences), and pragmatism, created the opposite situation which was to reduce or eliminate the number of genuine philosophical problems without replacing these genuine problems with a set of pseudo-problems. From the standpoint of Ockham's razor, it could be said that these were less harmful alternatives to the above description of linguisticism. It is not clear that this is the case, however, since the attempt to solve the new pseudo-problems arising in linguisticism's wake might bestir the linguistic philosopher to consider a real problem in the same fashion that Alexander Fleming, after being irritated that his bacteria culture was being destroyed by a mold, realized that this mold (penicillin) represented a cure for bacterial disease. By presenting a solution without the remainder of pseudo-problems, pragmatism, for example, as dispensed by some, despite its rich philosophical inheritance, might prove to be a philosophical sedative rather than an irritant.

Why has there been such an animus against metaphysics? In part, this can all be explained, as suggested earlier, as part of the empiricist reaction against claims to speculative knowledge, which did not appear to have any mode of verification. The Vienna Circle had done its work very well in vaccinating philosophers against metaphysical truth.

But, another reason for the bias against metaphysics is that metaphysics is identified, by and large, with systems of metaphysics, which lay claim to truth. In the words of Habermas, 'Every form of transcendental philosophy claims to identify the conditions of the objectivity of experience by analysing the categorial structure of objects of possible experience'.[14] The notion that there is not a system of metaphysics, but rather particular metaphysical truths, is not taken into account in this universal generalization of Habermas about transcendental philosophy. Also, in Habermas' definition of transcendental philosophy, the goal is identifying conditions of the objectivity of experience, not in discovering specific metaphysical truths. Habermas' definition resembles that of Kant's.

In the kind of phenomenological epistemology and phenomenological metaphysics which is the concern of this present work, no claims need to be made for any system of transcendental philosophy, and what is more, the main goal is neither in identifying conditions for objective experience, nor in analyzing categorial structures. The main concern at the outset of one's investigation is not in relating particular metaphysical truths to "reality" or the "objective world". Indeed, it is only if one's concern is strictly phenomenological in the first place that one can eventually arrive at a well based ontology.

While certain analogical relations will be suggested in terms of the relation of phenomenological truth claims to physical reality, these are posited as analogies of experience, and have the status of analogical possibilities, and not the status of necessary and universal truths. Such analogical relations that are posited are grounded first of all in the foundations of phenomenological knowledge. Such a foundation of certain and universal truth provides a bridge by which one may reach out and consider what implications might hold for the world at large. This is a bridge, which may be extended and/or modified in the future. All that the present work can lay claim to, for the time being, is to provide sound and firm phenomenological foundations for such a bridge. These phenomenological foundations may be taken as the first ingredients in the making of a transcendental attitude. Up until now it has not been at all clear what is meant by a transcendental attitude, since such a phrase normally connotes at worst some form of non-scientific mysticism, and at best some form of misguided idealism, or modified Kantianism. If this present work were to prove successful, the notion of a transcendental attitude will take on a new meaning and a definite content.

Once within a philosophical attitude, the particular philosophy must, (just as a work of art), be appraised on its own merits. The capability of adopting a philosophical attitude does not thereby license all claims to philosophy. It is a necessary, but not a sufficient condition for a true or great philosophic work. The strange but necessary test of history is required to fulfill the latter condition. That such a convergence arises is no surprise since the human mind is simply another example of the workings of nature. A successful biological species requires a span of time to demonstrate its hardiness. Intellectual species fare no better. In fact, if there were no such convergence of history (the "natural environment" of intellectual theory) and theory, it would be even more surprising. What is of importance is the recognition of philosophy as a valid source of knowledge in its own right, with its own special procedures and modes of validation, and it is to the realization of this unfashionable aim that the works of the present author are directed.

This aim will not be realized until or unless one is able to make the corresponding shift in consciousness. Mysticism has been much maligned because it is argued by non-mystical *cognoscentes*, (those outside of the privileged circle of mystical experiencers), that such claims that are brought forth by "mystics" are brought forth and appreciated only by members of the in-group. It is unquestionably true that some experienced change is demanded herein from the subject reader. Otherwise, what is set forth will appear to have a merely theoretical and hypothetical character. It does not follow from this that the call to embrace the respective new viewpoint is based simply upon an alteration of the quality or level of experience. The respective approach which is being proposed is not one in which it is being said that as soon as one participates in this "special experience", that the claims made therein are *ipso facto* certified. That is nonsense. That would be tantamount to saying that all that is required is that one assume (or experience) an aesthetic outlook to understand/appreciate the greatness of Picasso. It remains true, however, that in the absence of an aesthetic attitude, one will not be capable of appreciating the art of Picasso.

This present work offers itself as a modest aid to refurbish a lost glamour of philosophy. It is essential, for this, as a necessary condition, that one assume a transcendental attitude. To mistake the transcendental attitude for philosophical justification would be tantamount to a subject reader certifying that because in her or his experience, *Hamlet* is a "great work of art", and since this testimony coincides with the received opinion, *ergo*, it is a "great work of art". The positing of such a criterion of greatness in literature is no less absurd in literature than it is in philosophy. The certification or recognition of greatness is an act that cannot be reduced to the convergence of subjective experience with received opinion. What is involved in the act-recognition of the greatness of philosophical works is both a key shift of consciousness, and a level of epistemic verification. Unless subject knowers practise both a raising of consciousness, and discernment in recognizing truth, the entire project of restoring philosophy to its previous stature as a grand science is in serious jeopardy.

Philosophy is not and need not be poetry, (despite Heidegger's thoughts on this), although there are poetic philosophers such as Lao Tzu and Nietzsche. Philosophy is more like poetry rather than history in the Aristotelian sense that philosophy deals with the universal, not the particular. *If one were to consider philosophy as a whole, one could think of philosophy as a poetry of truth as if a poet were to write a poem about a painting in which truth were the subject of the painting.* This is not the same as the later Heideggerian vision of poetic truth as replacing truth in philosophy. It is crucial that if philosophy were to regain its role as Queen of the sciences that it be understood and appreciated as something other than a synoptic or grand empirical science. It is a different enterprise altogether. Philosophy is a map of an unexplored and entirely different kind of territory though it is possible to journey from such a territory to more familiar terrain.

Husserl was extremely helpful when he attempted to demarcate the phenomenological standpoint. However, this great achievement was marred by his preoccupation with perceptual realism and such empirical concerns as the method of variations. In this regard, although he was not as careful as Husserl was in demarcating a new standpoint, Hegel, among all other philosophers, was perhaps the most successful in demarcating the concept of a transcendental turn.

What is needed today is to return to the grand project of pure *philosophia*. No longer need philosophers be measured by the standards of empirical science. They must throw off these shackles. It is not enough, as Hartshorne says of metaphysics, that metaphysics need not find empirical confirmation, nor should it be discountenanced by the fact that there is no empirical disconfirmation, because 'every example counts for it'. What is more to the point is that there is an intrinsic mode of validation appropriate to metaphysics, and that one not only need not, but one must not borrow the model of truth-telling employed by the empirical sciences. This is very different from saying that there is no mode of certification whatever, except the standards of poetic reveries as appears to be the position of the later Heidegger or his self-appointed pupil, Richard Rorty.

Philosophy has been prisoner, for much of the twentieth century, the passing of which has just been witnessed, of Wittgenstein's concept that philosophical problems were the result of the distorting influence of language. In this sense, the twentieth century was Wittgenstein's century and philosophy was his prisoner. It is high time to free philosophy from its preoccupation with the illusory prison house of language.

Although Hegel and Husserl to some extent made attempts to set philosophy on its rightful path, such efforts have been for the most part, wasted efforts. Perhaps these grand efforts have gone to waste because insufficient attention was paid to the "how" by which particular truth claims came to be known. What is needed is the combination of the goals of such philosophers from the past and the provision of precise standards for how one knows what is true, the latter task of which has been the preoccupation of the analytic philosophers who dominated the twentieth century.

Philosophy must be encouraged to take the transcendental turn once again, and it is hoped in the course of this present work that an adequate justification for taking such a transcendental turn can be given. There is an incredible amount that both needs to be said and can be said. However, in light of the dominance of the model of science as the arbiter of knowledge and the preoccupation with the forms of language usage, in the manner of Locke, philosophy is mostly constrained to clear away the underbrush that obscures its vision. The underbrush is this present work is represented by a reverence for scientific methodology as the exclusive model for truth finding and an obsession with studying and highlighting language usage.

The fundamental problem and the one with which the work of philosophy proper can commence is the problem of justification, or, as it should more properly be called, the problem of validation or certification. This is what is inherited, as a residue, from empirical science and it is with this residue that one must begin. If the concept of certification can be explicated, a giant step will have been taken towards the restoration of the credibility of philosophy. This starting point, however, must be postponed for the time being in order that preexisting false images of epistemology and metaphysics can be thoroughly deconstructed such that the mind can be fully prepared for its new epistemological and metaphysical foundations.

For the present time, it is of great importance that philosophy be understood as a discipline in its own right with its own unique modes of validation. This is very different from saying that it has no modes of validation whatsoever, or that it is in the same domain as the arts or religious belief. But, it does not follow from this that it must be judged by the standard of the empirical sciences. This kow-towing to empirical science and its standard is the fatal error of philosophy.

Hsün-Tzu once spoke of *cheng ming* or the rectification of names. There is a need now, in the West, or, what is more properly a global region in which philosophy is to be carried out, to become aware of the existence of this essential philosophical activity of the rectification of names.[15] Philosophy is not empirical science. It has its own methods and its own peculiar modes of validation. Philosophy requires that a transition of consciousness take place in the subject appreciator, in order to be appraised as a discipline in the first place. It is easy to mistake such a transition for the poetic or religious temperament. It is for this reason that Hegel thought that philosophy was closest to art and religion. The evidence from poetry, music, art, religion and other transcendental domains must be called in to lend support to the notion that philosophy too, belongs to a transcendental domain. It does not mean, however, that thereby philosophy is a kind of poetry beyond repute. It means only that it is with these same concerns that philosophy is preoccupied and its task is to determine how one can know that which is most important to humanity. It is fitting at this point to conclude. In the spirit of T. S. Eliot's, *Little Gidding,*

> '... the end of all our exploring
> Will be to arrive where we started
> And know the place for the first time.'

Philosophy is a study that relates to the search for meaning in life and arrives at some deep level of response to that question. Whether the conclusion of the philosopher is that life is meaningless or meaningful, or sometimes meaningless and sometimes meaningful, that question never ceases to have importance for that individual. By this definition, Wittgenstein was certainly a philosopher *malgré lui*, whatever his reputation and symbolic authority as the destroyer of philosophy.

Notes

1. For Bernstein, the choice between foundationalism and non-foundationalism is a "dead option". *Cf.*, Richard J. Bernstein, *Philosophical Profiles*, Cambridge: Polity Press, 1986, p. 91. In that case, this present work falls into the category of philosophical vivisection or philosophical resurrection depending upon one's point of view.
2. At the end of a public lecture given by Rorty at Shaw College in The Chinese University of Hong Kong in March of 1993, in response to a direct question put to Rorty by the author, Rorty stated that there was no way to argue that his liberalism was objectively superior to Hitler's values. This is also Bernstein's conclusion (concerning Rorty's stance) in his "decoding" of Rorty, and he quotes from Feyerabend in a passage worth repeating: '"Objectively" there is not much to choose between anti-Semitism and humanitarianism. But racism will appear vicious to a humanitarian while humanitarianism will appear vapid to a racist. *Relativism* [emphasis in the original] (in the old simple sense of Protagoras) gives an adequate account of the situation which thus emerges.' *Cf.*, Paul K. Feyerabend, *Science in a Free Society*, London: New Left Books, 1979, pp. 8-9. Quoted from Bernstein, *Philosophical Profiles*, p. 83. The foregoing appears especially ironic when one considers that Rorty himself quotes Habermas' critique of Heidegger's "abstraction by essentialization": '... under the levelling gaze of the philosopher of Being even the extermination of the Jews seems merely an event equivalent to others.' (Habermas, 'Work and Weltanschauung: The Heidegger

controversy from a German perspective', *Critical Inquiry* 15, Winter, 1989, p. 453, quoted from Richard Rorty, *Essays On Heidegger And Others, Philosophical Papers*, Volume 2, New York: Cambridge University Press, 1991, p. 69). But, Rorty himself confesses that he is unable to distinguish one event as morally superior or inferior to another and in this respect, according to Habermas, Rorty's philosophy is equivalent to Heidegger's. If this is not coming full circle, it is not clear what coming full circle is. Rorty's philosophy is prospectively equally dangerous to today's society as Heidegger's was retrospectively to Hitler's. Rorty, it seems, is more confused than perverse. He calls himself a liberal, borrowing the definition of a liberal to be one who believes that 'cruelty is the worse thing we do', but couples this with being an ironist for whom the question 'Why not be cruel?' has no answer! (Given the earlier critique of this choice of a label, perhaps a more appropriate label would be an 'ironic liberal' rather than a 'liberal ironist'). *Cf.*, Richard Rorty, *Contingency, Irony, and Solidarity*, New York: Cambridge University Press, 1989, p. xv. Rorty has straddled himself with a powerless position from which he can only passively sigh when cruelty is done, but cannot speak up against it, except, presumably, in plaintive rhymes which are empty of any epistemic or moral suasion.

3. Aristotle, *Nichomachean Ethics*, 1098a10-12.

4. The philosopher Dummett reflects the mainstream view that *a priori* reasoning cannot afford substantive knowledge of fundamental features of the world. (*Cf.*, Dummett, Introduction to *The Logical Basis of Metaphysics*, Cambridge, Massachusetts: Harvard University Press, 1991, p. 1).

5. When one considers such incredible truths as the twin paradox where high-speed travel actually lengthens life span such that one twin can return to earth after 10,000 years have passed and his own 'era' rates only a few lines in an archaeological textbook, the notion of an event, once having happened, not necessarily having to have happened (yet) may also lose its aura of unshakeability. After all, the whole notion of a simultaneous happening is what Einstein has called into question. It is important to note that the twin paradox is not an hypothesis of physics, but has been proven by physical experiments by Emilia Picasso and an international team of physicists at CERN, the European high-energy laboratory near Geneva in 1977. *Cf.*, Nigel Calder, *Einstein's Universe*, New York: Viking Press, 1979, p. 91. *Cf.*, Lawrence Sklar, *Philosophy of Physics*, New York: Oxford University Press, 1992, p. 35, where the truth of the twin paradox is presented matter of factly, and the scientific evidence pointed to in support of it is the experiment in which fewer of unstable particles sent around the circular paths of accelerators decay than their compatriot particles in a group remaining at rest in the laboratory between the first moment when they coincide and the second moment at which they coincide. Hawking also refers to the twin paradox as a routine scientific truth. *Cf.*, Stephen Hawking, *A Brief History of Time*, New York: Bantam

Books, 1989, p. 36. The knighted Oxford mathematician and physicist, Roger Penrose also refers to 'the twin paradox' as an accepted scientific truth, although he does not consider it a paradox. *Cf.*, Roger Penrose, *The Emperor's New Mind*, New York: Oxford University Press, 1989, 1990, p. 197. Does the possibility that what has happened could not have happened (yet) require time reversal? If it did, such a consequence would not be acceptable to Sir Roger. (*Cf.*, Nigel Calder, *Einstein's Universe*, p. 125). Kurt Gödel, on the other hand, did not find this consequence unacceptable. In fact, he found it possible in principle, although empirically unlikely. Writing from the Institute of Advanced Studies at Princeton at the time, Gödel wrote that the implications of Einstein's theory were that '... it enables one e.g., to travel into the near past of those places where he himself lived. There he would find a person who would be himself at some earlier period of his life. Now he could do something to this person which, by his memory, he knows has not happened to him. This and similar contradictions, however, in order to prove the impossibility of the worlds under consideration, presuppose the actual feasibility of the journey into one's own past. But the velocities which would be necessary in order to complete the voyage in a reasonable length of time are far beyond everything that can be expected to become a practical possibility'. *Cf.*, Kurt Gödel, 'Relativity and Idealistic Philosophy', Paul Arthur Schilpp, (ed.), *Albert Einstein, Philosopher-Scientist*, Library of Living Philosophers, Vol. VII, La Salle, Illinois: Fifth Printing, 1991, pp. 560-561. Reichenbach recognized the theoretical possibility of time reversal as well: 'That Einstein's theory admits of a reversal of time order for certain events, a result known from the relativity of simultaneity, is merely a consequence of this fundamental fact.' *Cf.*, Hans Reichenbach, 'The Philosophical Significance of Relativity' *ibid.*, p. 303. Dummett appears to recognize the metaphysical possibility of time reversal as well, although he qualifies his position by saying that he is entering deep metaphysical waters: 'Why should the past not change after our consciousness has traveled through it, why should not the future now be in a different state from which it will be when our consciousness arrives at it?' *Cf.*, Michael Dummett, *The Logical Basis of Metaphysics*, Cambridge, Massachusetts: Harvard University Press, 1991, pp. 7-8. There is the grandfather paradox whereby one by traveling backwards in time meets one's grandfather and murders him and thus prevents one's own birth thus making it impossible to have traveled backwards in time in the first place. However, these and other imaginatively constructed paradoxes (which have generated even more imaginative solutions) may not be obstacles to the metaphysical possibility of time reversal, since there may be a difference between time reversing itself and an individual traveling backwards in time. Time reversal may only require a replay although no one may be aware of the replay. An individual may find it empirically impossible to travel backwards in time even though time reversal may be metaphysically possible. *Cf.*, David

Deutsch and Michael Lockwood, 'The Quantum Physics of Time Travel', *Scientific American*, March, 1994, pp. 50-55, Letters to the Editors, *Scientific American*, September, 1994, pp. 56-57; Michael Dummett, 'Causal Loops', in R. Flood and M. Lockwood, (eds.), *The Nature of Time*, Basil Blackwell, 1986; Kip S. Thorne, 'Do the Laws of Physics Permit Closed Time-Like Curves?', *Annals of the New York Academy of Sciences*, Vol. 631, August, 1991, pp. 182-193; David Deutsch, 'Quantum Mechanics Near Closed Timelike Lines,' *Physical Review D*, Vol. 44, No. 10, November 15, 1991, pp. 3197-3217; David Lewis, 'The Paradoxes of Time Travel', *American Philosophical Quarterly*, Vol. 13, No. 2, pp. 145-152, April 1976, reprinted in Robin Le Poidervin and Murray MacBeath, (eds.), *The Philosophy of Time*, Oxford University Press, 1993; Amos Ori, 'Must Time Machine Construction Violate The Weak Energy Condition?', *Physical Review Letters*, Vol. 71, No. 16, October 18, 1993, pp. 2517-2520; Graham Nerlich, *What spacetime explains, Metaphysical essays on space and time*, Cambridge: Cambridge University Press, 1994. For Hawking, the laws of physics do not permit time travel but he does not appear to consider it metaphysically impossible. *Cf.*, Stephen Hawking, *Black Holes and Baby Universes and Other Essays*, New York: Bantam Books, 1994, p. 154. The presumed imponderabilities of the grandfather paradox may one day be counted as equally insignificant as the once existing imponderability of the earth being round.

6. This account of analytic philosophy owes much to a seminar presentation on linguistic philosophy given by Rorty in a seminar for the Department of Philosophy held at The Chinese University of Hong Kong in March 1993 (the acerbic meta-commentary being provided by the present author).

7. One may well ask, how does one know this? Presumably, the answer is that it is a useful behavior not to consider that there can be a study of knowledge, and thus no act of knowledge is required. But, it seems that this simply does violence to language. One must have some awareness of one's claims. Even claiming that all knowledge is linguistic requires a knowing or a non-linguistic awareness of what one is claiming. Even if one claims only to know 'marks', that is still a kind of knowing. The analysts seem to be working very hard to remove the first person point of view. But, whether one has to think in the first person or not is not important. All that needs acknowledging is that one is capable of being aware, and one can be directly aware of one's awareness. This is as simple and as true as the fact that each husband can become aware of the image of his wife that he now images to himself. To describe this as only behavior is to edit out both the experiencing and the content of his awareness. If the price of excising consciousness is charlatanism, then the existence of consciousness is more acceptable than a fraudulent account of experience.

8. Psychologists working with higher primates have discovered value systems. For example, chimpanzees who had been taught how to sign showed a resistance to being put back in a cage with chimpanzees who had not

learned sign language. When asked what the sign users thought of the non-sign users, the sign users signed the word for 'insects'. While it may be alleged that it is only conjecture that this was an evaluation, one has to take the entire behavior in context. It should be considered that insects are food for chimpanzees and may well be considered as lower creatures. What is so terribly wrong with ascribing beliefs to people, anyhow? For a series of arguments that suggest that higher primates such as apes possess higher consciousness, one may be referred to Frans De Waal, *Good natured, The Origins of Right and Wrong in Humans and Other Animals*, Cambridge: Harvard University Press, 1996. Strictly speaking, apes and humans are hominoids as opposed to monkeys, who belong to a different branch of the evolutionary tree. *Cf.*, discussion on pp. 4, 25 of De Waal's fascinating book and p. 77 where an illustration implies chimpanzees have a sense of shame. Persuasive examples of the linguistic abilities of chimpanzees are provided by Eugene Linden. When seeing a swan for the first time, a chimpanzee signed the word for 'water bird'. When asked to give the name for watermelon (a fruit which had not been named), the sign for 'drinkfruit' was given. After having previously been taught the word for bracelet, when a ring was shown to a chimpanzee, the chimpanzee volunteered the sign 'finger bracelet'. A radish was referred to by the sign 'cry hurt food'. *Cf.*, Eugene Linden, *Apes, Men and Language*, New York: Penguin Books, 1974. Roger S. Fouts and Randall L. Rigby argue that the example of 'cry hurt food' provides evidence for the phenomenon of reconstitution, which, according to Bronowski and Bellugi is considered to be the evolutionary hallmark of the human mind. From this Fouts and Rigby conclude that it is possible that '... the capacity for language was in the repertoire of the species before the great apes split off from hominoid evolution'. *Cf.*, Thomas A. Sebeok and Jean Umiker-Sebeok, *Speaking of Apes, A Critical Anthology of Two-Way Communication with Man*, New York and London: Plenum Press, 1980, p. 285. Patricia Marks Greenfield and Sue Savage-Rumbaugh point out that their findings with Kanzi, a pygmy chimpanzee (*Pan paniscus*), provide evidence that bonobos can not only learn a simple grammar but moreover can invent new protogrammatical rules, that is, rules never demonstrated by any human or animal in the chimpanzees' social environment. *Cf.*, Sue Taylor Parker and Kathleen Rita Gibson, (eds.), *"Language" and intelligence in monkeys and apes, Comparative developmental perspectives*, Cambridge: Cambridge University Press, 1990, pp. 543-4. Certain higher primates, e.g., chimpanzees, orangutans and gorillas, can recognize their physical bodies in a mirror and know how to make use of the mirror for purposes of self inspection. It is but a short step from this to the possibility that reflective knowledge such as self-consciousness might possibly also exist. Is it too much to imagine that certain higher primates might even be conscious of their own mortality? If so, Heidegger's vaunted definition of the human being as the one being who is conscious of mortality may be in need of revision. If one places a sticker on the forehead of a chimpanzee and the chimpanzee sees his or her face in the mirror, she or he can then pull the sticker off her or his forehead. Thus, the chimpanzee knows that the reflection in the glass is a reflection of her or his body. The cat cannot make this connection. This gives rise to the consideration that human beings doubtless possess limitations in the capacity to know, the very existence of which limitations may be unknown to them. In other words, human beings may not be able to grasp something extremely obvious and at the same time be completely unaware that they fail to grasp what is obvious or even that there is something obvious to grasp.

9. It is of course true that one need not take up the question of what relationship language has to the world, but it does not then follow that no such relationship exists. If one does not choose to raise or answer such questions, the questions do not go away by themselves. In fact, if the consequence of ignoring such questions were that they would not be raised, this would be a serious consequence. For the loss of genuine philosophical problems is far more serious than the false confidence gained by pretending they no longer exist. If genuine philosophical problems are lost due to systematic neglect, then such systematic neglect is not benign; it is systematically malignant.

10. Even if one were to take up the position that language possessed only use value and not representational value, one would still have to know this. Knowledge cannot escape being part of the picture no matter how behavioristic one becomes. One must still become aware of behaviorism as a model; one can even raise questions about the truth or falsity of behaviorism as a model. If it were said that behaviorism is not true or false but only useful, even this must be something that is knowable and known. One can insist upon referring to this as another behavioral act, but this is to do much violence both to language and experience. At the very least, it is very inconvenient and therefore not useful in pragmatic terms. That one is forced to such excesses by the conventions of a theory is argument enough that the theory of behaviorism is false, especially when one considers that behaviorism presumably arose to exorcise bogeymen, not to create them. In any event, if one employs Ockham's razor, then it is far more simple and elegant to employ the language of consciousness for cognitive events than the language of behavior. On behalf of Wittgenstein, it would be to misrepresent Wittgenstein if only his behavioristic side were to be emphasized. *Cf.*, Timothy Binkley, *Wittgenstein's Language*, The Hague: Martinus Nijhoff, 1973, p. 136. The problem is, if all that really matters in human life is precisely what we must be silent about, then the speech of philosophers is not only trivial; it is distracting.

11. It may be that this is not to be entirely fair to Wittgenstein. He does say in *Culture and Value* that 'Man has to awaken to wonder - and so perhaps do peoples.' *Cf.*, Ludwig Wittgenstein, *Culture and Value*, Chicago: The University of Chicago Press, 1980, p. 2. It is not even fair to characterize

Wittgenstein's view as one which attributes all philosophical problems to the distorting effects of language. For Wittgenstein, there are other sources of philosophical confusion. In *The Blue Book*, he states, 'Our craving for generality has another main source: our preoccupation with the method of science. . . Philosophers constantly see the method of science before their eyes, and are irresistably tempted to ask and answer questions the way science does. This tendency is the real source of metaphysics, and leads the philosopher into complete darkness'. *Cf.*, Ludwig Wittgenstein, *The Blue and Brown Books*, New York: Harper and Row, 1965, p. 18. (The books were named for the colour of the wrapppers in which they were bound). Nevertheless, it must be taken into account that the characterization of Wittgenstein that is presented in the course of the work of the present author is based on the main influence of his ideas. Of course, this is a hazardous undertaking in which not the least difficulty is that there are two different Wittgensteins, the Wittgenstein of the *Tractatus* and the Wittgenstein of the *Investigations*.

12. The word 'intuition' has had a history of many uses. It should be noted that the use in the present work is not to be confused with either the popular meaning of the capacity for extra sensory perception (as a sixth sense) or the technical meaning found in Kant's definition of intuition in his first *Critique* (B 34). The capacity for extra sensory perception might very well involve a special mental talent. However the existence or non-existence of such a talent is an empirical question, not a philosophical one. Kant's technical definition in his first *Critique* of space and time as being pure forms of all sensible intuition (B 56) has been redefined in the present work and its sequel such that space and time function as pure forms of all plurality. There is no need to refer to intuition in this context. Intuition in the present work enjoys a meaning closer to what one would understand by a pure awareness, which may also be referred to as consciousness or knowledge. It corresponds most closely to what Aristotle means when he says that the knowledge of immediate premises must be non-demonstrative and that there is a starting point or originative source which enables one to recognize definitions (*Posterior Analytics*, 72b19-24). It is understood in the present work that by this Aristotle did not mean a special, occult knowledge, but a knowing of what is true immediately, without recourse to a deduction. Herein, 'phenomenological knowledge' has been used as the term of description rather than 'intuition' in order to avoid all the multifarious connotations that come to mind when the word 'intuition' appears, and so as to avoid such prolix explanations of its proper meaning as this one. The utilization of the term 'phenomenological' without the accompanying employment of the term 'intuition' might at first appear strange since Husserl employs the term 'intuition' freely in conjunction with the term 'phenomenology'. (*Cf.*, '... phenomenology ... claims to be nothing beyond a Theory of Essential Being developed within a medium of pure intuition.' This definition of Husserl's, ironically enough, appears

under his classification of 'Unambiguous terms' [was this tongue in cheek?] in *Ideas*, Part III, Chapter 7, 66). Be this as it may, if "intuition" were purged of all of its bad past associations, its "black ball" could be removed and it could once more be welcomed back as a valid member of the philosophy club. Such an argument as this one would fall under the classical Chinese category of the rectification of names (*cheng ming*). For a fuller explanation of the concept of the rectification of names, one may be referred to n. 15, below.

13. In a sense which perhaps Wittgenstein did not fully explore, his notion of picturing facts may contain a higher level of truth value in the sense that logical truth may be a representation of metaphysical truth in so far as the conditions for the necessity of logic are to be found in the very structuredness of the universe. To know the laws of logic would be to possess a reflection or a "picture" of reality. Of course, the knowledge of the laws of logic is not sufficient to know reality as a whole as the whole may not conform to the limitations of its parts. Wittgenstein did have his finger on something profound though the word 'picture' may have been misleading. For example, in Wittgenstein's choice of the example of the musical score and the music, it is true that the musical score is a sign of the music. Thus, there must be something congruent between the sign and the signified. The sign and the signified must share a common reality although each may also possess different realities. *Cf.*, *Tractatus*, 2.12; 2.16-2.17; 2.22-2.223; 3.21; 4.011-4.012; 4.014, 4.0141. Wittgenstein's view that sentences must possess logical form in common with reality in order to represent reality is a profound philosophical thesis. *Cf.*, *Tractatus*, 2.18; 4.12-4.1212. For an absorbing discussion of the matter, one may refer to, J.O. Urmson, *Philosophical Analysis, Its development between the two world wars*, London: Oxford University Press, 1971, pp. 87-93. This is quite apart from the fact that his theory may not have been well named (Urmson questions whether similarity of structure should be called 'picturing'), p. 88.

14. Richard Rorty, *Philosophy and the Mirror of Nature*, Oxford: Basil Blackwell, 1983, pp. 381-2.

15. *Cf.*, *Hsün-Tzu*, Book 22. To rectify a name, for Confucianism, was to return the name to its proper use, which meant, in accord with its ancient meaning. Of course this activity meant more than simply using language correctly, since its major emphasis was on orienting persons to engage in appropriate activities. *Cheng ming*, or the rectification of names, is not to be interpreted as the "ordering of names" as it has sometimes been translated since its function is to restore the ancient and proper meaning to the name and not to place the name inside of some kind of order or hierarchy. *Cf.*, Robert E. Allinson, 'Moral Values and the Chinese Sage in the *Tao De Ching*', (concluding chapter), *Morals and Society in Asian Philosophy*, Brian Carr, (ed.), London: Curzon Press, 1996. As an aside, it is interesting to reflect that the introduction of such a concept as *cheng ming* into

Western philosophy or as a critique of Western philosophy is an example of an Asiacentric biased direction and employment of cultural studies. The continuation of such an intellectual habit might constitute a healthy corrective to the preoccupation of cultural studies with the adaptation and employment of Western terms or methodologies to the critique of Asian traditions. In addition, the introduction of the concept of *cheng ming* into the activity of philosophizing in the West would also possess the benefit of encouraging a continual re-examination of the past and therefore provide a greater continuity with the past. Such a continuous re-examination of the past is not simply to provide a greater sense of tradition although this in itself is no small benefit. Such a continuous re-examination of past uses of language is a means to keep alive the possibility that previous modes of conceptualization may possess current validity. The custom of simply inventing new language possesses the deficit not only of losing a sense of tradition and continuity but also of discouraging the re-evaluation of the possibility that an ancient mode of conceptualization may represent a solution to a co-temporary problem. The importation of the practise of the rectification of names from the East to the West would represent a significant contribution to philosophical methodology in the West. It is ironic that the East, long associated with mysticism, would in this instance play a rationalistic role *vis-à-vis* the West regarded as post-Modern since in the post-Modern West words can mean anything at all and therefore would in no sense possess a proper meaning (which seems a fair definition of mysticism). In addition, since the rectification of names is an ancient Chinese philosophical practise and attempts to return words to their ancient and proper meaning, then the revival of such a practise in the West would be a renaissance of ancient Chinese philosophy and hence point back in an ancient direction rather than "forward" to a post-Modern (ahistorical?) direction.

PART I

THE NATURE OF METAPHYSICS

Andante espressivo
Slow and expressively

1 What is Metaphysics?

In philosophy, in *sensu stricto*, a proper definition of terms can only come at the end, and never at the beginning of an inquiry. That is why it may be that the great prefaces in philosophy, as Kant's two prefaces to the two editions of his first *Critique*, Hegel's preface to his *Phenomenology of the Spirit* and Merleau-Ponty's preface to his *Phenomenology of Perception*, were written after they wrote their books. Why a definition can only come at the end, and not at the beginning of an inquiry is itself a metaphysical issue, and one which it would be important to consider. Further discussion of this issue may be resumed toward the end of this chapter. For the moment, it can be pointed out that the approach taken here is very different from the approach taken in analytic philosophy, which insists upon a definition of terms at the beginning. When one is considering language usage for the purposes of the most immediate and the most unambiguous means of communication, it would be highly appropriate to insist upon a definition of one's terms at the outset of a discussion. If one's objective is instant communication which is likely to be understood in one and only one way, which is the type of communication normally attending the wish to elicit a single, desired response, frequently of desired behavior, it behooves one to let others know what one means by one's terms.

In philosophy, however, one's concern is not only, or perhaps not even primarily the urgency of communicating a single meaning instantly and without ambiguity with the intention of eliciting a desired behavior in response. As a result, linguistic clarity is neither the sole nor the primary concern of the philosopher. The philosopher's concern is primarily with the finding of truth and the obtaining of understanding of this truth and secondarily with the intention of eliciting new questions and answers to questions which have not been raised. While the distinguished figures who have argued for the pragmatics of communication in such elegant terms may have meant something quite different from what is said here, from the point of view of the present work, *the philosopher's chief concern is not with the pragmatics of communication.* The philosopher's chief concern is with the region of truth discovery and the terms with which the philosopher communicates are of secondary concern. The more the philosopher concentrates upon the terms of her or his discourse, the less the philosopher can concentrate upon the philosophical objective alluded to above.

On the other hand, when the voyage of discovery has reached its objective, the terms will by then have been given a meaning in use which will have enriched and empowered the understanding of the reader. It is for this reason that the words of a philosopher are only part of the means of the vehicle of discovery and their meaning can only take on a full and definitive multivocity at the end of the process of discovery. A few words that make up a definition may require an entire book to expound. The meaning of these few words that are enlisted at the beginning of a discourse to posit a provisional definition of something or other can at best only be signposted by the words themselves in the way that a person's name and signature is only a clue to a person's identity. After one thoroughly knows the life of Napoleon, one understands much more when one reads his signature than when one at first simply sees the famous signed N for the first time. As a result, the precision in a philosophical definition at the beginning of a philosophical inquiry can only be provisional. The more one explains these words, the richer and more universal the meaning of the words grow. From a few words, like scattered acorns, the meaning of the terms gradually expand to form a great oak tree.

If one has been successful in philosophizing, the definition with which one may begin, when later looked back upon, will be far more meaningful than it at first appeared to be. After the fully-grown tree has been seen, then and only then, can one comprehend the acorn whence it came. To ask then, for a full and totally clear definition at the beginning is to demand that the acorn provide the weary traveler a firm support on which to rest her or his back and ample shade to shield her or his eyes from the sun.

With this caveat, the dangerous work of the definition of terms may commence. If one wishes to remain in dialogue with the world at large, and not spend one's time in exclusive conversations with fellow philosophers, it is prudent to start with the popular definition of metaphysics. In popular language, metaphysics normally connotes a concern with spiritualism, or the realm of the occult. For the proverbial man or woman in the street, whoever is positing some system of spiritual thought which is outside the realm of scientific knowledge, or is concerned with a realm of phenomena which is not only outside of scientific knowledge, but which might actually refer to some dimension of existence of usually negative entities, normally discarnate, such as ghosts, or to other levels of existence such as etheric realms, astral realms, the afterlife, reincarnation, transmigration, karma, and/or a wide range of sundry psychic phenomena and psychic powers including precognition, retrocognition, clairvoyance, clairaudience, mediumship, telekinesis, teleportation, and psychic surgery, is a metaphysician. It is not altogether fair to rule out these realms as legitimate realms for the professional metaphysician. For the most part, however, the interest of professional philosophers in such domains has been restricted to such questions as the existence and nature of G-d, the soul, and the afterlife. However, if even these three are considered as legitimate areas of inquiry, it is difficult to know where, how, or why one should draw the line. It is important, therefore, to arrive at some criterion for deciding the legitimacy of these or other metaphysical topics.

For the moment, one should keep in mind an attitude of humility toward such extra-empirical subjects as possibly being beyond human understanding, and doubtless being beyond the competence of such metaphysical methods as may be elaborated in this present work. This, however, should not be construed as meaning that an interest in such realms is to be considered foolish, or that every sort of existential claim that might be posited about such realms is false. To rule out existential claims concerning metaphysical domains without a justification for such a ruling would be as arbitrary and bigoted as it would be to rule in existential claims concerning metaphysical domains without a justification for such a ruling.

Technical definitions of metaphysics are legion. The origin of the word is familiar to philosophers as a term invented as a title by an editor of Aristotle's lecture notes as taken down by students that followed upon his writings on physics, hence, metaphysics, or literally, after the physics. While many have therefore argued that this was only an editor's tool, the very fact that the writings came after the physics can be taken to possess some importance if one engages in a hermeneutics of textual placement. One may consider then that such issues to be taken up in metaphysics fall outside the bounds of physics, and in a sense, this is true, since most if not all metaphysical claims and issues are not ones which can be discovered or verified by scientific methods. This argument is a bit anachronistic and self-serving, since in

Aristotle's *Physics* many issues are discussed and methods of reasoning employed which would be considered metaphysical by today's standards.

Now, historically, of course, Aristotle considered some of what are now called metaphysical issues in his *Physics*, but hermeneutically this can be explained from the standpoint that in theoretical physics today certain borderline metaphysical issues are taken up (such as the limits or lack of limits of space, the origin of the cosmos and so on). It can still be maintained that Aristotle's *Metaphysics*, (which is not pure metaphysics either since it also contains arguments which would now belong to philosophy of logic and theology), is a mixture of what some would call ontology and others, metaphysics, depending upon the various definitions given to these terms. Aristotle himself used the words First Philosophy or Theology to label the concerns which he primarily addresses in these contexts, but such a self-labelling today would only serve to create more confusion since the term 'theology' is used to point to very different issues at the present time and 'First Philosophy' is a term which is not in use. Most of the commentators on Aristotle's works called 'First Philosophy', 'metaphysics'. According to Apel, since the seventeenth century, this was also called ontology.

In the main, the conclusion that may be drawn from the placement of Aristotle's *Metaphysics* with respect to the rest of his works, is that metaphysical issues somehow cannot be solved by the methods of science alone. In so doing, one defines metaphysics, at least provisionally, in a sense which corresponds with the popular definition of metaphysics, as that form of inquiry which concerns itself with issues that lie outside the province of empirical science as the limitations of scientific knowledge are understood today.

Someday, of course, the co-temporary version of science may alter. But, so long as science and scientists are bound to empirical discovery and justification of knowledge claims, most if not all metaphysical claims cannot be addressed from the standpoint of the empirical sciences. This does not mean that metaphysical claims are therefore not legitimate claims, although some famous early philosophers in analytic philosophy ruled out metaphysics as a valid discipline precisely for this reason. It is easy to understand why. If one cannot use scientific methods to ascertain truth-value, then what is to distinguish the claim of the metaphysician from that of the witch? But, this is a topic that falls under the subject heading of metaphysical method, which will be taken up below.

What of the relationship between the terms 'metaphysics' and 'ontology'? Some consider the term 'metaphysics' to be synonymous with the term 'ontology'; others make a distinction between metaphysics and ontology. It is not as if there were one "right" definition, but it is important in the use of a term to distinguish how it shall be used. The established usage of these two terms varies greatly among writers. This is the case regardless of what definition might be discovered in a dictionary or even a philosophical dictionary, as in Runes', *Dictionary of Philosophy.* Dictionary definitions are not legislative; they are only historical. A dictionary definition only records the uses a word has enjoyed in the past. It does not and cannot legislate how one should use the word in the future, or even if the past uses were justified or justifiable. A dictionary definition does have importance. But, in philosophical inquiry, its importance takes on a secondary status. This is why sometimes philosophers such as Whitehead and Heidegger coin new words and are reprimanded for their invention of strange sounding neologisms. Philosophers do this because they cannot find words for that which they wish to say.

One attempt to propose a distinction between the usages of the words 'ontology' and 'metaphysics' is to suggest that a concern with what exists may be taken to be the province of ontology (the study of being), and a concern with what really exists as opposed to what might appear to exist may be taken to be the province of metaphysics. This manner of forging a distinction is imperfect since existence, if constitutive of reality, is metaphysical. Thus, it is difficult to draw a clear distinction between ontology and metaphysics. Sometimes, the term 'metaphysics' is utilized when an existence is posited which transcends the means of scientific method to verify. In this present, respective work, the terms 'metaphysics' or 'metaphysical' will sometimes be employed to refer to the kind of truth which is known. Sometimes, the terms 'ontology' or 'ontological' will be employed to refer to that dimension of metaphysical truth that is constitutive of reality. Sometimes the term 'metaphysical' will be employed to refer to an argument as in Kant's sense of a metaphysical exposition that demonstrates an idea as *a priori.* Sometimes the term 'metaphysical' will be employed to refer to that ontological condition which provides the condition for the possibility of some epistemological truth being known. Sometimes, the term 'metaphysical' will refer to arguments, truths, ontological status and descriptions of reality that exceed the limits of scientific verification. Sometimes, the term 'ontological' will be employed to refer to metaphysical truths that possess existential status.

Some writers, such as R.G. Collingwood, consider that metaphysics should be a historical study concerned with what writers at a certain time period considered to be metaphysical. If one were to take up Collingwood's directive, then there would be no permanent metaphysical issues which all philosophers must address, but rather each age would develop its own metaphysical or anti-metaphysical positions. The Developmental view, discussed in fuller detail below, would see an interconnection between the view that metaphysics was strictly historicist and the view that there were Eternal Problems in Philosophy which remained the same through time irrespective of changes in history. In the Developmental view, the permanent issues would develop in history in part actualized by the metaphysicians themselves. This Developmental position falls in between and makes sense of the seemingly opposite purist 'Eternal Problems in Philosophy View', and a strictly historicist approach.

There are even tongue-in-cheek definitions that may contain a seed of truth whether or not they cohere with the philosopher's actual metaphysical practise. For example, one should be aware of F. H. Bradley's infamous definition of metaphysics as, '... the finding of bad reasons for what we believe upon instinct, but to find these reasons, is no less an instinct'.[1] It would be of value to meditate on this humorous definition and wonder if it does fit certain writers and perhaps even Bradley himself. In any case, jocular or not, this definition does imply something about metaphysics as an inquiry. What this definition implies about metaphysics is that whatever one feels about metaphysics, some or perhaps all people cannot keep from doing metaphysics, and this is also the conclusion that Kant reached in his first *Critique*. Kant, of course, wanted to leave metaphysics to the realm of faith, (as he defined metaphysical issues), but for some people, the desire or the need to create metaphysical systems is an impulse as difficult or impossible to restrain as the desire to possess metaphysical knowledge of certain things.[2] It is not altogether clear that these two desires or needs are to be identified with the desires or needs that are satisfied by the device of faith, although faith can supply answers which satisfy metaphysical needs or demands so long as such metaphysical needs or demands are not accompanied by a need to possess such answers on the grounds of knowledge.

There are overlapping disciplines such as theology, cosmology, cosmogony and theoretical physics. In cosmology, one is concerned with the cosmos as a whole, the origin, structure and workings of the universe. This differs from the domain of ontology which, in its common meaning, takes into account everything that there is and is not confined to the origin, structure and workings of the universe. In cosmogony, one is particularly concerned with the cosmos as an emanation of or creation by a Deity. In theoretical physics, there is an interest in the study of the very small (elementary particles) in addition to the study of the very large (cosmology). Of course, the application of these names is to some extent arbitrary. Some physicists posit realms of existence, or relationships to a Deity, or reflect upon issues of space and time in a way that is not very different from the practise of metaphysicians. It would be a mistake not to take account of their speculations simply because they are trained as physicists and not as philosophers. One philosopher who combined an expertise in both realms was Alfred North Whitehead.

While most philosophers have considered metaphysics as universal, some have considered only regional metaphysics to be valid. For example, some philosophers have thought that there could be a study of Pure Being as such. The most famous of these was, of course, Aristotle. Others have considered it legitimate to confine metaphysical inquiry to special realms such as the philosophy of man or the question of the self, or whether or not there is a G-d, or whether or not man possesses an immortal soul. It could be said that there are two different kinds of metaphysicians: universalists and regionalists. Of course, these two types can be compatible from one direction, but not vice-versa. The universalist can also be a regionalist, that is, can inquire into metaphysical regions, but the regionalist is not, by definition, a universalist.

Metaphysics, not epistemology, can be seen as the cornerstone of philosophy. During the eighteenth century, that part of the nineteenth century which fell under the influence of Kant, and the twentieth century, epistemology has been considered the center or the heart of philosophy. While in the present author's, *Space, Time and the Ethical Foundations*, the view that is to be presented will be that an absolute metaphysical/epistemological distinction is strictly speaking a pseudo-distinction, for the moment, metaphysics may be considered as the core of philosophy.

The emerging importance of metaphysics in philosophy may owe its origin to a reaction to the increasing control scientific knowledge has exerted over epistemology which itself is a residue of the history of the scientific critique of metaphysics. Another reason for the emergence of metaphysics is the fact that fashions change in philosophy just as they do in the lengths of skirts. Some of this development may owe its origin to the fact that the world is only now becoming more ready for metaphysics again, and some of this development may owe its origin to the fact that it is just now that a well founded metaphysics is appearing. But, it is an interesting and new development that metaphysics might now be becoming the new centerpiece of philosophy once more, and this marks an exciting beginning of a new era in philosophy.

It is important to reflect more deeply on the distinction between metaphysics and epistemology. Some consider that these are two separate sub-disciplines or branches of philosophy, and they are so treated in philosophy curricula. However, it may be that there are overlapping issues, and the possibility may be entertained that one cannot be done without the other. This question, too, can be taken as a metaphysical question. There are many questions considered to be epistemological questions, which can be treated as metaphysical questions, such as, 'what is the object of perception?' Is the obejct of perception a sense datum or a thing? What is the source of knowledge, is it intuition, inductive inference, deductive inference, none of the above, or all of the above? What is knowledge? These three questions are classical epistemological questions, but may also be considered as metaphysical questions.

When one reads a Platonic dialogue one cannot fail to notice that there are no self-dependent divisions of philosophical disciplines, since ethical questions necessarily imply epistemological questions, (as in *Meno*), and epistemological questions necessarily imply metaphysical ones, (as in *Republic*). In a sense, for Plato, one cannot be a philosopher without being a metaphysician, both from the standpoint that a philosopher has to know the whole of reality and thus the connections that obtain among all things, as well as reality as opposed to appearance (*Republic VI*, 485). Plato's version of the metaphysician straddles both the ontological and the metaphysical definitions.

One can also consider what can be labeled infra-philosophical metaphysics as metaphysical questions within each and every philosophical sub-discipline. Can one inquire into aesthetics without considering metaphysical questions such as the following: What is art? What is beauty? What is aesthetic experience? What is the art object? Can one attempt to construct a theory of knowledge without asking, what is truth? Can ethics be considered without considering, what is goodness? Can one inquire into the philosophy of man, without considering, what is the nature of man? All of these latter questions may be termed infra-philosophical metaphysical questions.

It seems that by asking the question, 'what is metaphysics?', one is inevitably moved in the direction of formulating answers or at least preliminary answers to the question. It seems that a further preliminary answer is that metaphysics must address the most basic or most fundamental question or questions that can be asked about something. In Platonic terms this is similar to asking the question, 'what is x?', or, 'what is the essence of x?' But, this answer still demands further refinement, because the answer that is desired, if it were to be considered as a metaphysical answer, must also possess some other characteristics. The answer must be universal, that is, obtain across time and across cultures. And the answer must also be in some important sense, necessary. It must be an answer that is inescapably true. Finally, the answer must relate to issues that are of significance to human beings. The issues must be substantive.

The task of defining metaphysics has not yet even properly begun. What has been set out can only be likened to the very first steps of a child. There are still important questions that remain. What is meant by necessity? Necessity for some will mean a kind of poetic necessity and not a logical necessity. Existentialists might consider that metaphysical necessity involves a kind of poetic experience. Mystics might consider that metaphysical necessity involves some kind of intuition given in a special state of mind or under very special circumstances. Religious metaphysicians might consider that metaphysics requires a kind of ultimate belief commitment. Or, there may be variations among these types as well. Poetic metaphysicians might consider that only an artistic element of taste is involved, not any kind of artistic necessity. Existentialists might say that the experiential component need not be necessary at all, but only dependent upon free choice. Every answer that one manages to discover only generates in turn an infinite set of new questions demanding answers with the same sense of urgency as did the original ones. The wider that one casts one's metaphysical net, the more elusive becomes the prey.

The budding metaphysician has marked out a difficult path to follow. Despite the fact that the time is now more ripe for the development of a new metaphysics, serious obstacles remain. If one employs an universalist framework, it will be countered that metaphysics is culture bound or that there is no metaphysics at all, that all truths and all frameworks of truth are relative. The advances of science and technology will be pointed to as evidence that a concern with metaphysical questions is retrograde. Given time, scientific advances will render most if not all metaphysical questions otiose. Advances in genetic engineering, for example, will possibly make immortality an empirical possibility. What possible relevance will there be in questions concerning the immortality of the soul or life after death?

If such worries seem premature, there are obstacles enough to make the life of the would-be metaphysician difficult. One of the most serious obstacles is that it may be that it is impossible to settle upon a definition of metaphysics in the first place. If a definition is insisted on before one proceeds, it may have to be allowed that in some sense that any definition elected is dependent upon some frame of reference or some philosophical system. Every attempt to define metaphysics is itself dependent upon a metaphysics, so that every definition of metaphysics as well as every metaphysical question is itself circular. This problem is what perhaps occasioned the development of system building in metaphysics, that is, the attempt to build a system that included everything within it. Whether or not one attempts to build a new metaphysical system, one must accept the fact that any definition of metaphysics that is posited is itself system or at least position dependent. But, this should not be a source of concern if it were to be recalled that definitions in philosophy only come at the end and not at the beginning of an inquiry. So long as one recalls this rule, one can stay out of trouble's way.[3] If through systematic metaphysics one finds that one's metaphysical inquiries form a systematic whole, whether a regional whole or a universal whole, this is a legitimate outcome. If one's inquiries culminate in the discovery that systematic relationships exist between the elements of one's inquiry, one has not thereby imposed a metaphysical system on the world.

It might be said, with Hegel, that philosophy is a circle and it does not matter where one begins. Every question will lead to another question until all questions are raised. From this perspective there is nothing wrong with beginning with definitions since it will not matter if one begins at the end since there is no real end to a circle. Since the twentieth century was so influenced by the need for definitions, if one now begins with a search for a definition, at the very least, such a beginning will point up the limitations of this approach to philosophy, and will also serve to demonstrate that questions cannot even be asked about metaphysics without the questioner becoming a metaphysician. In other words, one cannot begin to learn about metaphysics without doing metaphysics.

To what point has this inquiry progressed? Although, one can hardly be said to have learned how to walk, some preliminary conclusions can be drawn which can and must be amended in the sequel. A preliminary definition of metaphysics may be taken to be: that discipline which addresses the question of what is reality, and in so doing demands that an essential sub-set of one's answers consist of necessary and universal knowledge. In a later inquiry, such a statement must be qualified to include knowledge that is analogically related to universal and necessary knowledge. But, it is important not to underemphasize the role of questions, and thus to be attentive not to confine the definition of metaphysics to the kinds of answers that are being sought. This is, of course, not the final answer. This is only a very broad, generic definition.

The tentative answer that is suggested above requires further explanation, and without such explanation is at best only a computer without a program. The context of answers given and questions raised is of great importance. If, without explanations, one appears to speak too generally, one will be accused of making context blind statements. Questions of culture, questions of hermeneutics, questions of scope, questions of what kind of necessity is referred to, and questions of what constitutes metaphysical knowledge will all have to be considered more comprehensively before any definitions offered will possess any significant meaning. *A definition of metaphysics is obviously not a sentence long.*

It might well be that in the end the result would not appear to be greatly different from what is stated above. But, metaphysics is not defined only by the character of the *answers* at which one arrives, but, as has been emphasized, by the nature of the *questions* that one raises. Indeed, metaphysics may be defined by the special kind of *questioning* that leads one to a certain kind of answers with which one will ultimately and only be satisfied. It may well be that it is only after a long, sensitive and arduous process of questioning that one is ready to appreciate an answer that may have been available at the outset. Diotema's ladder of love in the *Symposium* may be extended to be a ladder of understanding. It is only after the right kind and the right order of dialectical purification that one can attend and understand the mysteries of metaphysics. *And it is only after reaching an understanding of the answers that one can understand the questions themselves.* Metaphysical knowledge only emerges at the end of a process and at the same time includes the process within it as part of what it knows.

This provisional attempt at defining metaphysics is only a picture or diagram of metaphysics. It remains to find the reality of which the previous set of statements is the picture. This metaphor is different in intention from Wittgenstein's notion of picturing. It is a new suggestion. It is only meant as a means of suggesting that whatever definition is posited as a definition of metaphysics, the definition is only a guide to inquiry. One only understands the beginning of philosophy at the end. This is of course a paradox. One must begin at the beginning to reach the end, but one cannot understand the beginning (properly) until the end. But, the paradox is not something that should put a stop to attempting to understand metaphysics. It is only meant to alert one to the fact that metaphysics, like other realms of philosophy, is not learned step by step, but rather in quantum leaps. So, one must be patient and wait for some quantum leaps to occur. By the time the end is reached, one will be able to start once more at the beginning and understand the beginning for the first time.

In a way, Hegel's definition of philosophy as a circle is correct; in another way, the circle should be seen as one which is three dimensional since knowledge grows deeper and deeper inwards as well as more thoroughly and intricately interconnected. Similarly, the model of the circle as a circle that also deepens inwards is also an answer to the problem of the hermeneutic circle, a topic that will be considered later on. The so-called problem of the hermeneutic circle is that one cannot escape one's starting points. But, in philosophy and especially in metaphysics, the problem that one cannot escape one's starting point or points is not a problem, because the destination that one desires to reach is deeper and deeper inside one's questions, and not simply laterally or horizontally in knowledge outside of one's questions. In philosophy, one is not trying to escape one's starting points as much as one is involved in becoming more deeply aware and understanding of them, and in what presuppositions one's starting points themselves are rooted. In a certain sense, the study of metaphysics is the hermeneutic circle because the unceasing raising of the question 'why?' must at some point lead to a metaphysical question. The human condition is a reflection of the hermeneutic circle, and the most fundamental human metaphysical condition is one of questioning.

The good metaphysician is both one who teaches how to continue asking questions, and also one who teaches how to reach a point where the questions can be shown to be answered, and in so doing teaches how one may reach the end of the hermeneutic circle. There is a certain resemblance between this and the philosophy of Ch' an or

Zen Buddhism. Metaphysical knowledge is a perfect balance between question and answer. Of course, that balance is a delicate balance, and once it is disrupted, the questions will emerge once again. The metaphysician's task is both to understand the balance between question and answer, and to see how that balance can be achieved: that is, both to understand the nature of metaphysics and to do metaphysics.

Notes

1. F. H. Bradley, *Appearance and Reality*, Oxford: Oxford University Press, Ninth Impression, 1930, preface, p. x.
2. Kant of course attempts to restore metaphysics in a different sense, as the metaphysics of experience but his attitude concerning traditional metaphysical concerns is to remove them from the province of pure reason.
3. In a discussion of Kant's theory of definitions, Lewis White Beck remarks that, 'Thus (if he is fortunate), the philosopher ends where the mathematician begins, to wit, with the indefinable elementary concepts and definitions of the concepts given at the beginning. Definitions in philosophy, therefore, are not the conditions of knowledge; they are what we hope to conclude with, not the raw material with which we begin'. Molte S. Gram (ed.), *Kant: Disputed Questions*, Chicago: Quadrangle Books, 1967, p. 224. In Kant's words, 'In short, the definition in all its precision and clarity ought, in philosophy, to come rather at the end than at the beginning of our enquiries' (B759). It is fitting that Kant's own treatment of definitions occurs near to the end of his first *Critique*.

2 A Typology of Metaphysics

One approach to the study of metaphysics is to divide up metaphysicians or metaphysics into different types. While the following list of types is by no means logically exhaustive, it is of interest to take a brief journey through an assortment of the different varieties of metaphysics that are possible which provide the greatest contrast or similarity to the metaphysics of the present work. Such a journey may be of assistance to the reader in understanding how or where the present work fits or does not fit into this spectrum of types. It also may be instructive in pointing out how or why other, competing approaches have not been chosen and why they represent inadvisable routes to take.

It must be borne in mind that each type is described in only the scantiest of terms and the purpose of this discussion is not to do full justice to each type, but rather to give the reader a bird's eye view of the range of different possible types for the sole pedagogical purpose of better enabling the reader to be aware of the similarity, difference and the distinctiveness of the respective work of the present author in relation to the work of the philosophical past, present and future. It is hoped that such a brief outline will serve to avoid confusing the respective philosophy of the present work from similar seeming approaches. While it is difficult to tell the dog from the wolf, it does not follow that the two species are identical.

The Metaphysics of the Mystic

Mystical metaphysics may include some of the other types to be discussed below within it as some of these types are overlapping. To put it briefly and far too broadly, mystical metaphysics takes both the subject matter and the mode of verification of metaphysics to lie outside the sphere of ordinary empirical experience but allows that the subject matter and the mode of verification to be within the realm of the mystical experience. The mystical experience is both the identification of the proper subject matter of metaphysics, and is the necessary key to open the door to the work of mystical metaphysics proper. Without the mystical experience one can neither come into contact with the realm of metaphysics, nor can one further the work of metaphysics, not to speak of verifying the truth claims that have already been made.

The commonplace critique of the mystical is basically that such an experience is beyond the scope of the ordinary person's capacity to enjoy, and, as a result, is considered suspect as a genuine state that can be experienced. Similarly, since there are no clear-cut indicators of how to achieve the mystical state, nor how to identify if one is in it, and what criteria apply within it, (such as the normal criteria that one might apply, e.g., logical consistency or empirical justification), many, if not most philosophers discount mystical claims. The major fear is that if the mystical were to be admitted as a legitimate state, then, 'anything goes', or, any claim can be valid so long as it is experienced within a mystical state. The problem with this critique of the mystical is that it is made without a close analysis of the major claims of most if not all major mystical traditions, which, upon analysis, disclose a common if not identical group of core truth discoveries. Even to acknowledge that this is so, however, does not make the mystical claims more acceptable to the non-mystical philosophers, since to verify even this common core of "truths" requires that one experience the mystical state, which, to the non-mystic philosopher, by its very nature, already disqualifies any truths so discovered, since any putative truths are only capable of being discovered while inside the privileged and perhaps inaccessible mystical state. Why ordinary experience is to be taken as the criterion of truth or of valid discoveries, and not mystical experience, is not itself ever justified by the non-mystical philosopher. However, since mystical truths by their very nature cannot be experienced within the ordinary state of experience, the truth claims of mystical philosophers (or perhaps more fairly labeled, philosophers of mysticism) are ruled out of court.

Theistic Metaphysics; Theistic, Religious Metaphysics; Non-Theistic, Doctrinal, Religious Metaphysics; Non-Theistic, Non-Doctrinal, Religious Metaphysics

Theistic metaphysics, as distinct from theistic, religious metaphysics, (although these types often overlap in certain respects), may be defined as that type of metaphysics that posits the absolute presupposition of some form of a metaphysical conception of G-d or occupies itself with the task of proving such a metaphysical type of G-d to be required by the system of metaphysics. It could be argued that theistic metaphysics could be further distinguished from theistic, religious metaphysics by stating that theistic metaphysics requires that the Deity is a metaphysical condition of the system and but does not necessitate a belief in the Deity or worship of the Deity. However, since theistic, religious metaphysical systems of the Western Middle Ages required both belief in the Deity and required the Deity as a metaphysical condition, such a distinction is difficult to make. Generally, theistic metaphysics and theistic, religious metaphysics will to a greater or lesser extent occupy themselves with the specification of the characteristics or qualities of the Deity as a prime concern. The category of non-theistic, doctrinal, religious metaphysics as distinct from non-theistic, non-doctrinal, religious metaphysics may be defined as that type of metaphysics which requires the belief in and subsequent analysis of various belief systems such as the number and type of heavens, reincarnations or dogmas; i.e., beliefs in the efficacy of types of prayer, chanting, meditations, religious observances, holiness of certain relics, books, places, rituals in the absence of a Deity. Both theistic, religious metaphysics and non-theistic, doctrinal, religious metaphysics can be distinguished from non-theistic, non-doctrinal, religious metaphysics in that non-theistic, non-doctrinal, religious metaphysics may not primarily or at all require belief structures, practises, or dogmas of any kind. Non-theistically and non-doctrinally oriented religious metaphysics may consider that speculation upon the nature or qualities of Divinity, an afterlife, or belief in the authority of any scripture, or revelation as either being impossible or inappropriate. With these classifications in mind, one might consider that Theravada Buddhism in general fits under the definition of non-theistic, non-doctrinal, religious metaphysics while Ch' an or Zen Buddhism in particular, rightly understood, fits under the definition of non-theistic, non-doctrinal, religious metaphysics.

Theistic, religious metaphysics had its heyday in the time of the Middle Ages in Western philosophy, and reached its height in the philosophies of St. Augustine and St. Thomas Aquinas. In fact, Medieval philosophy can be characterized as a series of attempts to prove the existence and define the nature of the Supreme Being. Surprisingly, derivatives of theistic metaphysics survived into the twentieth century with such figures as Alfred North Whitehead and Charles Hartshorne. The process philosophy of Alfred North Whitehead requires a unique, metaphysical concept of G-d for the metaphysical system to function and provides a description of that Deity. Hartshorne, initially one of Whitehead's students (in addition to having been a student of Husserl's), was proud to show to his graduate students in a graduate seminar on Whitehead in which the present, respective author was indeed fortunate to participate, a letter which Whitehead had written to him. Later, Hartshorne was to become one of the present, respective author's doctoral advisors. Hartshorne's metaphysics is equally dependent upon a metaphysical concept of Divinity, and his own radical definition of the nature of that Divinity. Both of these major philosophies of the twentieth century are examples of theistic while non-religious metaphysics, although the theology is very different from that of the philosophers of the Middle Ages.

Mystical metaphysics must not be confused with theistic metaphysics, although in some instances the two can combine in a single metaphysics, for example, in the case of St. Bonaventura. There is also the case of Heidegger to be considered. In 1991, in a private conversation with the respective author in Breitnau in the Black Forest, Max Müller, Heidegger's last surviving colleague who was for many years the Ordinarius for Philosophy at the Freiburg University and who claimed to be the only one who stood by Heidegger in the time of his disgrace and who assisted Heidegger in regaining his post from which he had been deposed, argued that Heidegger's philosophy was a theology. Heidegger's philosophy does not seem to fit the definition of theistic metaphysics introduced above. What did Max Müller mean? Was he suggesting that Heidegger's philosophy was tantamount to a non-theistic theology in which Being or Nothingness in certain respects usurped the position of the Deity in traditional theistic metaphysics? Müller did put forth the explicit suggestion that because of the fervour with which Heidegger presented his ideas as a solution to the problems of German society at his time (as he, Heidegger, perceived them) that his philosophy took on theological proportions. It may be that in this sense Müller meant that Heidegger's philosophy functioned in much the same sense as the new religions do today and thus religious metaphysics might have been a better term to describe Heidegger's project than theological metaphysics, but Müller chose theology as a term of description. In addition to the fact that Müller interpreted Heidegger's philosophy as a theology, he conveyed the impression that Heidegger himself perceived of his philosophy as a theology. On another note, Müller also reminisced that the night before the American occupation, Heidegger and his wife took down the pictures of Nazi heroes that decorated the walls of their home. Such was the practise of the times. But as Levinas has noted, while one can forgive others, it is difficult to forgive Heidegger.

Hartshorne would not have any sympathy for mystical metaphysics, although his philosophy as well as the philosophy of his teacher, Whitehead, both depend upon their own brand of theistic metaphysics. Hartshorne in particular seems to place special stress upon a very rigorous logical and analytical approach to metaphysics. In this respect, Hartshorne's metaphysics, while theistic, according to this classification scheme, is also a species of rationalist metaphysics, (to be discussed below), since there is no special mystical experience which is required for the acceptance of Hartshorne's metaphysics.

Rationalist Metaphysics

Rationalist metaphysicians rely exclusively or nearly so upon the use of rational arguments to advance the cause of their metaphysical systems or definitions of metaphysics. The most famous examples of rationalist metaphysicians were of course the rationalists of the seventeenth century in Western philosophy such as Descartes, Leibniz and Spinoza. Of course, the label is misleading when one considers such philosophers more closely. Spinoza's intellectual love of G-d can hardly be considered under the category of 'rationalist' any more than Descartes' discovery of the truth of the *cogito*.

Many other metaphysicians, moreover, have also relied upon the power of rational thought including Idealist metaphysicians such as F. H. Bradley and McTaggart who are often classified as neo-Hegelian philosophers. It is not entirely misleading to maintain that even though Bradley and McTaggart shared some of the same assumptions and methodological proclivities of Hegel, that they strongly favored the road of rigorous logical deduction to metaphysical conclusions, whereas

Hegel did employ other forms of persuasive techniques such as the poetic, edifying and transformative use of language.

It will be recalled that Aquinas thought that there was a unity of truth such that nearly all truths could be reached equally by reason or faith. Aquinas excepted three major tenets which could not be reached by reason and required a pure act of faith. But, the principle of the parallelism between different paths in reaching metaphysical truths with which this present work is concerned is not dependent upon these exceptions which are unique to Christian theology. In this present work of metaphysics, if it were to be found to merit such a label, Aquinas' principle might receive an altered formulation such that a natural unity of truth must exist in order that the truths of metaphysics can be experienced within a phenomenological experience (as yet to be defined), but that such truths would also have to be coherent with a rational and scientific account of the world.

The Metaphysics of Appearance and Reality

A very classic type of metaphysics is the type that contrasts two worlds, a world of reality and a world of appearance. Plato can be taken to be the archetype of appearance-reality metaphysics in the West. Besides the classical appearance versus reality dichotomy, there can be other variations of appearance-reality metaphysics. For Kant, the reality behind appearances cannot be known, or at least it is not supposed to be known via the categories, so that it could be argued that appearances assume the importance of reality in classical metaphysics although this is not a consistent position that Kant adheres to throughout his first *Critique*. Kant's central arguments such as his Transcendental Deductions are designed to show how his categories are necessary for knowledge of phenomena not noumena. For Hegel, appearances are instantiations of reality, and are not opposed to reality, but are the only way in which reality can manifest itself.

Reality and appearance metaphysics, then, do not have to involve a dichotomy between reality and appearance. In Hegel, there is a collusion between reality and appearances; in Kant, insofar as attention is directed to the world of phenomena, appearances constitute the world of reality with which one should properly be concerned. In another sense, as will be discussed in the sequel, things-in-themselves are presupposed as realities - despite Kant's strictures against such an interpretation of the *ding-an-sich* - and in this case, appearances cannot be said to usurp the function of reality. For a rigorous philosopher of epistemological direct realism, empirical things (which are appearances for Kant) would be directly perceived, such that there is not a separate perception of a general realm of appearances. It could therefore be said that epistemological direct realism is not a species of appearance-reality metaphysics since the contrast between reality and appearance is lost.

For phenomenalists, appearances, on the contrary, are all that there are, such that there is no other reality to contrast with the realm of appearance. For this reason neither epistemological direct realism nor phenomenalism can be considered as species of reality-appearance metaphysics since one of the terms collapses into the other. With epistemological direct realism, especially in versions which are naïve or simple, there is no general sphere of appearances with which to contend. With phenomenalism, the apparent other of epistemological direct realism, there is no sphere of a "reality" with which to contend, since all that there is is what appears.

The Metaphysics of Transcendental Conditions

Kant employs transcendental exposition and transcendental deduction (in his sense of these terms) to establish what he considers to be transcendental conditions, a tradition which in the present time has been brilliantly revived by such a distinguished figure as Karl-Otto Apel with respect to the use of the argument for transcendental conditions, although in this case, applied to discourse. To limit discussion to a necessary minimum, it can be said that for Kant transcendental exposition explains concepts as principles, which form the possibility of other *a priori* synthetic knowledge. Kant also employs the language of metaphysical exposition that for him demonstrates concepts as *a priori*. It appears to follow from his employment of metaphysical expositions that the concepts, which are demonstrated as *a priori*, are at the same time proved as necessary for possible experience. For example, Kant provides what he calls metaphysical expositions to prove that space is an *a priori* concept. As every reader of Kant knows, his mode of proof assumes the form of demonstrating that space cannot be learned empirically. In the course of his arguments it becomes obvious that for Kant outer experience would not itself be possible without the employment of the *a priori* concept of space. Hence, in the course of his metaphysical exposition of the concept of space, while perhaps Kant does not employ this vocabulary, space is also shown to be a "transcendental condition" of outer experience. It is interesting that while Kant himself inveighs strongly against metaphysics as it has been practiced by certain rationalist metaphysicians, he himself makes use of what he calls transcendental and metaphysical expositions. The critique of Kantian transcendental conditions is that one must assume the reality of that which Kant takes as "the experience of all subject knowers". If this experience is itself illusory, it is not at all clear that the transcendental conditions are conditions of anything at all. But, this only shows that Kantian metaphysics is perhaps not thoroughgoing enough or is, ironically, too pre-Critical, not that the argument from transcendental conditions or metaphysical expositions which establish transcendental conditions do not qualify as metaphysical types.

The Metaphysics of Experience

Once again Kant can be held up as a paragon of this metaphysical type. Paton's famous commentary on Kant was actually entitled, *Kant's Metaphysic of Experience*. In the argument above, Kant employs the term 'metaphysics' to describe the style or type of exposition he renders. However, the ultimate products of his arguments are for Kant the necessary concepts without which one could not have the experience that one does have. This would then appear to be the origin of the title of Paton's commentary. Again, the key problem for Kantian metaphysics (or metaphysical exposition) is the validity of this experience which is accepted for the most part without raising the fundamental Cartesian question about its reality. In the very few sections of the first *Critique* where Kant raises the issue of the reality of the empirical world, his treatment amounts to question begging as in his 'Refutation of Idealism'. But, this does not disqualify Kant as a metaphysician. It only points to the difficulties in attempting to do metaphysics from a strictly epistemological standpoint. Kant, of course, is not setting out to do metaphysics, but in certain sections of his first *Critique*, it cannot be said that he is doing anything but metaphysics of a certain type.

Revisionary and Descriptive Metaphysics

These terms were made famous by P.F. Strawson in his book, *Individuals*. Descriptive metaphysics would propose to set out the structure of reality in the way that it appears to the metaphysician without altering it in any way. Revisionary metaphysics would propose to alter the framework of reality in the very act of description. While it is difficult to imagine any metaphysics that has been purely descriptive, it is conceivable that one could say that Aristotle's metaphysics was of this variety. However, Whitehead, who would argue strongly that process and not substance was reality, would say that Aristotle was revising reality and not describing it. Philosophers who would have more obvious revisionary tendencies would be those like Leibniz who would substitute another reality for that which one previously would have thought to have been reality. It is difficult, however, to accept the notion of a descriptive metaphysics even when it is so self-described. In the approach taken in this present work, it will be argued that the revisionary-descriptive distinction is not a sound distinction, and that all revision involves some description and that all description involves some revision. The terms 'prescriptive' or 'normative' can also be used in place of the term 'revisionary'.

The Metaphysics of Absolute Presuppositions

The notion of Absolute Presuppositions is associated with the work of R.G. Collingwood who set out a brilliant description of his definition of metaphysics in his *An Essay on Metaphysics*. According to Collingwood, the work of the metaphysician consisted of exhibiting what absolute presuppositions had to be made in any historical epoch. While it is difficult to take exception to Collingwood's definition of metaphysics, Walsh in his book, *Metaphysics*, argues that the practise of metaphysicians was never confined to this, as metaphysicians frequently wished to do more than simply exhibit existing presuppositions. According to Walsh, they wished to argue that certain presuppositions were absolute and others were not. Collingwood could, of course, simply argue that whatever set of presuppositions were being argued for were those which that metaphysician found to be absolute, and the set which were truly absolute, (for at least his own historical epoch - although Collingwood does not clarify whether or not his own metaphysics is historicist), could be discovered by the proper application of metaphysical reasoning such as he himself, for example, practiced in his *The New Leviathan*. Rather than Walsh's critique, a critique that might have more force would be to inquire if the idea of Absolute Presuppositions encompasses or allows for metaphysical insight. It could be that the limitation of the idea of Absolute

Presuppositions lies in its being a variation, albeit an extremely subtle one, of conceiving of metaphysics as being concerned with statements or propositions of a certain type, (in this case of presuppositions which are themselves propositions not yet or not usually propounded, which underlie scientific or other propositions), and thus not of having to do with the obtaining of certain types of insights.

Hegelian-Dialectical Metaphysics or Developmental Metaphysics

While it might seem arbitrary to select Hegel's type of metaphysics for special attention, the emphasis need not be placed on the Idealist character of Hegel's thought, but may be placed on the dialectical process. In what may be termed Hegelian-Dialectical metaphysics, instead of focusing on a set of metaphysical concepts, one emphasizes the relation between those concepts so that any further concepts to be discovered must bear a dialectical relationship to the previous ones. In this way, all new metaphysical ideas must bear some relationship to previous metaphysical ideas, whether or not the relationship is dialectical in Hegel's exact sense of that term. In fact, the term 'developmental' may be preferable to 'dialectical' but the concept of development is strongly influenced by the concept of the dialectic. As will be noted below, even 'developmental' is not a competely suitable adjective since at times the process may appear to regress rather than to develop although the regression may nonetheless constitute an advance given the circumstances of the historical epoch. The key to this type is the understanding of the role of past, present and future philosophers as collaborating over the centuries in producing whatever metaphysics is considered to be the best metaphysics of the day, as over against a strictly Absolutist type of metaphysics which would appear to have no relationship to previous, present or future philosophers or philosophies. For Hegel himself and perhaps for Hegelians, the process of the dialectical progress might have appeared to have come to its culmination in the thought of Hegel, but this idiosyncrasy of thought need not be retained. In the next chapter, this type of metaphysics will undergo further refinement.

The Metaphysics of Hartshorne

It is of especial interest to examine the metaphysics of Hartshorne, who, at the present writing, enjoying the wonderful age of over one hundred years, may certainly be perceived as the dean of American metaphysics. The present, respective author was privileged to be his student. For Hartshorne, who appears to be Leibnizian in this regard, a metaphysical truth is defined as a truth which will be true in all possible worlds.[1] In this respect, Hartshorne ties the notion of metaphysics to the notion of conceivability rather than to the notion of phenomenological verifiability as is presented herein. From the standpoint of the present work, the notion of whether a metaphysical truth is true in all possible worlds is either unanswerable - as it transcends experience - or it is arbitrary if it utilizes the criterion of possibility in this world to legislate what is possible in all other worlds.

If one veers away from Leibniz's/Hartshorne's fascination with conceivability as a criterion for truth in metaphysics, and heads toward phenomenological certification, then the issue as to whether metaphysical truths are true in all possible worlds becomes immaterial. From the phenomenological standpoint, the notion of other worlds is inadmissible. One may be free to conjecture about other worlds, but such conjecture is not part of phenomenological knowledge.

Similarities between Hartshorne's and the Present View

Hartshorne accepts that metaphysical truths must be verifiable, and only insists upon a wider notion of verifiability than that which applies to science.[2] Such a view is similar to that of the present work, in that it is the verifiability of particular propositions that becomes important and fundamental instead of the need to appraise entire philosophical systems for their coherence or completeness. If one employs the criteria of the comparative coherence and completeness of metaphysical systems, one could argue that the "truth" or "falsity" of one's metaphysics rests upon whether one's system offers a more total and comprehensive system of explanation than other systems, or whether one's system includes others inside of it and adds its truths to them - or shows itself to actually understand and fulfill the limited truths of the other systems. But, this, so it would seem, must await the exposition of an entire satisfactory system. And, even then, there is no guarantee that the most coherent, complete and inclusive system nonetheless is a faithful portrait of reality. It may be the case that the metaphysical approach or method that tends to yield both a greater number of and more significant individual metaphysical truths is a preferred approach.

In Hartshorne's case, individual metaphysical propositions become important again. In the case of the present work, all metaphysical truth in the strict sense consists of the truths of individual metaphysical cognitions. To think that metaphysical truth resides in systems is to commit the fallacy of misplaced abstractness. One cannot or should not, however, confuse a metaphysical system with a systematic metaphysical methodology.

For Hartshorne, verifiability resides in the meaningfulness or lack of meaningfulness of a metaphysical utterance. For the present view, verifiability is connected to how one becomes aware of the truthfulness (in this context, not the meaningfulness) of a metaphysical utterance. For Hartshorne, the truthfulness of the metaphysical proposition is discovered in the discovery that its opposite is logically inconceivable or the fact that one cannot empirically discover a counterexample. In the present view, the truthfulness of the first order metaphysical proposition is discovered in the very act of its being perceived as universally and necessarily true in the epistemological act of understanding it. In contrast, for Hartshorne, it is important to maintain a distinction between 'formulations of metaphysical truth and the truth itself'.[3] This again shows the tie that Hartshorne's metaphysics has with the traditional metaphysics against which Kant applied his critique.

In the phenomenological approach taken herein by the present author, the very notion of metaphysical truth (of the first order) is discovered in the act of understanding it. For phenomenological metaphysics, the distinction between epistemological and metaphysical truth is blurred. For Hartshorne, metaphysics is still an attempt to describe reality as it exists in itself. In this sense, Hartshorne's metaphysics is pre-Critical.

A Comparison between Specific Metaphysical Truth Claims in Hartshorne's and in the Present Work

It would be of interest to see what would happen if one examined from the standpoint of the present approach one or two putative individual metaphysical truths taken from Hartshorne's system. For example, one may take the proposition 'something exists' which Hartshorne presents as a metaphysical truth since, for Hartshorne, it is impossible to state its opposite coherently. From the point of view of the present work,

Hartshorne's argument that it is conceptually impossible to deny that 'something exists' represents a confusion of linguistic and conceptual orders with the ontological order. The linguistic unstatability and/or the conceptual incomprehensibility of the contrary of an existential proposition are no guarantee of the truth of the existential proposition. Reality may or may not precisely or comprehensively conform to either the limits of language or the limits of comprehensibility.

Furthermore, 'something exists' is a contingent truth. Whether or not it is possible in language or in thought to state or think that 'nothing could exist' is irrelevant to the possibility that nothing could exist. That 'there might have been nothing' is not a 'fine example of what Wittgenstein called "language idling"'.[4] In many remarkable ways, Hartshorne's metaphysics is very Leibnizian. (The present, respective author was privileged to attend Hartshorne's seminar on Leibniz and Spinoza). Leibniz thought that the question, 'why is there something rather than nothing at all?', was a metaphysical question requiring a metaphysical answer. From the present standpoint, the fact that there is something is purely circumstantial. That there might have been nothing is an empirical possibility, not a metaphysical one.

Even if one were to consider that the order in the Universe makes it unlikely that there is no Divine purpose, there is nothing incompatible with a belief in Theism and the fact of the existence of something (however trivial, such as flotsam or jetsam) which would not necessarily require a Divine origin. That there could have been nothing until or unless a Divinity considered that human creation was something significant is a different standpoint from the standpoint that the existence of anything at all required a Divine origin. For Plato, the Demiurge works with pre-existent materials. Theism does not need to be identified with creation *ex nihilo*.

For Hartshorne, it is logically impossible to deny that something exists for the denial would appear to require the existence of something. This account is less precise and less persuasive than that of Descartes and Augustine who argue that denial requires the existence of a denier, not simply 'something' in the abstract. In any event, the case of whether or not it is logically impossible to deny the existence of something is not relevant to the possibility that at some point, either past or future, it might have been or might be the case that nothing exists and yet there could be no one to either assert or deny the existence of something. The fact that someone exists now to assert or deny that something exists is a contingent fact and nothing significant follows from this concerning the metaphysical status of 'something exists'. All that follows from the statement of 'something exists' is that the assertion or denial of this statement requires some kind of existence, hence the statement implies existence. But, the existence implied by the statement is only a contingent, empirical existence, and not a metaphysical one. And, the necessity of the statement depends upon the contingent existence of the statement maker.

In the point of view being presented in this work, the closest analogue to 'something exists' is 'consciousness exists'. From the standpoint presented herein, Hartshorne's abstract 'something' is simply a *cognoscendum* included in consciousness and thus 'something' is hardly a primordial or even a primitive datum. Even if Hartshorne did not intend the abstract 'something' to be abstract and meant rather that it should always be instantiated as a concrete particular, nonetheless, this concrete particular would also always be embedded in consciousness, and would in no sense be a primordial or primitive datum. From the point of view that 'something' was a concrete particular, there would be no necessity in any concrete particular existing, and thus there would be no metaphysical necessity that this or that concrete particular would have to exist. The existence of any concrete particular could in no sense represent an ultimate datum, that is, a datum that could not not be and without which nothing else could be.

If the 'something' represented simply the abstract possibility of some concrete particular or another existing, and did not represent any concrete particular, then to say that 'something' would always exist would be to commit the fallacy of misplaced abstractness. For 'something' in the sense of an abstract possibility could not and never does exist. By definition, possibility is not actuality, even in Hartshorne's own terms. Furthermore, the logical impossibility of denying an abstraction coherently still does not entail that that abstraction or, (what would make more sense - its concrete representative), existed. To think this is to think that reality must conform to the laws of logic, and there is no reason to assume that this must be the case.

From the point of view of the present, respective work, the criterion of metaphysical truth is not that its opposite is self-contradictory to state or think, but simply that its affirmation is inescapably true. First order metaphysical truths in the present, respective approach are one and all necessary truths in their certification and ontologically contingent in their existence. For Hartshorne, metaphysical truths must be unconditional and existential.[5]

From the present point of view, metaphysical truths are incontrovertible within phenomenological consciousness, but there is no necessity either that the content of the phenomenological consciousness must consist of currently discovered content or that phenomenological consciousness itself must exist.

All that is maintained at the outset of the present work is that phenomenological consciousness is the primary datum. That is all that is asserted and all that one needs to assert as an inital necessary truth of metaphysics. In a strict sense, it is not an assertion except as a by-product, since its reality arises from its discovery, not from its status as an assertion. But, this distinction must be attended to later. What can be stressed is that from the phenomenological standpoint, the criteria of universality of apprehension and the epistemic certainty that attends apprehension are the most apposite criteria of first order metaphysical truth. If existence means something more than that which is an object of phenomenological consciousness, then existence as a category of necessary first order metaphysical truth is inappropriate.

From the phenomenological standpoint, one begins with experience and seeks to find the most ultimate datum within experience. Whether experience itself must exist in the first place is not a question that is decidable from the phenomenological standpoint, and its decidability is both irrelevant and incapable of verification. To begin with the self-imposition of the satisfaction of such criteria - such as the legislated impossibility of the non-existence of experience - is to begin from a weak standpoint in metaphysics. If rationalistic metaphysics is construed as taking logical possibility as a criterion of what can exist, then, it is this kind of metaphysics which Kant quite rightly railed against. However, rationalism may perhaps be credited as one of the inspirations for the writing of his first *Critique*, i.e., the provocation of his criticism of the powers of reason alone to discover truths about reality. In this respect, one must be grateful for the historical existence of rationalist metaphysics.

What is important to note is that the criticism to which rationalist metaphysics is liable is not necessarily a criticism that applies to any and all metaphysics whatsoever. The phenomenological standpoint carries its own source of correctability within itself without making the further assumption that reality must be rational or that what is rational must be real. That Hartshorne appears to be applying Hegel's criterion of the relationship between logic and reality as a criterion of metaphysical truth may seem surprising but may nonetheless be true.

When considering the issue of metaphysical truth from the phenomenological standpoint, no assumption is to be made concerning the relationship between logic and reality. If any relationship between logic and reality is to be drawn, it will be drawn only after one departs from the phenomenological standpoint and considers the ontological conditions for metaphysical truth. But any such conditions are transcendental conditions and are not to be assumed as existing without reference to being conditions for truths which are independently established as truths.

Categorial Contrast

The area of categorial contrast is another area where Hartshorne's scheme and the present one can be fruitfully compared so as to see the contrast between traditional metaphysics and phenomenological metaphysics. For Hartshorne, polar contrasts are logically irreducible.[6] Each polar contrast requires the other for its very meaning. But, in the present work, as will be discovered, polar contrasts require different levels of interpretation.

For example, in Hartshorne's scheme, the absolute and the relative are correlatives. In the present work, when one is considering the meaning of the relative from the standpoint of the relative, the absolute is implied; when one is considering the meaning of the absolute from the standpoint of the absolute, however, it must be remembered that the relative is not implied. Thus, the relation of absolute to relative is only asymmetrically relative, not correlative. While this might appear opaque or even untrue, a simple example will suffice to make its meaning clear. Consciousness is the absolute term; object is the relative term. From the standpoint of an object, there must be consciousness; from the standpoint of consciousness (despite Husserl), there need not be an object. An object cannot exist (phenomenologically) without consciousness; consciousness can exist (phenomenologically) without an object. All objects are relative to a consciousness; consciousness does not exist relative to objects. The relativity of the relation is only one-way, or asymmetrical.[7]

From another level, the entire relationship of relative to absolute only exists from the standpoint of the relative. From the absolute standpoint, there is no relative standpoint (there is no absolute standpoint either as the entire concept of a standpoint can only emerge from a relative standpoint). This might appear to be a trick, but the fact is that even the concept of the absolute is a distinction made from the relative side. The absolute does not describe itself as absolute.

Hartshorne's 'Principle of Asymmetrical Relations' is a correct principle, but not for the reasons that he has given and not in the sense in which he intends. For Hartshorne, the asymmetry (though conceptually symmetrical) is ontologically biased in favour of the concrete. In the present work, the asymmetry is phenomenologically biased toward the positive term, rather than the privative term. The concrete-abstract distinction is not relevant in phenomenological awareness since all phenomenological awareness is particular and universal at once.

The entire issue of relations is resolved differently in this work than in the two options presented in classical metaphysics. In classical metaphysics, generally speaking, one is either an extreme monist, in which case all relations are internal, or an extreme pluralist, in which case, all relations are external. In phenomenological metaphysics, all relations are internal from the standpoint of the lower or privative standpoint, and external from the higher or positive standpoint, when the higher or positive standpoint is viewed from the standpoint of the lower or privative standpoint, and non-existent when the lower or privative standpoint is viewed from the perspective of the higher or positive standpoint (which is a non-existent standpoint).[8]

Degrees of Metaphysical Truth

The ordering of metaphysical truths in the four classes which are specified below represent a hierarchy of degrees of metaphysical truth. There appear to be four such categories. The first class of metaphysical truths consists of certain propositions that can be found in certain kinds of mathematics. (This will be detailed later on and the reasons for such qualifiers will become evident). It is interesting that for Hartshorne, at least in some places, mathematical truths are also classified as metaphysical truths as well, although the presenting reasons for this are not the same as the reasons adduced in the present work. This will be discussed in detail below.

According to the present, respective work, metaphysical truths that are just above pure mathematical truths are pure phenomenological truths, which are about space and time, which are in turn the phenomenological foundations of mathematics. The reason why metaphysical truths which take as their content the foundations of mathematics are considered closer in degree of truth to what is absolutely true, is that those truths are more universal in application than the particular truths of mathematics.

Above both classes of truths is the awareness of the truth or truths of these truths. Such an awareness, which is aware of the truth of both of these classes of truth, is a philosophical awareness that comprises the set of the third class of truths. The fourth class of truths, which is experienced only rarely, consists of those truths which are seen to be true of all of these types of truths and indeed even of other types of truths, nay, even of the understanding of the existence of falsities, taken together, and contains glimpses of what truths may transcend all of the above. Such a fourth class of truths is evidenced, for example, by the capacity of being able to become aware of Plato's Fourth and Plato's Fifth. These four classes of truths stand to each other from lower to higher as representing the incorporation of higher and higher universality and thereby greater and greater degrees of metaphysical truth.

In Hartshorne's scheme of things, the distinction between mathematical truths and metaphysical truths has mainly to do with existence. His distinction is similar to the classical Aristotelian distinction. For Aristotle, mathematical truths do not exist separately and therefore are not metaphysical.[9] Metaphysical truths, for Hartshorne, must be existential whereas mathematical truths need not be, and therefore, mathematical truths are not metaphysical. Both classes of truths for Hartshorne are unconditionally necessary.

However, Hartshorne also seems to suggest that mathematical truths may also be metaphysical. By that he means (according to his own distinction that he draws between mathematics and metaphysics) that mathematical truths presumably could exist, and when they did, they would qualify as metaphysical truths. To paraphrase Hartshorne, according to this understanding of him, mathematical truths need not have existential correlates; mathematical truths could not exist. Metaphysical truths, for Hartshorne, could not not exist. When mathematical truths have existential correlates, they become metaphysical. This treatment of the relationship between mathematical and metaphysical truths is flawed, because a metaphysical truth, which, according to Hartshorne, could not not exist, should not be capable of changing its status from the status of not having existed to having existed necessarily.[10] In any event, this is very different from the present distinction between mathematics and metaphysics, which again differs from the Aristotelian distinction based on independent (or separate) and dependent existence. The present distinction between mathematics and metaphysics relates to the levels of awareness involved in the process of coming to an understanding of the respective truths. In this sense, the distinction between metaphysics and mathematics in this present, respective work bears a closer resemblance to the Platonic distinction of levels which is presented in the divided line analogy in the *Republic*, than it does either to the Aristotelian distinction of non-separate existence/separate existence or to the Hartshornian distinction of existence and non-existence. Of course, if one takes into account that Aristotle's description of metaphysics also involves truths of higher and higher generality (first and highest principles and causes), then the present, respective view may be said in this sense to bear some resemblance to Aristotle's description. However, the chief distinguishing feature of the present view has to do with its focus on ascending hierarchical levels of awareness which is closer to the Platonic view (which Plato identifies as philosophical rather than metaphysical) than it is either to the Aristotelian or Hartshornian one. It is also true, according to the present view, that if mathematical truths can be shown to be necessarily true because they are characteristics of the structuredness of reality, then mathematical truths may be said to possess existential correlates.

Hartshorne's rationalism shows itself in that his metaphysical categories, despite his attention to asymmetry, are not distinguished in any ontological sense. Cosmologically, Hartshorne distinguishes one category from another. For example, he may distinguish the actual from the possible by saying that what is actual subsequently delimits what is possible.[11] But, this is not a true metaphysical distinction since it distinguishes only logically between empirical possibilities. In the classification offered in the present author's, *Space, Time and the Ethical Foundations*, in which the ethical sphere is discussed, love, for example, is distinguished as ontologically prior to hate and fear, which are ontologically derivative. This is not a logical distinction merely among empirical possibilities, but an ontological distinction in principle among empirical possibilities. In Hartshorne's classification, the distinction between actuality and possibility is a logical distinction between metaphysical terms. The distinction between love and fear, which is introduced in the sequel, is a distinction between ontological levels among empirical possibilities.

While Hartshorne would appear to value asymmetry, in his metaphysical scheme the asymmetry has no ontological or phenomenological justification; it is purely logical. He may claim that it is ontological, but it is only logical, because his starting point is the starting point of the rationalist metaphysician that in its particular Hartshornian version, is the starting point of process. He is a process philosopher, but he is a rationalist metaphysician who happens to begin from process, rather than substance. Thus, his asymmetry is a logical asymmetry that is given no phenomenological but only an assertoric justification within his system.

What further distinguishes what is presented here from Hartshornian metaphysics is that Hartshorne's metaphysical postulates are just that, postulates, and are not phenomenologically grounded. For example, the putative case of a metaphysical truth that is discussed above is the example that 'something exists'. Hartshorne argues that this is a metaphysical truth because its opposite is logically inconceivable. However, this metaphysical truth is, according to the approach taken here, an empty truth, because there is no way of knowing *what* that something is.

In the approach presented in this work, it may be said that an example of a metaphysical truth is that awareness exists. One may easily possess an idea of what this means, since the subject knower is intimately acquainted with awareness. It is also the case that with the claim that awareness exists; its opposite is literally inconceivable. Additionally, however, in the approach taken in this work, there is a *presenting content* to whatever first order truth claims are lodged. The truth claims lodged herein are not assertoric or propositional: they are descriptive of a phenomenological content or deductive from that content in the case of second order metaphysical truths.

To sum up. There are two basic ways in which the approach taken here differs from Hartshornian metaphysics. The first way in which the present work differs from Hartshornian metaphysics is that while Hartshorne pays surface attention to asymmetry by giving it priority as a metaphysical category, his metaphysics of asymmetry is logically and not phenomenologically grounded. Thus, Hartshorne's metaphysics is still the metaphysics of a rationalist metaphysician, although his metaphysics is that of process rather than that of substance. The second way in which the present work differs from Hartshornian metaphysics is that the content of what Hartshorne states as examples of metaphysical truths is empty, that is, is not phenomenologically verifiable. Hartshorne's claim that 'something exists', for example, because no experience can count against it, is empty because the content of what that something is, is unknown. In the case of the present work, the claim that consciousness exists is not true simply because its opposite is inconceivable, but because it is necessarily true every time it is phenomenologically certified to be true. The method of certification will be discussed in the sequel.

Regional Metaphysics

One of the problems with metaphysics in the past, whether 'descriptive' or 'revisionary' in Strawson's categories, was that it attempted, by and large, to reach conclusions that described the whole of things, or described reality as a whole. For example, a metaphysical system might be devised to show that reality as a whole was process rather than substance or vice-versa. While these approaches are not devoid of merit, one of the more obvious difficulties with such "rationalist" approaches is that the difficulties of verification are magnified with the addition of each new empirical territory over which the metaphysical system raises its flag. One of the results of this is to place metaphysics under the great pressure of being compelled to prove or in some way to establish credibility for its results over an increasingly wider domain of truth territories. This becomes more and more difficult to accomplish, and results either in the adoption of an abstruse technical terminology for the metaphysics so as to define the claimant's area in such a way that it can apply to the whole, or in the restriction of the claimant's area (a road normally not taken by the metaphysician, but which forms part of the present approach).

If the choice is the adoption of a technical terminology to define the ever widening scope of application of the metaphysics (such as is the case with Leibniz, Spinoza, and Whitehead), two kinds of problems ensue. The general philosophical reader becomes disenchanted with the prospect of having to move under the bulky encumbrance of such concepts and begins to move away from metaphysics altogether. This has the effect that those who continue playing the metaphysical language game find themselves talking with an ever more narrowing audience, a specialist audience in metaphysics, or, what is even more common, a specialist audience devoted to a particular metaphysician, a factor that contributes substantially to the lack of interest on the part of the general audience in reading metaphysical works. Metaphysicians who choose to stay within the confines of their technically denominated systems find themselves in the position of being obliged to talk only among themselves, that is, with those equally familiar with the idiosyncrasy and the abstruseness of their terminology. In this respect, in the final analysis, they do not find themselves in a different situation than the equally technically bound analysts who can also only talk among themselves, except that the metaphysicians laded with technical terminology are in a sense more guilty of being in an ironical position, since their knowledge, while presumably designed to be of the most general, would appeal, similar to the technically circumscribed analysts, to an equally small audience. To add to the irony, it must be considered that in point of fact their audience is even smaller since those philosophers who are attracted to metaphysics in the first place tend to be more rare.

Here, the proposal is to return once more to the domain of necessity which is part and parcel of philosophical truth, but which is not restricted to the forms of ways of knowing (Kant) or language forms (speech patterns). The method for doing so is what may be termed philosophical restriction, but not philosophical destruction. While necessity once more becomes a prime object of concern, this necessity is restricted to phenomenological knowledge, and is not extended to things-in-themselves. This gives philosophy a proper domain of objects, which is not in competition with the domains of other disciplines. Phenomenological description is to be carried out only in regional domains, not in the unrestricted domain of reality as such or reality as a whole.

Notes

1. Charles Hartshorne, *Creative Synthesis and Philosophical Method*, La Salle, IL: Open Court, 1970, p. 162. (The author of this work had the good fortune of participating in Hartshorne's graduate seminar that formed the basis of *Creative Synthesis and Philosophical Method*).
2. *Cf.*, Nancy Frankenberry's excellent discussion, 'Hartshorne's Method in Metaphysics,' in Lewis E. Hahn (ed.), *The Philosophy of Charles Hartshorne*, The Library of Living Philosophers, Volume XX, La Salle, IL: Open Court, 1991.
3. *Op. cit.*, p. 18, 31. *Cf.*, *Ibid.*, p. 296.
4. *Ibid.*, p. 297.
5. *Ibid.*, p. 295.
6. *Ibid.*, p. 303.
7. *Cf.*, Robert E. Allinson, *CHUANG-TZU For Spiritual Transformation: An Analysis of the Inner Chapters*, Albany, NY: State University of New York Press, 1996, Sixth Impression, (especially Chapter Eight).
8. *Ibid.*, Chapter Eight.
9. *Met.* 1064 a28-b6.

10. For the set of implications this point has both for Anselm's ontological argument and modal logic, *Cf.*, Robert E. Allinson, 'Anselm's One Argument', *Philosophical Inquiry, An International Quarterly*, Vol. 15, No. 1-2, Winter-Spring, 1993, pp. 16-19. (*PHILOSOPHER'S INDEX*, Vol. 28, No. 1, Spring, 1994, pp. 92-93). Kant's disallowance of mathematical truths as philosophical is based on the point that for Kant, while both mathematical and philosophical knowledge contain synthetic *a priori* judgements, in mathematical knowledge, as opposed to philosophical knowledge, an *a priori* intuition is available. *Cf.*, Kant's 'Transcendental Doctrine of Method' in his *Critique of Pure Reason* (B 741-743). That would qualify mathematical knowledge, in Kant's terms, as metaphysical knowledge in terms of the vocabulary of the present work. From the point of view of the present work, the only difference between mathematical knowledge for the mathematician and mathematical knowledge for the metaphysician is in terms of how it is understood, and the uses to which it is put. The content of the knowledge is the same in both cases. For the mathematician, a mathematical truth, for example, may be simply assumed to be true and it may serve as the axiom of a mathematical system. For the philosopher, the same mathematical truth must be understood and therefore known as necessarily true in order to be true, and upon analysis, must be understood to be true for the right reasons, e.g., must be understood *as true* and therefore to be a different kind of truth than a conceptual truth. Thereafter, such a mathematical/metaphysical truth for a philosopher can serve as an example of metaphysical truth both for the purposes of pedagogy in teaching how truth may, nay, indeed must be ascertained, and for the purposes of linking such truths in analogies to higher truths.

11. The discussion could be enlarged. It could be argued that the actual does not exhaust the real or the existent since what is possible could become actual (as with Aristotle). Whitehead distinguished merely logical possibilities (possible possibilities) from real possibilities from which something might happen. Traditionally, Western philosophy understood possibility and actuality as ontological rather than logical in status. Kant initiated a movement away from this approach by construing the modal categories as not being concerned with content but only the relation of knowledge to the mind. For Kant, they became transcendental and not merely logical but still removed from the issue of content. In addition, for Kant, existence became the only real mode. In his schematism of the modal categories, they all involve existence with the addition of a time quantifier. Possibility is existence at some time; existence is existence at this time; necessity is existence at all times. Existence does not exhaust reality. It is obvious from this analysis why for Kant the Divine is not a necessary existence because necessity would belong to the logical inference. For all of the comments in this note, and for all of his gracious assistance, the present author is indebted to the distinguished John E. Smith, Clark Emeritus Professor of Philosophy at Yale University.

Allegro deciso
Rapid and well marked

3 Pedagogical Approaches to the Study of Metaphysics

Metaphysics can also be considered from the standpoint of pedagogical strategies. One can approach the study of metaphysics through the history of systems; one can approach the study of metaphysics through the study of selected metaphysical topics or problems; one can approach the study of metaphysics through the application of a metaphysical perspective; one can approach the study of metaphysics by plunging directly into one system and studying metaphysics in the midst of doing metaphysics.

The History of Systems

The study of the history of metaphysical systems can take the form of studying each Great Philosopher as presenting a system in isolation, or it can take the form of linking metaphysical systems together in such a way that the history of philosophy itself forms a system in the manner of thinking about the history of philosophy as is presented by Hegel. It is more common to study systems in isolation from each other. In this fashion, one studies the system of Plato, and then the system of Aristotle, and then the system of Spinoza, and so on. Of course, it is impossible to study Aristotle without reference to Plato, so that a completely purist approach to systems as isolated entities is difficult if not impossible to carry out. The study of metaphysics as a history of systems, however, belongs more to the study of the history of philosophy than it does to metaphysics proper.

The Approach by Topics

To set this present work in the light of an additional perspective, one may also consider approaching metaphysics via the selection of metaphysical topics. One may select major topics which have been concerns of metaphysicians in the past, and treat each topic severally either from one's own metaphysical perspective, or, one may discuss each topic as it has been treated by selected figures from the past. This approach, however, suffers from not being able to take sufficient account of the systematic connections that might obtain between different metaphysical topics. For example, a treatment of space as a different topic from time might result in a kind of metaphysics that would not take into account the interrelationship between the two. However, one can treat topics separately such as the reality of the self, space, time, the reality of the external world, the reality of other minds, theism, immortality and so on. In so doing, however, one might in the end possess some metaphysical understanding of certain metaphysical questions, but one would lack understanding of any possible systematic connection between these various topics that might exist.

The Approach by Problematic

A further pedagogical approach to the study of metaphysics is to study selected metaphysical problems and their attendant solutions. In this way one may study the mind-body problem, the problem of the proof of the external world, the problem of the existence of G-d, the problem of the immortality of the soul, and so on. There is a strong similarity between this approach and that of the approach by topics. The difference lies in the fact that in the problems approach, each topic is seen not only as an area to be investigated, but as a problem to be solved, or, if unsolvable, to be considered inherently problematic. If the problems appear to recur over time and in one form of another are perceived to reappear as problems in a variety or in all philosophies, the problems approach may be considered to be a study of the 'Eternal Problems of Philosophy'. This approach would, similar to the approach by topics, select problems from the systems of philosophers and treat them individually. The problems approach possesses the same limitation as the approach by topics, since it would not become evident why any one metaphysical problem should have any relationship to any other metaphysical problem. Of course, it can be argued that the problems need not have any systematic connection with each other, but this is a *petitio principii.*

The Approach by Perspectives

A perspective approach to the study of metaphysics would be to approach the subject matter of metaphysics through a metaphysical perspective such as, process philosophy, the dialectic of concepts, a single system perspective, the perspective of hermeneutics, or comparative philosophy. While there is merit in such an approach, with respect to how the approach by perspectives is defined in this present work, the limitation is that one's metaphysical perspective has been arbitrarily chosen. The approach by perspectives strongly resembles the approach of studying metaphysics by doing metaphysics, and differs from it only by not grounding or justifying one's perspective. One is then left with the question as to why this particular perspective has been selected rather than another perspective. There is but a short step between the approach by perspectives to the study of metaphysics and the practicing of metaphysics, and the step largely consists of a thoroughgoing grounding of one's thematic perspective.

Cyclical and Dialectical Progression

To select one perspective for review both because of its novelty for Western philosophers and for its special illumination of the present approach, it is of interest to contrast the cyclical progression of *Yin-Yang* philosophy with the dialectical progression of Hegelian philosophy. In Hegelian dialectics the new concept replaces the old concept as the old concept is negated, although some of it is preserved in the new concept. New concepts replace old ones whilst including parts of the old ones within themselves.

In *Yin-Yang* progression, the two concepts exist simultaneously with each other, and while one gradually replaces the other, the replacement is only temporary, and the one which has been replaced, itself gradually regains its ascendancy. The image of the progression is a circle in which the top and bottom halves rotate in terms of their respective ascent and descent, but each half is never entirely replaced by the other half. The progression therefore is the rotation of a circle and not the ever upward movement of the dialectic.

A further difference is that in the Hegelian dialectic, the two concepts are in warlike opposition to each other such that there is an antagonism between the two concepts. In *Yin-Yang* progression, the two concepts are not antagonistically opposed, but are both necessary to each other's existence and complement each other's existence. In Hegelian dialectic, there is an infinite succession of new concepts replacing old and inadequate ones (leaving open the fascinating question as to whether Hegel's own system achieved the final progression and hence in a way negated the concept of the infinite process); in *Yin-Yang* progression, there is a constant rotation between two sides of the same concept revealing the necessity of both halves to form a greater whole, which at certain times emphasizes one of its aspects, and at other times emphasizes the other. The *Yin-Yang* progression follows a phase of expansion and contraction like the phases of the moon, where one side of the concept reaches its fullness and thus reaches its fruition, and then must descend to allow the other side of the concept to dominate for a time. In Hegelian dialectics, there is a constant onward progression of new concepts, and there is no corresponding notion of cyclical phases of ascent and descent. In *Yin-Yang* progression, the two sides are not replaced by a third, but each side requires the other side for its own completeness; the two sides gradually replace and are replaced by each other in terms of ascent and descent; there is a phase or a period during which it is correct that one be at the zenith, and a natural time for it to recede to the nadir and to be replaced by its other half.

Hermeneutics

Since there has been much discussion of hermeneutics in recent times, there is reason to briefly discuss this perspective separately. While hermeneutics has not been considered a metaphysical approach, but rather an approach to the interpretation of texts, one can incorporate the idea of hermeneutics into one's metaphysics. One mode of incorporating hermeneutics into one's metaphysics would be to take metaphysical concepts from one philosopher and adapt them to a different use within one's own metaphysics. For example, one might take the concept of space, which is treated by Kant, and one might take the concept of time which is treated by Kant, and one might relate these two concepts to each other in a manner which is relatively or completely unknown to Kant. One might refer to this as an act of hermeneutic metaphysics in that one is taking concepts from the system of one philosopher and interpreting them in a different way. This notion of hermeneutics is not necessarily tied to a conviction that each interpretative act is limited by its historical framework such as is the view of Gadamer. One can provide a grounding or a justification for one's hermeneutic act that has universal application. There are certain parallels with this approach and the approach taken in this present work.

Modified Hegelianism

Instead of having recourse to the idea of Hegel's Absolute making use of human history to work out its own development, one can understand all philosophers on a higher level, as collaborating with each other in the work of truth discovery. This study of metaphysics would be to first take the perspective that all great philosophers are collaborators and that each system can be seen as contributing a part of a whole. The philosophical collaborators may or may not be conscious of such a collaboration. The systems are not taken just as they are but are treated hermeneutically, so that one is not incorporating whole systems, but rather one is interpolating certain features from each system and collecting them together so as to form an approach rather than another system.

Modified Hegelianism is not the same as eclecticism since eclecticism would borrow ideas here and there and assemble an aggregate of such ideas, the ideas themselves remaining relatively intact. In modified Hegelianism, the borrowed ideas are not simply borrowed but they are interpolated such that after being borrowed they no longer possess the same meaning as they did when they were part of the system from which they had been borrowed. In addition, in modified Hegelianism, there is some attempt to show a relationship between ideas as employed in the systems from which they have been borrowed and the new approach of which they form a part. For example, the idea of space-time that plays such an important role in the sequel to this present work is strongly related to the treatment of space and time that one discovers in the philosophy of Kant and has thus been "borrowed" from Kant. However, it was not simply borrowed from Kant since it also underwent some development after its treatment by Hegel. Such a work, thus, could not be considered simply eclectic.

Chinese Modified Hegelianism

Instead of adapting the Hegelian dialectic *simpliciter*, one can adapt the *Yin-Yang* concept as well such that the new approach might itself be composed of two distinct halves which rotated in a cyclical progression. By adapting the *Yin-Yang* model of progression, the two halves would complement each other and over time, one aspect would naturally dominate and the other would naturally recede (and vice-versa) as the needs of history gradually change. At the time of the presentation of the approach, however, it may appear as if both halves are being presented horizontally as if they coexisted on an equal plane. This however, is only a feature of presentation. In the actual use of the approach, each half of the approach would dominate in turn.

This approach itself is perceived as having progressed developmentally from previous systems, so that with regard to its genetic origin, the approach itself may be perceived as having evolved in a progressive direction. With respect to the content of the approach, one aspect of the approach may dominate and the other recede in a cyclical or circular direction depending upon the needs of the time. In this respect, after evolving, the approach itself may be perceived as remaining constant while internally reversing itself to meet the demands of history. The concept of the *Yin-Yang* rotation is that both halves will always be considered to be necessary. In this sense there is a combination of the Eternal Problems approach with the notion of historical change. With respect to the alteration of dominance of the aspect, the approach does not appear to progress in history. However, in another sense, the change of dominance follows history - or leads it as the case demands - and in this sense does represent progress - as it addresses the needs of the time - although to the observer, it may seem at certain times to retrogress in history. The present work is offered as an example of a part of, if not a whole metaphysical approach of this kind.

The general point of such a 'one substance, two aspects' approach, or, to utilize an Eastern metaphor, a *Yin-Yang* approach, is that the approach is not weighted permanently in one direction. It is more like a philosophical medicinal chest the medicines and the dosage of which will vary with regard to the incidence and degree of the mental or cultural disease of the times. With respect to the particulars of the approach presented herein, the two aspects are the phenomenological foundations on the one hand, and the analogies to metaphysical realities on the other. As suits the needs of the time, it is obvious that more attention is paid in this work to the phenomenological foundations, (what traditionally would be construed as an epistemological focus), than is paid to the metaphysical constructions. However, it should be understood that such a concentration is purely of co-temporary interest, and should not represent a tendency that will be of relevance or interest in every historical epoch.

Which aspect of the approach will be emphasized or further developed is a function of the ability of the philosopher to diagnose the problems of her or his time and to prescribe solutions that can cure those problems. All too frequently philosophers dazzle audiences with their comprehensive reading of previous philosophers and co-temporary philosophers, their mastery of difficult and highly technical arguments, their capacities for lucidity and eloquence, and their brilliant word jugglery. While these skills are important in a philosopher, the most important skills are frequently the most neglected, namely, the diagnostic ability to ferret out the problems that most need correcting, and the prescriptive ability to offer philosophical medicines that cure those problems while producing as few undesirable side-effects as possible.

Where is the philosopher as diagnostician and prescriber? Are such skills taught in the academies? Of the two skills, diagnosis is the most fundamental and should be the first to be developed. If the diagnosis of a problem is mistaken, then the possibility of a solution being helpful is virtually nil. Even when, by chance, a solution presented is correct, if the diagnosis of the problem is unknown or mistaken, the solution will be disregarded. One may think of the diagnosis as knowing the target and the solution as the arrow. If the target is unknown, there is little chance of hitting the target or even knowing when the target has been hit, no matter how many arrows are shot.

Of all skills that need to be developed in the philosopher today, the skill of diagnostics is the skill that most needs development, and is the skill that is not only the least attended, but perhaps is nearly unrecognized as a philosophical talent in the first place. A diagnosis of the need for diagnostic abilities is needed in the first place. Such a diagnosis of the need for diagnostics is implicitly supplied in the introduction to this work.

The present approach may be regarded as a kind of philosophical pharmacy. The two major aspects of the approach, the phenomenologizing of the concept of truth and the analogical pointing to the structure of reality may be conceived of as the two areas that require the most attention in the future. Which of these areas will require the most urgent attention at any particular moment in history will depend upon the progression or the remission of the disease.

Allegro non troppo, ma con spirito
Not too lively, yet with a swing

4 Metaphysical Principles and Metaphysical Insight

It is important, for the proper understanding of this work, to distinguish between metaphysical principles and metaphysical insight. The identification of the business of metaphysics with the production of metaphysical principles is one that is made in Walsh's classic book on metaphysics, *Metaphysics*. For Walsh, at the center of each metaphysical system there is a series of categorial principles that are treated as possessing unrestricted validity. These 'Categorial principles are not read out of, but read into, experience ...' He ends his chapter on metaphysical assertion and argument with the following statement: 'The study of metaphysical texts may exercise our intellects and even sharpen our wits; what it cannot do, on this view of the matter, is to improve our understanding.'[1]

Walsh appears to be saying that metaphysical statements (substituting this phrase for his "categorial principles") are *a priori*, and therefore are not empirical generalizations from experience. Further, while *a priori*, they do not play any informative or transformative function. While it is not obvious why Walsh has formed this view of metaphysical statements, this view of metaphysics may arise in part from his characterization of metaphysical statements as *a priori*, and in part from his having formed a view of metaphysics by attending to its outward and visible product, namely, statement forms. That metaphysics ultimately issues in statements is a fact of language using animals. From the point of view of this present work, what is of interest are metaphysical insights or metaphysical truths, not the statements in which they are housed. But, the focusing on statements is also characteristic of the language obsessed age in which philosophers live and which to a large extent they have created. In this work there will be much reference to statements as well, in the spirit of Prince Hal in *Henry IV, Part I* who could speak the language of royalty when in court and could '... drink with any tinker in his own language ...' in the tavern. Thus, in order to communicate when in the linguistic tavern, one must use the *patois* of those besotted with language.[2] It is useful to bear in mind that when the phrase 'the truth of metaphysical statements' is employed in this present work, the truth to which one is referred is not that truth which arises from the linguistic form of the statement or the truth of the *statement*, but that truth which exists as an objective truth or *noema*, which is but signified by the statement form.

Now, if a statement is *a priori*, it is easy to see why someone, like Walsh, would conclude that one cannot arrive at such a statement by an empirical generalization. With this view one cannot help but agree. However, it would not seem to follow that one would necessarily have to read metaphysics back into experience. Even Kant, that arch antagonist of metaphysics, has stated in his famous B1 formulation, in the first *Critique*, that, '*Wenn aber gleich alle unsere Erkenntnis mit der Erfahrung anhebt, so entspringt sie darum doch nicht eben alle aus der Erfahrung*'.[3] 'But though all our knowledge begins with experience, it does not follow that it all arises out of experience.' One might consider the value of modifying Kant's phrase to read, 'while all knowledge arises in experience [which does not imply that the knowledge begins with experience, but only that experience is the occasion of its arising], not all knowledge originates from experience', [which implies that while experience is the vehicle for the conveyance of knowledge, or the venue for its appearance, it is not its source].

It seems that Walsh may perhaps be misled by having focused his attention on the outward form of metaphysical thinking, namely, the statement form of its conclusions, and not having attended sufficiently to either the discovery of metaphysical truths or the function that such truths can play in one's life. While his description might be true of the practise of some metaphysicians, it does not characterize the type of metaphysics practiced here, nor does it characterize the type of metaphysics practiced by such classical figures as Plato, Spinoza or Hegel.

As shall be observed in the course of this present work, metaphysical statements, while *a priori* in character, are not read into experience, but are rather discovered in moments of insight. Those moments of insight always take place experientially. For example, it can be phenomenologically detected that anger is derivative from fear or hurt, and such a statement is true, if and only if, it is first found to be true in the depths of one's own experience. It is not an empirical generalization from experience, since, according to the "rules" for empirical generalizations, any one experience of this nature would not justify making a universal claim. An empirical generalization is only allowed as an inductive inference from a repeated number of experiences. But, according to the kind of phenomenological metaphysics outlined in this present work, unless such a truth is initially found in subjective experience, one does not thereby possess the right to use it as an interpretative principle of experience. And, one example of such an experience is sufficient unto the day thereof. If one requires further examples, such further examples do not make it more legitimate to induce an empirical generalization; they merely illustrate and remind one of the universality experienced in the first experience. How it is possible to find the universal within the particular is difficult, if not impossible to explain, but it does not follow from the difficulty or impossibility of providing an explanation that it is impossible for the particular to betoken the universal in some sense. If there is no sense at all in which the particular can exemplify the universal, then metaphysics is bankrupt and has no legitimate claim to anyone's allegiance.

It is allowed that the universal is symbolized by the particular in other disciplines as in mathematics in which the truth claim that $1 + 1 = 2$ is not perceived as true and only true of each person's private formulation of it. When the truth of the mathematical relationship is perceived, it is granted that a universal relationship is perceived, and not a relationship which is limited to the example that is in front of any one particular subject inquirer.[4] It could be argued that this is but a hollow discovery. What is important to remember is that it is both a discovered relationship' which is and can be seen to be true, and one which is not something that can be said to have been an article of knowledge before it was seen to be true.

Perhaps there are metaphysicians who are guilty of what Walsh describes as reading their principles into experience, but such a practise is simply bad metaphysics. Metaphysical insight always initially takes its rise from within some experience. After one has garnered some metaphysical insight, one may use it to guide one's practise, but this is legitimate only after one has discovered it. Otherwise, one is applying principles to experience without the slightest concept of whether it is correct to do so.

Walsh's two statements are tied to each other. That he would say that one does not increase one's understanding by arriving at metaphysical knowledge follows from his concept that metaphysical knowledge is simply being read into experience. In this case, metaphysics is simply a giant chess game in which one can sharpen one's intellectual skill by seeing how experience can be organized or co-ordinated by classifying it in accordance with a set of basic metaphysical principles.

But, the ultimate purpose of metaphysics is to give mankind some increased understanding and wisdom. To think otherwise is to trivialize metaphysics and make it unworthy of pursuit. Walsh may perhaps be misled by the fact that metaphysical insight may appear to be packaged in a universal, propositional statement form, but this is only the package and is not a record either of how that metaphysical knowledge came to one in the first place, or how it can function in one's life.

When Plato says that all evil-doing comes from ignorance, this is most certainly a metaphysical statement. No superficial analysis of an empirical experience can countenance the formation of this conclusion. But, Plato doubtless had some profound experience, which he described as having insight into a Form, which led him to this conclusion. Leaving aside Plato's form of description of the moment of truth discovery - a description that appealed to Plato, but caused others untold grief - Plato, it may be conjectured, underwent some profound experience of the relationship between evil-doing and ignorance. He did not simply make up his theory as an intellectual rule that he advised should be read into, and thereafter relied upon, to interpret experience. Nor did he simply unthinkingly repeat what he had learned from Socrates. Surely, Plato must have undergone some deep experience or set of repeated experiences which led him to a moment or a collection of moments of insight that whenever human beings chose that which was truly harmful for themselves, they did so from a lack of understanding.

It is likely that Plato came to the realization that in the midst of a moment or a series of moments of insight or understanding, a human being did not make the choice that she or he did at other moments when such insight or understanding was lacking. In other words, one's understanding affects or can affect one's choice. Since moments of high understanding are fleeting, it is of course helpful to enter one's daily life armed with such insights, which can be turned to for guidance whenever one is distraught or in a quandary. Ethical rules, when employed in this way, could be said to be cases of applying categorial principles to interpret experience. If no such application were to be made of ethical principles, it would appear that a large class of discovered metaphysical principles would serve no purpose.

Now, it is entirely possible that Walsh does not accept that Plato or any philosopher such as Spinoza could have experienced such moments of insight that would increase understanding or wisdom. Walsh states that, 'There is no such thing as a special stock of knowledge accessible only to metaphysicians nor is it the case that some metaphysicians have a grasp of fundamental truths of fact which are unaccountably lost sight of by others'.[5] In this case one has nothing to learn from metaphysicians (or poets or sages) that cannot also be rediscovered by any lay person. So much for the brilliant insights of Plato in his *Republic*, his *Symposium* and his *Seventh Letter* and Spinoza in his *Ethics*.

But, on what grounds can Walsh or others rule out the possibility of having such moments of insight? And, when the non-philosopher or non-sage has such a moment of insight, is the non-philosopher or non-sage not a philosopher or a sage at just such a moment? Can all such possibilities be ruled out on the grounds that no particular experience can allow anyone to make a universal judgement? Even Walsh himself does not appear to go so far as this, as some truths of fact, as he puts it, are not 'unaccountably lost sight of by others'. If no one can possess any kind of universal insight or wisdom, then not only philosophers of the wisdom tradition, but also poets, artists, novelists, religious thinkers and ordinary humans, to take Walsh's example, who have reported such moments in their lives, must all have been mistaken.

That such experiences of meaningfulness cannot be entirely accounted for on the grounds that all experience is empirical, is either grounds for thinking that all experience is not only empirical, or grounds for thinking that one can possess certain truths, even though no empirically satisfactory accounts for how such truths are possessed can be rendered. Indeed, without some theory of how experience transcends the empirical, one could make no sense of Victor Frankl's accounts of meaningfulness which he was able to experience even during his captivity in Nazi death camps, which he later related in such books as *Man's Search For Meaning*, or the experience of Anne Frank, written down in her diary to perceive of life as meaningful, nay, even worthwhile during the darkest days of persecution by the Gestapo.[6]

Another approach to explaining how Plato could possess certain truths is to say that Plato had access to some other form of experience, namely an otherworldly experience, and it was from this experience that Plato derived his conclusions. This would appear, in general, the tack that Walsh himself takes in his interpretation of Plato. The problem with this depiction of Plato is that whether or not it corresponds with Plato's own self-description, the consequence has been to lead many philosophers to simply brand the revered Plato a mystic, and therefore to restrict the validity of his discoveries to those privileged to share his mystical framework or experience. In effect, such a restriction is a universal one since the insights of any fellow mystics would be further discounted simply on the grounds that they were gathered by mystical means.

Plato described in very metaphorical terms a set of experiences and discoveries that do not seem to be readily available in ordinary experience. But, the set of experiences and insights that he described does not therefore belong to a realm that is inaccessible to the rest of mankind. It is entirely possible that ordinary experience, when understood on a deeper level, is capable of yielding up such insights as Plato garnered.

The absolutely common experience of anger, for example, when it is observed and reflected upon, can always be seen as derivative either from fear or hurt on the one hand, or a sense of injustice or a desire to protect, on the other. This does not require any kind of mystical insight or divine intuition. It does require a willingness to allow the phenomena of inner experience to show themselves and a willingness to reflect deeply upon one's own experience. If one is reluctant to trust the data of one's personal experience, one may be referred to documented examples from the work of psychoanalysis. In the course of psychotherapy, the patient can at an appropriate moment come upon an insight of how her or his behavior is governed by some principle learned in the past, and in so doing free herself or himself from such governance in the future. If such moments were not possible, then the work of psychoanalysis would be totally fictional and every psychoanalyst or psychotherapist would either be a charlatan or a dupe.

There have been critiques of Freud which argue that his principles (and there is no reason to defend everything which Freud thought to be true) were non-falsifiable, and therefore had no truth-value. But, this is not to understand how the truth-value of such principles is validated, which is only in the appropriate context of psychotherapeutic self-discovery. Most if not all of the theses of psychoanalysis are metaphysical, but it does not follow that they possess no means of validation. The same can be said to be true of all genuine metaphysical principles. Not every metaphysical principle is a sound one. But it does not follow from this that all metaphysical principles are unsound or incapable of validation.

Sometimes the ways in which metaphysicians in the past have attempted to describe the criteria for coming to see their insights as true have not been entirely helpful. For example, when Descartes attempted to put forth his famous principle that whatever can be clearly and distinctly conceived must be true, he was attempting to say something about the depth level clarity that a phenomenological introspection or a moment of insight can bring with it. But, this description by itself, outside of the context of discovery, appears inadequate and suspect. It would appear that any so-called truth might appear to the subject knower to be clear and distinct, and yet could nonetheless be one about which the subject knower might very well be mistaken. If one takes the Cartesian description of the criterion of truth too literally, and out of context, it appears to be seriously flawed. Walsh himself comments on the Cartesian criteria of clarity and distinctness that, '... despite much effort they [the rationalists] were not able to specify what distinguishes an acceptable from an unacceptable intuition in metaphysics: the criteria of clarity and distinctness were not themselves sufficiently clear and distinct'.[7] From this account one might well imagine that rationalists were first stumbling upon various possible candidates for metaphysical truth, and then applying to such candidates the rather vague criteria of clarity and distinctness. With such a description of the metaphysician's practise of truth discovery, one cannot help but reject the validity and the employment of such criteria.

The above description of the practise of metaphysicians is most likely a misdescription. It is a description that abstracts from the moment of discovery and the context of truth. It is far more likely that Descartes achieved some metaphysical insights and during those moments of discovery, realized their truth-value, (this is not to say that every insight that Descartes came to was a valid one). It was only after his discoveries and his realization of the truths of his discoveries that he attempted to explain the process by which he had come to know that the truths that he had discovered were true. His attempt at an *ex post facto* explanation was a clumsy one; it suffered, as had Plato's, from inexactness and inadequateness. But, if one interpolates his description, (or Plato's), more carefully and more in depth, then one will not be tempted to form too literal an interpretation of the description.

What Descartes was describing was the powerful quality of the moment of truth. The moment of truth must have appeared to him with such a compelling quality that he could only use the language of clarity and distinctness to describe it. In a moment of introspective isolation, the truth that accompanies the experience that 'I and my consciousness are one', appears to one with a terrible clarity, and in the absence of other interfering information, as very distinct. This is not to say that any and all such insights are valid ones. It is only to say that when such an insight presents itself, one must at least pay serious attention to the possibility that the insight is a true one. One must also bear in mind that the sourcing of the insight must also be taken into consideration. Contrary to Walsh's opinion, a practiced and mature thinker who has learned how to distinguish between empirical observations and metaphysical insights is in a better position to evaluate the importance, and/or the truth of an insight than someone with little or no experience in philosophical introspection.

The problem with Descartes' criteria is that they are not to be externally applied to independently discovered and truth neutral candidates that have been isolated and abstracted from the conditions of their discovery. The truth criteria, when abstracted from the knowledge situation, have no truth discovering or validating power of their own. The truth criteria are always context specific and context bound. To put it another way, the validity of the criteria are themselves "proven" by the truth of the content of what has been discovered. In the sequel, it will be more fully explained how and why truth "criteria" are the results of the truth of the discovered distinctions, and not the other way around. It is the discovered truth that brings with it such clarity and illumination that it appears as if these attendant features are themselves responsible for the truth that is discovered. *The truth criteria are not selectors, but are rather reflectors or reflections of the truth content.*

Perhaps, metaphysicians have not expressed themselves in the best of all possible fashions. But, they have been attempting to leave certain clues behind them. If no attempt is made to interpret such clues, because the clues by themselves appear fraudulent, much of that of which they are clues may be missed. In order to appreciate Descartes' clarity and distinctness criteria, or Plato's "insight into the Form criterion", one must not take these criteria literally, or examine them by themselves for their validity in isolation from the context of the truth discoveries or reported truth discoveries that the metaphysicians were making.

At another juncture, the truth-value of Descartes' discovery of the identity of himself and his consciousness may be treated. For the time being, attention only needs to be drawn to the issue that for Descartes, the *cogito* was a moment of metaphysical insight. It was not a logical conclusion from an argument.[8] But, neither was it an "intuition", for this description seems to imply that one possesses certain intuitive faculties, and that the content of what is to be considered to be true or false is subject to the inspection and the vetting of such resident faculties.

One does not first possess a neutral truth content that is then subject to inspection by an intuitive faculty. If in the description of the knowledge event, one employs the word 'intuition', this is only to attempt to explain that what was seen to be true (or more accurately, what was discovered as true) came to one in a flash of insight. But, the insight is actually part of the knowledge situation and cannot be abstracted from it and then hypostatized and made into a knowledge faculty by itself. If this is done, then it is fair game to question the existence of such a faculty. The only way to discover the possible validity of a metaphysical insight is to recreate the conditions of the claimed discovery so as to see whether or not one can have a similar if not identical knowledge experience. There is and can be no other court of appeal.

In the case of Descartes' discovery (and, again, one is not thereby committed to saying everything that Descartes or any other metaphysician discovered was true) of the identity of self and consciousness, such a thought experiment must be individually performed by every would-be subject knower in the privacy of her or his phenomenological consciousness. This is the only crucible of metaphysical truth. The act of discovery and what it is that is discovered, form one whole. There is no separate datum and separate act of intuition that is brought to bear on that datum. In Aristotelian language, the object of thought and the thinker become one. This is itself a metaphor, and if taken literally, will also be misleading. It is a description, as with Descartes' clarity and distinctness criteria, which is constructed after the fact. It is a metaphorical attempt of explaining what has already happened, and as a retrospective description, cannot be taken as a rule that is to be applied to future truth candidates.

All that one can do is to attempt to recreate the context of the metaphysical discovery to see if one can also experience the same insight. After such an experience, one can then understand how these truth criteria are both true in a sense and also how they very much clumsily miss the mark. *They are true only as post-cognitive descriptions which are attempts to highlight a dimension of what has already occurred, in language forms that are no longer appropriate to what has occurred, and which taken by themselves make very little sense.* Descartes attempted to portray the moment of profound insight in less metaphorical terms than had Plato and Aristotle, but his attempt was no less a misdescription than their attempts at retrospective descriptions. Just as Aristotle's criteria are less metaphorical than Plato's, so Descartes has attempted to state his criteria in terms that would be even more acceptable to those who would demand a less metaphorical account of the conditions of subjective truth discovery. But, even his description, as non-metaphorical as it may appear on the surface compared to the descriptions of the ancients, is nonetheless a metaphorical description, which can only hint at the self-certifying qualities which are fleetingly present during an experience of truth discovery.

Truth criteria cannot be understood too literally. They are stage directions or clues for future enactments. If analyzed by themselves, their only valid claim to status is as *ex post facto* accounts, and attempts to capture in linguistic and conceptual forms that which has formed a unitary whole wherein content and knowledge of that content has come to one in an instantaneous moment of discovery. If one concentrates on the epistemological side, one will miss the element that makes, or more precisely, *that has made* the cognitive moment a moment of cognizing truth. That which is true is the content of what it *was* that had been discovered. In the case of Descartes, what he discovered was the identity of himself and his consciousness. But, the truth of this discovery cannot be known apart from the moment of the discovery, and what precisely he did discover also cannot be known apart from the moment of the discovery, or more precisely the rediscovery of this by each subject knower in the magnificently revealing private moment of self insight or insight into the self.

To sum up. All of the foregoing is not to say that all metaphysical insights are valid, and one only needs to recreate the conditions of the moments of their discovery for the possibility of rediscovery. But, those insights that have lasted through history as important philosophical discoveries deserve a sincere attempt at rediscovering whether or not they are true. This is the treasure that metaphysicians from the past have left behind. It is to be ignored only at one's own peril and at the risk of the consequent impoverishment of one's life.

There is no need to be overwhelmed by the fear that one will be besieged with a host of claims that mystics and madmen will gainsay to be true. If any and all claims to truth are subjected to the rigorous conditions of subjective (not intersubjective) truth discovery, the wheat can be discerned from the chaff. If a claim is set forth as an empirical truth claim, it is a simple matter to test its validity. If a claim is set forth as a metaphysical truth claim, even though one cannot appeal to the same set of methods as the empirical scientist to establish its truth or falsity, it does not follow that there are no criteria at all to which one may turn. It is only the metaphorical nature and the retrospective timing of the application of the criteria that require proper understanding.

To conclude. Metaphysical truth selection criteria are not to be found outside of the conditions and the actual moments of truth discovery. As stated above, the criteria are at best *ex post facto* clues to what has already transpired in a passing moment of metaphysical insight. It does not follow that everything that every metaphysician has claimed to be true, is in fact true. It may be that, for example, Bradley's statement that, 'The Absolute enters into, but is itself incapable of evolution', is not true. Perhaps, it may not be corroborated in the crucible of each subject's introspective consciousness. It does not follow from this, however, that the subject knower possesses no internal capacity for the recognition of truth.

In the present work, the gauntlet is thrown down that each metaphysical claim lodged herein must be put to an internal truth test. The only metaphysical truth claims that may be vouched for are the ones that can meet the test of transcendental introspection. It is up to each subject reader to discover the truth or falsity of the claims set forth in this work. There are no tools or equipment available other than these moments of metaphysical discernment. Bishop Butler once said, when we sit down in a cool hour, we can discern moral good and evil.[9] The implication was that such discernment was possible. Here, what is being said is that metaphysical truth and error can also be discerned. If it were denied that a capacity for such discernment or insight is possessed without first attempting to practise with it, this present version of metaphysics is being rejected with prejudice. Every metaphysical truth that is claimed herein to be true may turn out upon deeper and more careful inspection to be false, but the ability to discern that is also dependent upon the same internal court of appeal. It is not to be claimed that the truth claims to be set forth within are one and all eternally true, but it is suspected that the method for discerning their truth value is one which is available to all, and not restricted to professional metaphysicians, who are teachers only in Homer's sense, in which where two walk together, one walks in front only because she or he has trod this path before.

Notes

1. W. H. Walsh, *Metaphysics*, London: Hutchinson University Library, 1963, p. 170.
2. William Shakespeare, *Henry I, Part I*, Scene IV.
3. Immanuel Kant, *Kritik der reinen Vernunft*, Hamburg: Felix Meiner Verlag, 1956.
4. For the noted Oxford mathematician Sir Roger Penrose, who is Rouse Ball professor of mathematics at the University of Oxford, who together with Stephen Hawking, was the winner of the 1988 Wolf Prize for physics, when one sees a mathematical truth one is making direct contact with the same externally existing world of mathematical concepts that existed for Plato. *Cf.*, Roger Penrose, *The Emperor's New Mind*, New York: Oxford University Press, 1989, 1990, p. 428.
5. Walsh, p. 169. Such a view as Walsh's is not reinforced by Descartes' interesting comment that it is dangerous for a person of ordinary intelligence to embark upon a reading of the *Meditations*.
6. *Cf.*, Viktor E. Frankl, *Man's Search For Meaning: an introduction to logotherapy*, New York: Pocket Books, 1972. For Frankl, there are three categories of meaningfulness in human life: the meaningfulness that derives from creative productions; the meaningfulness that derives from experience; the meaningfulness that is the result of one's means of coping with suffering. According to his own account he was able to survive the Nazi death camp because of two factors: one, pure chance (that he was not selected to be shot); two, that he had resolved that he would live to write a new theory of psychotherapy which would endow the world with meaning. In the case of Nelson Mandela, it was the reading of *The Diary of Anne Frank* that was the means that enabled him to survive his long years in prison.
7. *Op. cit.*, p. 168.
8. *Cf.*, The argument put forth by Errol E. Harris in *Fundamentals of Philosophy*, that [Descartes] insists that *cogito ergo sum* is not a syllogism or conclusion drawn from a major premise ...', p. 161. The '*cogito, ergo sum*' formulation, which appears in the earlier *Discourse*, (Part IV), but not in the *Meditations*, does possess the appearance of a propositional argument. In the *Meditations*, the *cogito* makes its appearance in the formulation, 'this proposition, I am, I exist, is necessarily true each time it is expressed by me, or conceived in my mind' (*Meditation II*). This would appear to be a more mature formulation. In the formulation of the *Meditations*, the fact of existence is known as true in [and only in] its moment of conception. This appears to be a different mode of knowing truth than knowing the truth of an inference. The debate on this point is itself an interesting one and one may be referred to the now classic article of Jaakko Hintikka, '*Cogito, Ergo Sum*: Inference or Performance?' *The Philosophical Review*, Vol. 71, 1961, pp. 3-33. Hintikka seems to be

making a different point than that of this present, respective work since Hintikka's view is based on a performatory view of truth and not an insight or discovery view of truth. Hintikka's explanation would appear to be truer of Vico than Descartes. However one considers that Descartes himself construed his discovery, from the point of view of the present, respective work, its significance does not arise from its being a logical deduction. In addition, from the point of view of the present, respective work, the significance of the discovery of Descartes is the awareness of the certainty of self-knowledge, with the emphasis on the *knowledge* portion rather than the *self* portion of self-knowledge. The discovery of self-knowledge is not original to Descartes. It appears earlier in the work of Augustine as a logical argument and despite its appearance did not seem to create strong waves in the history of philosophy. While such a fate has been implicitly ascribed to the lesser status to which Augustine consigned his argument (for Augustine, the proof of the certainty of self-knowledge is only incidental to his discussion of the nature of the Trinity whereas for Descartes it becomes the foundation for the whole of his philosophy), it may be that the fame and influence of the Cartesian legacy also derives from its more unique epistemic origin. *Cf.*, W.T. Jones, *A History of Western Philosophy*, New York: Harcourt, Brace and Co., 1952, pp. 355, 662. In any event, the argument of the derivativeness of the Cartesian argument is not a novel one. In his essay, 'Arnauld and the Modern Mind', Peter Schouls has pointed out that "Arnauld's very first comment on the *Meditations* is that he finds it 'remarkable' that Descartes has laid down as the basis for his entire philosophy exactly the same principle as that laid down by St Augustine', namely, that 'you yourself exist'..." *Cf.*, Elmar Kremer (ed.), *Interpreting Arnauld*, Toronto: University of Toronto Press, 1996, p. 40. Schouls, in his extremely accessible essay, does proceed to emphasize that for Descartes, unlike Augustine, 'systematic doubt' is the basis for the individual's reconstruction of knowledge. Bernard Williams points out that in a letter to Colvius, Descartes makes the point that Augustine utilizes the argument to prove the incorporality of the soul, which he, Descartes, does not. *Cf.*, Bernard Williams, *DESCARTES, THE PROJECT OF PURE ENQUIRY*, Harmondsworth: Penguin Books, 1987, p. 106. Descartes has also been the subject of criticism because his entire argument assumes the existence of an external world and other minds before he "proves" it in that his language is already socially, culturally and historically based. It should be clearly noted that this objection confuses existential and phenomenological relevance. While his argument of course depends upon the prior existence of language and other minds, the validity of his proof is not dependent upon that existence any more than it is on the fact of the physical existence of his own brain. Phenomenologically speaking, he can be certain of his own consciousness without being phenomenologically certain of other minds or of language. Of course he is presupposing the existence of a world (and an audience), but these existences are not part of the phenomenological certainty of consciousness or of the validity of the argument for its discovery even though they are physical conditions of its capacity for communication. For further discussion of these and related issues in Descartes, one may be referred to Part II., Chapter 2 of the work of the present, respective author *et passim*.

9. *Cf.*, Sermon III, Henry Sidgwick, *Outlines of the History of Ethics*, Boston: Beacon Press, 1960.

PART II

THE NATURE OF KNOWLEDGE

Moderato, non troppo
Easily, but not too slowly

1 The Modes of Knowledge, the Case of the *Idiot Savant* and How Many Angels Can Dance on the Head of a Pin?

Prelinguistic Knowledge

The phrase, 'If one knows something, one must be able to put it into words', is a phrase with which philosophy professors intimidate students. Whether it is true that if something is known, it must be able to be put it into words, is debatable, but it is important not to simply accept this dictum at face value. If one is not able to put something into words, it does not follow that one possessed or possesses no knowledge of it. One may have known or know something, but not know how to speak about it. When Lao Tzu says in the first sentence of the opening chapter of the *Tao De Ching*, or *The Way of Life*, that the Tao that can be spoken about is not the constant Tao, the implication is that one knows, or at least knows about something that cannot be spoken about. Knowledge exists which cannot be put into words.

      While it is not that one must accept the authority of Lao Tzu that knowledge outside of language is possible, it is important to consider that in classical Chinese culture such an idea was considered plausible.[1] Knowledge outside of language was not simply ruled out of court. Historically, such a position was held and considered intellectually respectable. The message, as delivered by Western philosophers, that knowledge outside of language is *per impossibile* is contradicted by the empirical example that at least one philosopher, philosophers, that knowledge outside of language is *per impossibile* is contradicted by the empirical example that at least one philosopher, representing a tradition, did not consider it to be an impossibility. So, at the very least, one should remain open to examining the possibility that knowledge can exist which cannot be put into words. One cannot as Rorty simply legislate that all knowledge is linguistic.

It is also important to consider the implications of the need to use language to express knowledge. It does not follow, for example, that knowledge depends upon language for its origin. In fact, if one follows the train of thought in Augustine's, *De Magistro,* it is argued that one must first know before one can use language to refer to the known. If Augustine's arguments are correct, it must be the case not only that one can, but that one *must* know something before one can put it into words.

Consider Augustine's argument applied to the common appellations for the female parent. In all languages, a word is evolved to name the female parent, e.g., mommy, mom, ma, mummy, mama. But, in order to know that this word refers to the female parent, one must also have access to a non-linguistic datum, namely, the female parent. One cannot know if the word applies to the object described, unless one has linguistic-independent knowledge access to the object described. In Medieval philosophy in the West, the classic example given was that one could not know that the name 'Hercules' applied to the statue of Hercules unless one were first (or independently) acquainted with the person (or representation) of Hercules.

If one considers the case of the development of civilization, it also is the case that one can now put into words many things that could not be known before. Perhaps, what cannot be put into words now will be able to be put into words in the future. Thus, the fact that something cannot put something into words now does not mean that knowledge of it is impossible. It might mean that knowledge at the present moment is not linguistically available in actuality, but when it becomes available, it will imply retrospectively that knowledge was potentially possible.

One also should ask what parameters are of not being able to put something into words. While Augustine taught that nothing could be learned through the use of language, it may be the case that in an extended sense that language may nonetheless be of partial use. Language, for example, may be inadequate to convey some or all of a *cognoscendum,* but it may be capable of affording a partial glimpse of the *cognoscendum.* In other words, language might be partially adequate to render some aspect of what is known. Thus, not to be able to offer a precise and comprehensive definition of the *cognoscendum* is not the same as not being able to speak about it at all. A clumsy explication is still an explication and implies the possibility of the transmission of some knowledge, no matter how vague or inchoate.

It is also important to take into account the manner of putting something knowable into words. Some items of knowledge may not be capable of being described, but words, or a sufficient number of them, might serve the purpose of pointing to or signifying what is known. In the special case of edifying discourse as opposed to descriptive discourse, words function so as to transform the consciousness of the reader such that it is only when the reader reaches a certain state of consciousness that the knowable becomes known. This is true whether one is reading philosophical, spiritual dialogues or *mondo* in Zen literature, Kierkegaard's, *The Purity of Heart is to Will One Thing*, or Hegel's, *Phenomenology of the Spirit*. In these cases, there may not be any parity between the meaning of particular sentences and the temporal moment during the reading of the work that the knowledge is obtained. There is also no parity between the literal meaning of the words and the level of knowledge or insight that is obtained. (It could be said that the latter could be put into another set of words, but this will lead to a *regressus*).

Even in cases in which it might appear that one can put what one knows into words, one may not really be capable of doing so. For example, if one draws a circle on the board and then comments that the image that one has drawn on the board is a circle, one has spoken falsely. The outside of the circumference is further away from the center than a point on the inside of the circumference, and thus one has not drawn a circle after all. When one attempts to state in words that a circular image is a circle, one discovers that one cannot communicate such a thought in language. This is a more radical claim than that of post-Modernism. For post-Modernism, words can take on an infinite variety of meanings. What is being said here is that in a strict sense no word by itself can take on any meaning at all. If a word cannot take on even a single meaning, then *a fortiori* it cannot take on an infinite variety of meanings. Words can only point to what one knows; words do not and cannot encompass what one knows any more than the chalk image can encompass or embody the idea of a circle. If a circle cannot be represented by a chalk image, neither can it be represented by a mathematical symbol, a verbal sound or a written word. In this manner, no knowledge, when the matter is thought about deeply, can really be put into words. However, univocal knowledge may still be possible even though it may not be possible to express it linguistically. There is also an interesting case in which what is known does not appear to be related at all to discursive thinking, and this is the case of the *idiot savant*.

The Case of the *Idiot Savant*

Any epistemology worthy of its name must be able to solve or at least address the problem of the *idiot savant*. To discharge its proper responsibility, epistemology must consider whether knowledge is possible and how it is possible. What then of the knowledge of the *idiot savant?* Since it is possible, how is it possible? If epistemology does not concern itself with this case, then it is radically incomplete, since it refrains from considering one kind of knowledge. Strangely enough, it seems that epistemologists have neglected the knowledge feats of the *idiot savant*, and, as a result, epistemology remains not only incomplete, but retarded in its development since it cannot benefit from the consequences for theories of knowledge that may follow from a thoroughgoing consideration of the case of the *idiot savant*.

It is most instructive to consider the example of the *idiot savant*. There is scientific evidence that there are those who know by means which cannot be duplicated by others. Large mathematical multiplications, divisions, and square roots can be carried out in an instant by these *idiots savants*, the truth of the results of which can be verified by those using slower, more plodding means or by those making use of computers.[2]

Two questions then arise. First of all, can one know (as the *idiot savant*) without knowing that she or he knows? If it is considered that the *idiot savant* does indeed know the right solutions to amazingly difficult mathematical puzzles, then the *idiot savant* possesses knowledge without being able to discourse upon it in discursive terms. If the *idiot savant* does not know that she or he knows the right solutions to difficult mathematical puzzles, then the *idiot savant* knows without knowing that she or he knows. It may be argued that she or he does not know that she or he has hit upon the right answer until her or his answer is verified by the mathematician employing ordinary, acceptable means. It may further be argued that even after having been informed, she or he actually does not even know that her or his answer is correct; she or he simply accepts the authority of the mathematician, (or the person with the computer), who testifies that the *idiot savant* is correct. If it is argued that she or he does know that she or he knows, prior to being informed, then it could be argued that it comes to much the same thing for if she or he does know that she or he knows, she or he knows without being able to put how she or he knows into words. It is suggested here that regardless of which position one takes on the matter, that the *idiot savant* possesses knowledge without being able to speak about the knowledge that is possessed in a manner that is normally consonant with the possession of such knowledge. Secondly, what are the transcendental conditions for such knowledge, that is, the possibility of the possession of knowledge without being able to elucidate how such knowledge has been acquired? What are the transcendental conditions for knowledge which can exist, but which cannot be explained by any known means?

To the first question. Can the *idiot savant* know without knowing that or how she or he knows? The fact that such knowledge (as possessed by the *idiot savant*) does exist itself possesses enormous significance. Is it the case that knowledge hosts discover and possess knowledge which can be verified independently of the host, but which the host neither knows to be true nor how to prove its truth? One might argue that if outside verification is required to prove that the answers offered by the *idiot savant* are correct, then the *idiot savant* herself or himself does not know that she or he knows. If outside verification is considered to be a prerequisite for knowledge, then it could be said that one knows without knowing that one knows. It is difficult to avoid the conclusion that she or he did know or at least did possess knowledge when others utilizing acceptable means verify her or his answers. Should it not be said that the *idiot savant* possesses the right answers without knowing that these answers are correct? Is this a knowledge of something without a knowledge that this knowledge is in fact knowledge? Is this a knowing without knowing that one knows? How is it possible that one can possess knowledge without knowing that one is in possession of it? It may be objected that this example does not show that one can have knowledge without knowing that one has it, because it is only a second party, e.g. someone other than the knowledge holder, who knows that the first party (the *idiot savant*) possesses true knowledge. But, whether one knows through a first or second party, it is a fact that the first party possesses true knowledge which cannot be justified by that first party to be true knowledge. If it is known to the first party to be true knowledge, then the *means* by which the first party knows this is manifestly a means which is incapable of being explained. If it is known to the first party, then it is possible to have true knowledge without being able to adequately, precisely or comprehensively state in words the manner by which such knowledge is acquired or possessed. If that which is claimed to be known by the first party is said to be known only by a second party, this state of affairs only reflects that the first party possesses knowledge without knowing that she or he does and without knowing how she or he does. If it is considered that the *idiot savant* knows that she or he knows but cannot explain how she or he knows, then the knowledge of the *idiot savant* can be likened to the knowledge claims of the psychic. The possession of knowledge of the psychic is also inexplicable. However, since the documentation of psychic knowledge is subject to disputation, this example, however important, will be deferred.

The *idiot savant* can put knowledge into words since the *idiot savant* can give voice to or write down the mathematical answer. However, it is to be expected that if one can put one's knowledge into words or symbols, that one understands the words or symbols that one is articulating. If the *idiot savant* can give no account of the answer that she or he articulates, can this count as understanding the answer? A lack of understanding of the origin or the meaning of one's answers or even if one's answers are true answers is similar to possessing knowledge in a language that is unintelligible to the speaker. If the *idiot savant* does not comprehend the answers that she or he gives, then the *idiot savant* can speak but in a language that she or he does not comprehend.

The second question is, how is it possible to possess knowledge without knowing the manner by which such a possession has come about? The only conceivable answer is that the knowledge that one possesses is somehow built into the subject knower as pre-reflective knowledge. Some, like *idiots savants*, (without knowing how and perhaps without knowing that they do) can tap into such knowledge. Outside verification proves that *idiots savants* have access to such knowledge without knowing that or how or why they do. Thus, the transcendental conditions for the existence of knowledge that is not known by the subject holders of that knowledge to be knowledge, is the existence, or, since it is not possible to be known by empirical means, the metaphysical existence, of pre-existent knowledge. The term 'pre-existent' knowledge is perhaps not totally accurate since one may consider that some form of innate talent is at work. Nevertheless, this innate talent must be capable of knowing something which is not accessible by ordinary means.

By giving up the search for metaphysics and showing it to be impossible on the first level of knowledge, one once again finds metaphysics to be possible, indeed to be necessary, in order to account for second level knowledge, that is, knowledge which cannot be shown to be possible by empirical means. Just as Kant gave metaphysical arguments (expositions) for the existence of (the *a priori* "concepts" of) space and time, and thus brought in metaphysics, albeit of a different kind, through the back door (the concept of a metaphysical exposition or argument), here, metaphysics, taken in this context to mean the ontological existence of necessary conditions is shown as necessary for the actual existence of knowledge which cannot be shown to be possible by empirical means.

The same argument can be applied to the condition that the *idiot savant* knows without being able to adduce any proofs for how what she or he knows is true. This suggests that a subject knower possesses access to knowledge that is direct. The capacity to possess direct access to knowledge shows that pre-reflective knowledge must pre-exist in the subject knower. The knowledge of such mathematical truths, which are true of the universe, is pre-existent in the subject knower. This can only mean that the subject knower as the microcosm of the universe is the knowledge center, as it were, of the universe. What is true of the universe exists, in knowledge form, in the microcosm, the subject knower. This is the only way to explain how mathematical truths that are internally known to *idiots savants* can also apply to the universe.[3] Even if it were to be alleged that it is through a kind of mysterious and rapid calculation and not through an access to pre-existent knowledge that the *idiot savant* can arrive at her or his answers, one would still be left with the circumstance that such truths as are discovered apply to the universe. Thus, even a mysterious and rapid calculation is a calculation of something that possesses an objective correlate. The *idiot savant* possesses access to truths of the universe.

Why any one individual with lowered mental capacity (in other areas) can possibly possess such remarkable ability and not another such individual and what brain capacities or functions can be detected to be different is an empirical question, and while assuredly should be of great interest to the empirical scientist is of no special importance to the philosopher. The *transcendental conditions* (in Kant's sense) and the *implications* of the fact that she or he possesses this ability are of stupendous consequence. To quote from Rilke's 'Song of the Idiot': "How good!"

Can further light be shed upon the discovery that transcendental conditions must exist in order to account for knowledge which cannot be known by any empirical means? Can it simply be said that built-in pre-reflective knowledge or abilities appear to exist? This seems to be reminiscent of the doctrine of innate ideas. It might be that there is a difference between the discovery that is made here and the doctrine of innate ideas. The condition for the possibility of the existence of such transcendental knowledge as has been referred to above is that the subject knower contains or possesses direct access to in microcosmic intellectual form the laws that govern the universe as a whole. Is this a doctrine of innate ideas? It is a metaphysics that includes the universe as well. It is a doctrine of the subject knower as connected to the world, and as the pre-reflective possessor of the laws that govern the universe. If the doctrine of innate ideas treats the subject knower in isolation from the cosmos, then what is presented here is not a doctrine of innate ideas.

The notion of the subject-knower as containing in embryonic form the macrocosmic laws of the universe makes it more plausible why ideas that are known internally can also apply to the universe at large. It also makes it more plausible as to why such ideas should be capable of being known internally in the first place. If the subject knower is the intellectual pre-reflective and post-reflective agent or instrument of the universe - the mind is the window and the mirror of the cosmos - then it makes more sense as to why it should be possible to know internally from self reflection and/or self-discovery the ideas which upon empirical application are also discovered to govern the world of physics. A doctrine of innate ideas which did not possess a connection with the cosmos would make it seem somewhat arbitrary that human beings possessed ideas *a priori* that applied to the cosmos. The notion advanced here suggests that it is not surprising that such pre-reflective knowledge exists; it would be more surprising if it were not to exist.

Philosophical Debates

Intentionality Versus Behaviorism

Are there irresolvable philosophical debates? What of the position that the mind is a Cartesian theater, for example, as opposed to explaining or describing all that occurs from a behavioristic standpoint? From the standpoint of assuming the mind is a Cartesian theater or magic lantern show, one can, like the audience of a mental theater, become aware of a toothache as an item of prelinguistic knowledge. For behaviorism on the other hand, any description of a pain as a toothache is linguistic, and one cannot really experience a toothache as a toothache without making use of a language system. For the linguistic analyst or behaviorist, there can be no phenomenological reduction, as one is always operating within a world of signs and concepts. This conflict, it appears, cannot be resolved. It cannot be resolved because the entire debate is taking place within a linguistic and conceptual world. One possesses no access to a prelinguistic world.

It is only if one attempts to consider an abstract level of knowledge such as that which is represented by space and time, which is a phenomenologically reduced spectrum, that there is any hope of penetrating to the issues involved in understanding the difference between prelinguistic, linguistic and postlinguistic knowledge. In the reduction, or transcendental reflection, if one prefers this description, one employs language while one attempts to burrow beneath its surface.

In the example of pain, it seems that the behaviorist and the one who argues that there are intentional states, are at loggerheads. This is because one side is arguing about a description of a particular experience which in its view it possessed prior to its being expressed linguistically. From this side of the argument, the particular experience does not require the employment of language since the experience was prelinguistic. From the other side of the issue, to meaningfully possess this experience in the first place would already have required a linguistic act.

The example of pain is not a fruitful example for comparison. In order to approach the limits of language, one must take up examples that are at the beginning or the end of the limits of language that are examples of putative linguistic or prelinguistic data employed by subject knowers capable of utilizing language. Otherwise, the discussion can degenerate to a shouting match. One participant insists that pain (or the experience of red or blue) is an irreducible particular. The other argues that this irreducibility is a function of a network of conceptually understood relations and an understanding of a world system.[4]

The question of reducibility or irreducibility does not arise, strictly speaking, for the phenomenologist, since the phenomenologist is concerned with phenomenological data and not with the theoretical object of an irreducible particular or a reducible particular. However, with that qualification, it may be said that the view presented here finds a greater agreement with the position of Thomas Nagel, that there are irreducible particulars, rather than with Rorty's view that experience who argue that language systems and world systems are required for experience by citing the examples of putative, irreducible particulars. In order to best persuade those who argue against the possibility of prelinguistic or postlinguistic knowledge, one must employ examples known to language users at either end of the spectrum which are *a priori* truths, and not matters of contingent experience. Thus, if one were to argue that space could not be understood purely conceptually, one would be on better grounds than if one were to argue that pain could not be understood purely linguistically, as perverse as this situation may seem.

The One and the Many

For the Greeks, the One and the Many was an, if not the, essential distinction. This remains true today, although what is meant by the One and the Many may require modification. An analysis of the One and the Many - or the Essence of Number - may prove fruitful for the understanding of the question of how knowledge that transcends language is possible.

If one were to begin with mathematics as Plato was insistent upon doing, a better understanding of the One and the Many could be achieved. While it may be debatable whether every particular number is or possesses an essence, it may be the case that there is an essence of number itself. The embodiment of such an essence is the number one. Every other number can be understood and can only be understood as a derivative of one. One itself cannot be defined by any other number or as the sum of any other numbers as it is absolutely primitive. This is important to understand even though it has been thought that the concept of number altered with the introduction of the zero from India. (The remarkable and distiguished Professor Fred Sturm was kind enough to inform the present author that the Olmecs also discovered the zero). However brilliant a contribution to mathematics the invention of zero is, it does not alter the fundamental definition of number stated above. Zero is a derivative concept since it represents the absence of any and all ones. Similarly, negative numbers are derivative concepts. Negative one is the presence of a one that counts against one. All other numbers can be defined as the sum of ones. It is not necessary, of course, to define number in terms of the sum of its ones. Seventeen, for example, can be defined as one more than sixteen. But, any such definition is logically derivative from and reducible to a form of a sum of ones. The sum of ones is the basic or core essence of number, of ones. The sum of ones is the basic or core essence of number, because every other definition is based or grounded on this essential definition. The independent invention of zero by the Indians and the Olmecs did not alter this, for zero must still be defined in terms of being the absence of one in general. Zero is the logical privative of one. One does not need to be and cannot be defined in terms of zero. Zero is the absence of which one is the presence. One is the positive existence of something; it cannot be defined by its absence, whereas zero is precisely the absence of any and all ones.

One is inescapable because it is the most primitive boundary of embodiment, which is why it is chosen as the symbol of Unity. It is impossible to proceed from the One to the Many without employing a form of plurality. The two forms of plurality, (to speak in a provisional fashion), which are discussed below, are space and time. Space and time are the conditions that make it possible to proceed from the One to the More than One. Strictly speaking, space and time are required even to represent One in the first place.

Space in the Philosophy of Kant

Kant's brilliant metaphysical exposition of the concept of space in which he puts forward his four arguments for the *a priori* character of space are still valid if they are understood not as arguments for the *a priori* character of physical space (which is not what he intended in any case), but if they are understood as arguments which explain on the level of phenomenological knowledge, the difference between conceptual and preconceptual forms of plurality.[5]

While what is to immediately follow will be treated in a more detailed fashion in the present author's *Space, Time and the Ethical Foundations*, some of what is to follow may be anticipated here. The following descriptions of Kant's arguments are to a certain extent interpolations of his arguments and are not intended to be purely expository accounts. They are intended is some respects to make the points that he was making and in some respects represent interpolations beyond those points.

In his first argument, Kant argues against the empiricists that space cannot be learned from outer experience, because, in the interpolation posited by the present, respective author, one must bring the inside-outside distinction with one to experience. It may be that he could also have included topside-bottom side and between two sides in his attempt to characterize spatial relationships. It is interesting to note that he does include alongside, an inclusion that supports the present interpretation or interpolation. Whether or not one agrees with Kant or the empiricists here, what the argument can be understood as saying is that space is a different way of obtaining a plurality than a conceptual plurality, and that every *representation* of even a conceptual plurality requires the form of space. Every word must be represented as spatially distinct from every other word. Alongside, inside and outside are not different merely conceptually. In order to understand the difference between alongside, inside and outside, one must have access to a prelinguistic, aesthetic awareness whether ostensive or kinaesthetic.

One cannot employ spatial imagination without recourse to the specific form of pluralization that is given by space. While this may appear, on the surface, to be like the medieval definition of why opium puts people to sleep, i.e., opium puts people to sleep because of its dormitive powers, there is a decided difference. The circular definition of opium is purely conventional and linguistic. The circularity of spatial definition in Kant's first argument is evidence of its prelinguistic character. Space cannot be understood on a linguistic level; one must possess access to the mode of a prelinguistic, kinaesthetic or ostensive form of pluralization.

Whether or not this means that other animals must also be able to do this - which is sometimes argued as a *Reductio ad Absurdum* of Kant - is beside the point. What is relevant for human philosophers is whether the animal man can become aware of this kind of distinction. *In order to become aware of this distinction (conceptual versus non-conceptual), a transcendental reflection is required, that is, a reflection which takes place inside of consciousness and which cannot be learned empirically.* The awareness of the distinction between conceptual and non-conceptual knowledge requires a third kind of knowledge which must be neither conceptual nor non-conceptual in the sense in which the representation of space and time are non-conceptual. This third kind of knowledge is non-conceptual in its own unique sense.

For pedagogical reasons, it is advisable to proceed directly to Kant's third argument. One cannot picture space without placing every example of space inside or within a greater space. If one attempts to separate space into two or more parts, it cannot be separated save by itself. Every part of space is part of one and the same space. Hence, there cannot be more than one space. Space is manifestly not a concept.

Kant's fourth argument is closely related to his third argument. His fourth argument is another illustration of the prelinguistic character of space. Whereas no empirical concept can be infinitely complex (or else no conceptual understanding would be possible); space is infinitely divisible and extensible, and thus cannot be a concept. While an empirical concept, such as 'dolphin', can be understood without grouping every dolphin inside of another dolphin, space cannot be understood without the form of spatial imagination. Concepts gather their instances under themselves. The instances of space exist within itself. Every example of a concept is not a part of a concept but every example of space is a part of itself. It is not simply that space is something physical, and thus cannot be a concept. It is that whatever physical space may be, *there can be no conceptual understanding of space*. (This explains why Augustine could not understand time, which, like space, is not conceptual and hence is not comprehensible conceptually). For purposes of this argument there is no need at this point to refer to the inter-definability of space and time which is another matter which will be taken up in the present author's *Space, Time and the Ethical Foundations*, and does not affect the truth at issue here.

It is now pedagogically appropriate to consider Kant's second argument. Kant's second argument, which has been vilified for being psychologistic, is also a reflection of the prelinguistic or preconceptual character of space in that one cannot accomplish the act of representation without making use of the plurality given by space. Whereas, for many readers, Kant may appear to have been proposing that one perform a psychological experiment here, the important implication of his argument is that all representation requires preconceptual pluralization. What, for many of Kant's readers, may appear to have assumed the form of a psychologistic argument was in fact a simple test of phenomenological introspection. It is not truly liable to the critique of being psychologistic because the thought experiment that he proposes (if one reads between the lines of his argument) is not an empirical thought experiment. Whatever his thought experiment might prove, it can be understood as another illustration of the impossibility of representation without spatial imaging. It can also be argued that Kant's second argument is a phenomenological test that demonstrates that one can experience consciousness without an object.

How Many Angels Can Dance on the Head of a Pin?

How many angels can dance on the head of a pin? While this question most frequently is posed facetiously to indicate the utter fatuity, futility and hilarity of philosophical investigations, what are the implications of such a question? While one normally answers, equally facetiously, that it depends on the size of the angels and the size of the pin, such answers are, of course, misleading. If angels are to be understood as lacking all materiality, then could it be possible that an infinite number of angels could dance on the head of a pin? But what would it mean to say that that which was not corporeal was capable of dancing? And while it seems tempting to argue that an infinite number of angels could dance on the head of a pin, if angels are lacking in materiality, then in what sense can one place on the head of a pin or otherwise represent any number of angels, much less an infinite number? Indeed, without a body, how can one represent even one angel? It seems that the concept of number is dependent upon representation and representation appears to require extension. But if angels are non-extended, how is it possible to represent angels as possessing numerical distinctness?

What one has discovered is that one cannot represent number, whether one or many, if one were to refer to a non-material realm. To put this another way, conceptually, every angel *qua* angel is the same. However, it seems that one is able to speak of and to imaginatively conceive of more than one angel. The concept of an angel is insufficient to account for the human ability to enumerate angels. 'More than one angel' is not a conceptual distinction; it is a non-conceptual distinction. One must have recourse to a different sort of knowledge than that which is afforded by concepts in order to be able to become aware of a number of angels. *Since an awareness of a number of angels is possible, this represents a form of proof that there must exist an access to a source of knowledge that does not arise from concepts.* The *question*, rather than the *answer* to the question, 'how many angels can dance on the head of a pin?' reveals an important epistemological truth: that there are at least two separate and epistemically independent sources of knowledge. That one can ask such a question in the first place reveals that one possesses access to knowledge that does not arise from nor is deducible from concepts.

Such is the real meaning behind the wonderful story Leibniz relates concerning his declaration that no two leaves were exactly alike. While a gentleman of his acquaintance went about collecting leaves to prove him wrong, this amusing consequence missed the point. Even Leibniz was not totally aware of the genius of his claim.[6] It was not that empirically it was impossible to find two identical leaves (such a question is indeed an empirical one and would be based upon the length and the colour of the veins of the leaf and so on); from the standpoint of the present author, what Leibniz should have meant is that one cannot differentiate one leaf from another *qua* leaf on the grounds of conceptual difference. Since one can and does spatially and numerically differentiate between two or more leaves, the means by which one is able to do so are other than conceptual ones. Leibniz did not say all of this. His argument simply was that no two identical things could exist for there must be a sufficient reason why something exists in one place rather than another. His argument was based upon the principle of sufficient reason, and its validity depends upon whether or not one accepts the principle of sufficient reason.

The awareness that one can differentiate between two sources of knowledge is itself a non-conceptual awareness. Once possessed, such an awareness can be classified conceptually. But, the original possession of such knowledge is not through concepts. When Kant discovered that there are two sources of knowledge, in the vocabulary of the present work, such a discovery occurred as an act of non-conceptual, transcendental reflection.

Postconceptual Knowledge

Postconceptual knowledge lies on the other side of the spectrum from conceptual knowledge. Postconceptual knowledge is the kind of knowledge that may be possessed as emergent from or as a reflection upon conceptual knowledge. The condition for the possibility of the understanding of Plato's Fourth, for example, is the employment of postconceptual knowledge that emerges from and transcends conceptual understanding. The employment of postconceptual transcendental reflection is the condition for the possibility of the discernment of the difference between a spatial distinction and a conceptual distinction. The understanding that space and time are not concepts is not itself a conceptual understanding. For convenience's sake, one can choose to use the language of concepts as a short hand to refer to space and time, but the understanding of space and time may not be reached through concepts. The understanding that one possesses prelinguistic knowledge is itself an understanding that is obtained postlinguistically.

The Doctrine of Transcendental Reflection

One application of transcendental reflection consists of the discernment of conceptual and conceptual-spatial distinctions within consciousness.

In this case, transcendental reflection is not only an inspection of the contents of consciousness as in a transcendental introspection, but is also a discernment of the difference among the items in consciousness. It is best not to refer to this mental activity as intuition, since the word 'intuition' carries with it such untoward connotations as, for example, picking up extrasensory signals and so on. As a result, in the interest of employing a technical term to discriminate this sort of mental activity from other sorts of mental activity, the phrase 'transcendental reflection' is used.

While it may be suggested that what is being discussed herein could be referred to as second order thinking, this phrase does not precisely capture what is being indicated here, since second order thinking could be a kind of reasoning. But, what is indicated here is not ratiocination. It is a pity that up to now there has been a paucity of terms which can be drawn upon to demarcate different types of mental acts such that only very crude demarcations can be made, such as ratiocination versus intuition. But, even the very act of understanding the difference between reasoning and intuiting requires an act of transcendental reflection that is not a species of either ratiocination or intuition. The act of transcendental reflection which is required to understand the difference between ratiocination and intuition may be entitled 'transcendental understanding', or in the terminology presented here, 'transcendental reflection', a phrase that refers to the purely theoretical, disinterested understanding of a transcendental object, that is, an object the empirical embodiments or associations of which remain irrelevant and in which the grounds for the understanding of which are neither conceptual nor non-conceptual in the sense in which space and time are the non-conceptual grounds for certain kinds of distinctnesses. It is just this kind of transcendental reflection that Kant calls upon in the Transcendental Aesthetic when he states that one must isolate sensibility from any empirical conditions.

It is the opinion of this present author that those acts of transcendental reflection which discriminate among different types of knowledge such as the knowledge of concepts and the knowledge of space merit further inquiry. The type of knowledge that one employs when one knows that space is not a concept must be sharply distinguished as a different type of knowledge than that which is employed when one knows the very definition of space itself, i.e., that mode of plurality which is the condition for the possibility of the representation of existence of more than one in the same time. One's knowledge that *this* (the foregoing definition) is the definition of space is a very different sort of knowing from the knowing that ratiocination and intuition are different forms of knowledge. One's knowledge that this previous definition is the definition of space is an example of first order representational knowledge. First order representational knowledge is a type of knowledge that involves a necessary non-conceptual element. One cannot represent space to oneself without the non-conceptual ingredient. One's knowledge that one then knows the proper definition of space is an example of second order knowledge or post-representational knowledge.

One clue to what transcendental reflection is can be found in the study of Kant's Appendix to the Transcendental Analytic of his first *Critique* entitled, 'The Amphiboly of Concepts of Reflection'. Another clue can be afforded by the study of Plato's *Seventh Letter*. A further clue can be found in Kant's claim in the first *Critique* that there are two stems (*zwei Stämme*) or two sources of knowledge (*zwei Erkenntnisquellen)* (B29, B55). While Kant does not intend the same kind of meaning in these two different passages, in each passage he makes reference to different stems or sources of knowledge. In the first passage he refers to sensibility and understanding as two stems of knowledge. In the second passage he refers to space and time as two sources of knowledge. The question is, by which form of knowledge or which source of knowledge does he come to know that there are two different stems or sources of knowledge or what the different stems or sources are? Transcendental reflection is the condition for the possibility of understanding the existence of and the difference between the two sources of knowledge.[7]

The work carried out in the chapter, 'The Forgotten Fourth' is transcendental reflection. It is not sufficient to distinguish this to call this 'philosophy' or 'thinking' since these terms are very broad and can include pure deductive reasoning. This is the problem with Hegel's sometimes useful definition of philosophy as 'the thinking study of things'. Such a definition is too general and does not differentiate the kind of thinking that is unique to philosophical inquiry. When the object of knowledge is distinguished from the knowing of the object, this distinction is not obtained through concepts: it is a knowing that is not representational or conceptual, but is a direct knowledge. Intuitive knowledge or inferential knowledge is different from the knowledge of different orders of knowledge such as the knowing that knowledge in mathematics is different from knowledge in science. ('Intuitive knowledge' would be too vague a descriptive term; it would not differentiate this kind of knowledge from other kinds of knowledge.)

Knowing differences among different types of knowledge is not a knowing that can be reduced to either sort of knowledge and is an act of transcendental reflection. It should be observed that transcendental reflection can be sometimes be representational as in the knowledge of space or sometimes post-representational as in the knowledge that space is not a concept.

A key source of the difficulties, illocutions, endless linguistic innovations and transformations and finally the inventions of technical terminology that are seemingly entailed herein is that language itself is being pushed to its breaking point. All attempts to communicate must take place through the use of language. But, language must itself be understood to be an imperfect instrument of knowledge. The same language tool can and must be employed to point one both to preconceptual and postconceptual knowledge, but it can neither represent nor take one to these *loci*. One may not be able to communicate what a toothache is or even understand it completely oneself without a conceptual and a linguistic system, but there is an irreducible and obvious factor of experience which is not covered by the linguistic and conceptual system of description.

Is all of this, in the end, a difference that makes a difference? The simple and yet important answer is, yes. One's understanding is different when it is understood that language and conception have limits. One's ways of doing and understanding philosophy may also be different. In the very first sentence of the *Tao De Ching*, it is said that the constant Tao is the Tao that cannot be talked about. And yet, the rest of the entire work of the *Tao De Ching* proceeds to talk about it. For Wittgenstein, that of which one cannot speak, one must be silent. With Wittgenstein, silence appears at the end of his *Tractatus* and signifies, perhaps, the end of philosophy. For Lao Tzu, what cannot be talked about marks the very beginning of philosophy, and philosophy consists precisely of talking about that which cannot be said. For Wittgenstein, when one arrived at that about which one could not speak, one had reached the limits of language. For Lao Tzu, when one arrived at the limits of language, (which is his starting point) one had discovered the correct location for the commencement of the real work of language and philosophy. The present work possesses more affinity in this regard to that of Lao Tzu than it does to that of Wittgenstein.[8] *Philosophy can perhaps be defined as the art of talking about that which transcends the limits of language.* In this present, respective work, an attempt is made to offer an understanding of what is meant by the art of talking about that which transcends the limits of language.

What is intended herein is not naïve mysticism. For example, various forms of transcendental reflection are indicated herein and the distinctions between them are marked.

In this present work, it may be said that, that of which one cannot speak, one must evoke, and that of which one cannot speak, one can edify, and after the work of evocation and edification has been completed, one's understanding can never be the same. When one finishes reading and understanding Hegel on Hegel's level, one is not the same as one was before. It is not only on a conceptual level that one understands Hegel. In fact, if one's understanding is limited to a conceptual understanding, one cannot have understood Hegel. How could one possibly understand the last sections of the *Phenomenology of Mind* on the level of conceptual knowledge alone? In order to understand Hegel, one's own power of understanding must be first transformed and expanded in the attempt at understanding. One's power of comprehension is pushed beyond its conceptual boundaries to a place of higher understanding in which one understands that which earlier was referred to as the fourth class of truths. This is not the knowledge of mere concepts. Nor is it the pure reverie of religious ecstasy, the state that Hegel satirized as Schelling's, 'Night in which all cats are black'. One is stretched beyond the limits of language and conception to a level of understanding that is only possible in the act of stretching, and not possible so long as one remains conceptually and linguistically bound. In the edifying act, one can experience this power of understanding, and it is only by entering into this expansion of consciousness that one can begin to reach, as with Adam's hand in the panel of *The Creation of Adam*, in Michelangelo's fresco of *Genesis* on the ceiling of the Sistine Chapel, beyond the limits of language.

Space and Time

Space, or the characteristic of matter that is extension (rather than solidity, for example), seems to be a necessary feature of unity or plurality. One cannot speak of a 'oneness' or a 'more than oneness' unless one has recourse to space.[9] Knowledge of what is space and what is time is an example of prelinguistic or preconceptual knowledge. An example of conceptual knowledge is the ability to recognize a dog. A concept, such as the empirical concept, 'dog', (Kant's favourite example), is a rule for recognition. It is unclear what one's knowledge of a dog would be without language. Attempting to know what conceptual knowledge is like without language would be analogous to Kant attempting to know what the thing-in-itself was like without applying the categories. In the end, Kant goes so far as to say that the thing-in-itself must exist although even to say this is illegitimate according to his own strictures. For instance, in his first *Critique*, Kant states emphatically: 'Doubtless, indeed there are intelligible entities corresponding to the sensible entities ...' (B309) In various places Kant appears to attribute causal efficacy to the thing-in-itself as well. For example, he writes: 'Our mode of intuition is dependent upon the existence of the object, and is therefore possible only if the subject's faculty of representation is affected by that object' (B72). Here, both existence and causal efficacy are pointed to, albeit to the 'object' and not to the 'thing in-itself'. But in this reference the 'object' fulfills the function of the 'thing-in-itself' since otherwise Kant would be a subjective idealist. As Kant himself states, '... the object must be capable of being in some manner given. Otherwise the concepts are empty ... in this thinking we have really known nothing; we have merely played with representations' (B195). In order to avoid his own strictures of committing a transcendental misapplication of the categories, Kant should not be able to say either that the thing-in-itself exists or that it possesses causal efficacy. (Existence and Causality, to take the liberty of slightly condensing Kant's formulation without altering his meaning, are two of his twelve categories). But, he would not be the first philosopher whose practise violates his principles.

To return to the prosaic example of the household animal. Before one learns the name 'dog' to apply to the familiar household creature, one does have knowledge of something, though it would be somewhat difficult to put into words that of which the knowledge consists. It is, in a sense, analogous to the epistemological problem of attempting to say what the sensory materials are of which an object is made before one possesses the idea of an object. The idea of an object is doubtless a sophisticated idea and requires an act of connecting colour, line, solidity, extension, continuity and the like. It is impossible to grasp the idea of an object without first connecting the ingredients that are essential to its conception. However, one must be able to perceive something before one is able to achieve such a sophisticated conception. It is impossible, however, to intelligently discuss the concept of the "perception before conception of an object". In fact, each part of the "perception before conception", whether colour or solidity, itself represents an object that possesses a conception appropriate to it. The very notion of a sensory component is already an objectified concept. But perception at some point must be possible before conception, however unintelligible such a statement must appear to be. Thus the occurrence of "perception prior to conception" must exist even though it resists a coherent linguistic or conceptual description.

When something is understood about space and time, one makes use of that which is referred to as postconceptual understanding to understand an object that exists prelinguistically and preconceptually. Space and time are logically prior to empirical concept formation. When one understands the nature of space and time, the object of understanding is the reality of space and time which is not a conceptual reality but a preconceptual frame of representation.

Notes

1. It is not necessary to refer to classical Chinese culture as examples may be found in Western culture of those who have considered it to be possible that one may possess access to knowledge outside of language. One of the more famous examples that can be cited is that of Einstein who writes in a letter to Hadamard: 'The words or the language, as they are written or spoken, do not seem to play any role in my mechanism of thought.' Quoted in Roger Penrose, *The Emperor's New Mind*, New York: Oxford University Press, 1989, 1990, p. 423.

2. Sir Roger Penrose, the celebrated Oxford mathematician, cites the example of Johann Martin Zacharian Dase, an illiterate farmer's son, who lived from 1824 to 1861, in Germany, who was able to multiply any two eight figure numbers together in his head in less than a minute, or two twenty figure numbers together in about six minutes. *Cf.*, Roger Penrose, *The Emperor's New Mind*, New York: Oxford University Press, 1989, 1990, p. 7. Other examples of the feats of *idiots savants* are recounted in Howard Gardner, *Frames of Mind, The Theory of Multiple Intelligences*, New York: Basic Books, 1983, p. 155. One example he cites is that of L., an eleven-year-old who was studied by the neurologist Kurt Goldstein, who was able to remember virtually endless series, such as railroad timetables and newspaper financial columns. Another example is that of the Indian Srinivasa Ramanujan, the great natural mathematician, who, as he lay dying, told his teacher Hardy, who had just arrived in a taxicab, that the number 1,729 - the number of the cab - was the smallest number that could be expressed as the sum of two cubes in two different ways. (p. 166) While Gardner does not suggest that Ramanujan was an *idiot savant*, for all intents and purposes, his abilities were of the same order and equally inexplicable by himself or others. In other words, he knew without knowing how he knew. The knowledge of *idiots savants* is not limited to

mathematics. Gardner relates the case of Earl, who on his own, figured out how to make a windmill out of a clock and of Mr. A. who was able to wire his stereo, lights and television to a single switch. Perhaps the most astonishing case was that of Joe who according to clinical psychologist Bernard Rimland: '... put together a tape recorder, fluorescent light and a small transistor radio with some other components so that music from the tape was changed to light energy in the light and then back to music in the radio. By passing his hand between the recorder and the light, he could stop the music. He understands the concepts of electronics, astronomy, music, navigation and mechanics ... He reads Bowditch on navigation. Joe is supposed to have an IQ of 80. He does assembly work in a Goodwill store.' (p. 214) For further reading, one may be referred to H. L. Resnikoff, and R. O. Wells, Jr., *Mathematics and Civilization*, New York: Holt Rinehart and Winston, Inc., 1974, reprinted, New York: Dover Publications, 1984, W. W. Rouse Ball, *Calculating prodigies* in *Mathematical recreations and essays*, and S. B. Smith, *The Great Mental Calculators*, New York: Columbia University Press, 1983. One does not need to have recourse to the fabulous examples of *idiots savants*. The philosopher Köhler (better known as a psychologist) observed evidence of reasoning ability in chimpanzees that were not language trained. Köhler pointed out that even imitation required the insight that imitative behavior was being elicited. Human infants not yet capable of language show evidence of rational thought. *Cf.*, L. Weiskrantz, (ed.) *Thought Without Language*, Oxford: Clarendon Press, 1988. Adult deaf mutes who have not acquired American Sign Language show evidence of rational thought. *Cf.*, A. Montagu, *Touching: The human significance of skin*, New York: Harper and Row, 1986. Of course, as argued above, Augustine showed much earlier in *De Magistro* that thought must precede language.

3. According to Frege, the laws of number are laws of the laws of nature. *Cf.*, Gottlob Frege, *The Foundations of Arithmetic*, J. L. Austin (trans.), Evanston: Northwestern University Press, 1980, p. 99. If one knows the laws of mathematics, one knows that which governs the laws of nature and thus possesses knowledge that applies to nature.

4. In a public lecture at the University of Hong Kong in March of 1993, Rorty described precisely such a debate as one which would frequently arise between himself (taking the side of the network of language) and Thomas Nagel (taking the side of irreducible particulars, such as, the mind) the end result of which was in Rorty's words, an [intellectual] shouting match.

5. Phenomenologizing Kant's arguments for the *a priori* character of space would appear to solve Bennet's revival of Quinton's story of the hypothesis of one being inhabiting two spatial worlds which have no spatial relations to each other. (Bennett, p. 65) Phenomenologically, it would be impossible to represent two spaces that are not divided by one and the same space. According to Bennett, 'Kant, however, takes the Aesthetic to be showing

that ... outer experience must be of things which occupy Space.' Jonathan Bennett, *Kant's Analytic*, Cambridge: Cambridge University Press, 1966, p. 62. This reading of Kant would appear to suggest that Kant is treating space as a thing-in-itself. There have been a few attempts to take note of the possibility of treating Kant as a phenomenologist. *Cf.*, J. N. Mohanty, 'Kant and Husserl', *Husserl Studies*, Vol. 13, No. 1, 1996.

6.   Leibniz's *principium identitatis indiscernibilium* (the principle of the identity of indiscernibles) is: 'no two objects in nature can differ only in number'. *Cf.*, *Nouveaux Essais*, II, chap. 27, section 1. In his fourth letter to Samuel Clarke, Leibniz stated: 'There is no such thing as two individuals indiscernible from each other'. *Cf.*, H.G. Alexander (ed.), *The Leibniz-Clarke Correspondence*, New York: Philosophical Library, 1956, p. 36.

7.   Kant himself seems to recognize a need for developing such a theory of knowledge, but considers that it is beyond the scope of his inquiry. In his Introduction to his first *Critique* he writes, 'I entitle *transcendental* all knowledge which is occupied not so much with objects as with the mode of our knowledge of objects in so far as this mode of knowledge is to be possible *a priori*. A system of such concepts might be entitled transcendental philosophy. But that is still, at this stage, too large an undertaking' (emphasis in the original, Kemp Smith translation, B25). In one passage, Kant differentiates transcendental reflection from logical reflection: '*Transcendental reflection*, on the other hand, since it bears on the objects themselves, contains the ground of the possibility of the objective comparison of representations with each other, and is therefore altogether different from the former type of reflection' B319 (emphasis his). It may be the case that it is transcendental reflection, both in Kant's use of the term and in the use of the term employed by the present author that is responsible for sorting out the transcendental location of concepts. In Kant's language, 'Let me call the place which we assign to a concept, either in sensibility or in pure understanding, its *transcendental location*' B324 (emphasis his). For Kant, logical reflection takes no account of the faculty of knowledge and Kant emphasizes, 'Indeed they [logical reflection which is a mere act of comparison and transcendental reflection] do not even belong to the same faculty of knowledge' (B319). From this statement one may infer that Kant has implied that there is another unspecified faculty of knowledge. Earlier (B318) he described the faculty of knowledge as constituted by sensibility and understanding. Similarly, he identifies the two kinds of knowledge with sensibility and understanding (B318). However, transcendental reflection would appear to be a separate faculty of knowledge or to belong to a separate faculty of knowledge since he has stated that, 'The act by which I confront the comparison of representations with the cognitive faculty to which it belongs, and by means of which I distinguish whether it is as belonging to the pure understanding or to sensible intuition that they are to be compared with each other, I call *transcendental reflection*' (B317) (emphasis in the original). It seems that

for Kant, transcendental reflection may constitute a third source of knowledge.

8. P.M.S. Hacker has written that the reaction of the Vienna Circle as exemplified by Neurath's response to the last sentence of the *Tractatus* was that there was nothing to be silent about. In his opinion, this differed from Wittgenstein's view in the *Tractatus* that ineffable metaphysical truths were to be shown through the analysis of language. According to Hacker, in the *Investigations*, Wittgenstein repudiates even this and takes the stand that there is no philosophical knowledge at all. *Cf.*, P.M.S. Hacker, *Wittgenstein's Place in Twentieth-century Analytic Philosophy*, Oxford: Blackwell, 1996, pp. 44-45, 110-111. If one interprets the famous last line of the *Tractatus* from the standpoint of Hacker's understanding of the *Investigations*, then there is nothing to be silent about.

9. Number represents a mixed case in which a rule for recognition represents that which is non-conceptual. This fact is what has given rise to such confusions as whether number is intuitively or analytically known or whether number possesses an essential nature or is simply a symbol of pure external relations. For example, when Rorty attempts to show the futility of finding the essence of number 17, this illustrates the problem that arises when one does not distinguish two sources of knowledge. (*Cf.*, Rorty's 1st Romanell Lecture, *Anti-Essentialism in General: The Number Seventeen as a Model for Reality*, 1992). Searching for the essence of 17 is futile, since only different concepts are conceptually distinguishable from each other. (Rorty proceeds to apply his anti-essentialism to all concepts, which obfuscates the essential difference between conceptual and non-conceptual sources of knowledge). Such confusions that arise from not sufficiently or not at all distinguishing two or more sources of knowledge are illustrated by the enormous complications that attend the attempt to define number as revealed in Frege's, *The Foundations of Arithmetic*, in which one of his most penetrating definitions is: 'Abstract number is the *empty form of difference*' (emphasis his) (p. 56). While Frege thinks that number is an analytic concept, the above definition illustrates how a concept is utilized to stand for that which is non-conceptual.

2 Descartes' Legacy and Exorcising the Ghosts of the Cartesian and the Hermeneutic Circles

Preface to the Cartesian Legacy

The primary legacy of Descartes is the legacy of direct knowledge that is both certain in status and universal in application. Descartes' proof of the existence of consciousness is an example of direct knowledge that is both certain and universal. It is not necessary to follow Descartes in thinking that he has proved the existence of the self. However, it cannot be denied that he has proved the possession of knowledge that is on the level of certainty of the existence of consciousness.

When something is present before the mind of the subject knower, the fact of this presence cannot be known by inference; it must be known directly. That something were present to mind could never be known to be present to mind if it had to be inferred that something were present to mind before it could be known. The capacity to become aware of the immediate data of consciousness is a natively perfectible and perfected power. Just as the power of reasoning must be perfected by example and training, the capacity for the discernment of immediate data and for making distinctions between types of immediate data must be perfected just as any other mental skill.

One may take as an example of an item that is known by immediate awareness the example that the subject knower is aware that she or he is experiencing. The awareness that one is experiencing cannot be known by inferential reasoning. *What it is to experience cannot be known by inferential reasoning*. That something is present to mind is not and cannot be an item of inferential knowledge. What would permit or entitle one to infer that what is present to mind is present to mind? One can infer that item x or item y must be present to mind. But, this is different from knowing that something right now is present to mind. To be able to infer that something is present to mind implies that one already knows what it means for something to be present to mind. Knowing that something is present to mind cannot be known by an inference. How would one even know what the expression 'present to mind' means? Knowing that something at this very moment is present to mind requires an act of transcendental introspection. The knowledge that something is present to mind is a knowledge that is a certain truth and is not and cannot be based on any inference.

What is the locus of any certainties that may be discovered as certain truths? Is necessity an internal quality of certain propositions? It may be that *in certain cases*, as in the example of one becoming aware that one is experiencing, the grounds for certainty lie not only in the object grasped, but also in the very act of grasping itself; i.e., the non-refutability of the moment, the fact and the mode of apprehension. In these cases, the necessity derives from the apprehension and the realization of the certainty of the state of apprehension, and does not derive solely from the truth of a proposition or from a proposition as a revelation of intuition, and manifestly not from a deduction. Of course, the truth of the proposition is, as is argued below, what provides the source of the apprehension and realization of the certainty of the state of apprehension. But the point at present is that beyond the immediate state of truth-certainty, all further "proof" is derivative: consequent and dependent upon this apprehension. Self apprehension is not an empty luminosity which the subject knower provides which, cat like, awaits the entrance of equally epistemically blank items to seize upon them and recognize them as being either necessary or contingent truths.

Descartes' *cogito* is not a proposition that presents itself to a mind that then is seen as a necessary proposition. The *cogito* is not the contemplation of a proposition or the contemplation of an object. It is not the first principle of a science. It is not a proposition; it is not an argument; it is not an inference. It is the knowledge of the subject knower's special capacity for self-revelation. The subject knower can and in fact does reveal herself to herself or himself to himself in immediate, direct awareness. Consciousness, or the *cogito*, is not a thought; it is one's identity. The *cogito* is not a simple idea or the conclusion of an argument. Self-knowledge is simultaneously the means of knowledge and what is known.

Since the human being is classified as a type of ape (the only surviving member of the family *Hominidae*), one may characterize the Cartesian announcement of the *cogito* as an intellectual beating on the chest: it is the announcement of the realization that the capacity for incorrigible knowledge by direct acquaintance, on which all other knowledge claims must rest, must be derived from self-certification. The proclamation of a knowing subject: 'I think; I am' is the statement of one's own status, and at the same time the revelation of the grounds which are self-supplied. Epistemology equals ontology in this one unique instance although the epistemological and the ontological dimensions can be logically distinguished. The being of the subject knower is realized only through this private act of recognition of one's being. In this way, one is the architect of one's own being. The recognition of this fact and of this power brings with it a special delight. Through reflection and only through reflection can one come to knowledge of oneself and therefore to one's self, proper.

The primary legacy of Descartes is the legacy that one can possess certain and universal immediate knowledge. If one remains in doubt as to the legitimacy of this legacy, one may consider a different and more homely example of immediate knowledge. Suppose one is asked to turn the lights off, and after one performs this act successfully is then asked if the lights went out. One can answer that she or he is certain that the lights went out, but she or he cannot prove that this sequence occurred. If one can be certain without proof, then proof is not a criterion for certainty. Both immediacy and immediate certainty are conditions for the existence and the intelligibility of any kind of proof. Without consciousness there can be no proof. How, then, can one prove that consciousness exists by an inductive or a deductive proof? In fact, how can one prove that proof exists? How can one prove that any particular proof is valid? One cannot provide a proof for proof. Ultimately, the mind is satisfied and that is the criterion of a successful proof. Ultimately, it is the mind which approves of proof. Thus, proof must always be proof for a mind.

Immediate certainty cannot be proved. For Aristotle, one could not be mistaken that one is sensing, although one could be mistaken about the content of what one is sensing. For Descartes, one cannot be mistaken that one is imagining, although, of course, one could be mistaken about the content of what one is imagining. For all the power of the potentially omnipresent and omnipotent evil daemon, it could not surpass or derogate from the power of the human imagination. The proper conclusion to Descartes' dream argument is that while in any particular instance, one cannot demarcate whether one is awake or dreaming, (Descartes' argument from coherence that he proposes in *Meditation VI* falls prey to his arguments in *Meditation II*), what one cannot be mistaken about is the immediate fact of consciousness. A close reading of one passage in Descartes reveals that Descartes allowed himself to doubt even his own existence, unless he could be certain of the existence of a non-deceiving Deity. In *Meditation III* he states that '...without a knowledge of these two truths [whether there is a Deity; whether He may be a deceiver] I do not see that I can ever be certain of anything'.[1] Here, 'anything' can include the existence of the *cogito*. Such an implication provides an additional path, one that is normally not taken, to the presumed conundrum of the Cartesian circle, to be discussed in the sequel. However, despite Descartes' disclaimer, it is difficult to understand how the *cogito*, understood in the sense of this present work, is dubitable under any conditions. For as per Descartes' own argument and that of Augustine before him, there must be an awareness of something even if that awareness be fraudulent. Descartes' argument is impervious to his worry that without a good Deity, he cannot be certain of anything.

While Descartes does not prove an 'I', he does establish the phenomenological existence of consciousness. The phenomenological existence of consciousness is not established by an argument: its existence is immediately observable. In fact, it is not quite correct even to speak this way, for consciousness is not observed as if it existed apart from the subject knower. Consciousness is not perceived as if it were in a mirror. The subject knower, or, more precisely, the act of consciousness of the subject knower is the very same consciousness that is known. *The subjective knowingness of the consciousness of the subject knower is consciousness itself in its active mode. The very act of the awareness of consciousness is the same as consciousness becoming aware of itself.*

There is no difference and there can be no difference between consciousness as an act and consciousness as an existence. Consciousness is, as it were, completely self-transparent. Even this way of speaking is inaccurate, because it implies a bifurcation between consciousness as an epistemological existence, and consciousness as an ontological existence, or a knowingness that is subsequently aware of a separate ontologically existent consciousness. The subjective awareness of consciousness - which is the only mode of awareness of consciousness that is possible (consciousness is not and cannot be an inference) - is at once an establishment of the independent ontological existence of consciousness, for, *if awareness of consciousness is only possible if consciousness becomes aware of itself, then consciousness must exist in order to become aware of itself.* This is no more than to say that awareness must exist prior to self-awareness. But the existence of awareness is not the existence of an ontologically separate item. Self-awareness is awareness that becomes aware of itself. The consciousness that must exist in order to become aware of itself is not a different ontological existence from the consciousness that becomes aware of it.

Descartes, while thinking that he has established the thinking subject, has not really established the "thingness", the subjecthood, or the identity of the thinking thing. In a more sophisticated version of the dream argument some two millennia prior to Descartes, Chuang-Tzu points out that one can never be sure whether the thinking self is a butterfly or a human being, and thus opens up the possibility that thinking or consciousness is not reducible to a human thinking substance.[2] From the standpoint of the present author, while for Descartes consciousness is irredeemably established, it is an open question as to whose consciousness or what kind of consciousness it is. It is not clear that consciousness is a thing or a substance type existence at all. It might be a process rather than a substantial existence. It is not clear that consciousness is a subject. It might be that all that exists is an event, which contains the fraudulent concept of subject within it. But, while Descartes has not proven what he thinks he has proven, the insight that he bequeaths is that consciousness is the ultimate datum. This cannot be established by deductive argument, but can only be something of which one can become aware by becoming aware of the nature of consciousness.

As has been argued above, consciousness cannot be an inference. The subject knower cannot infer that she or he is aware of herself or himself. The subject knower must first be aware in order to become self-aware. Self-awareness is a species of awareness; it is not something separate from awareness. Even the word chosen to describe self-awareness reveals this, since one calls self awareness, 'reflection'. When one reflects upon something that is known, the word 'reflection' reveals that awareness is a reflection of something. That reflection arises from the subject knower; it cannot arise from any other source. A mirror can catch an image because it is a reflecting glass. The consciousness of the knowing subject remembers images because the images are reflected in it. While Descartes referred to consciousness as the natural light, this image may not be the most apposite. For, the image of a light implies that that which it illuminates is first in darkness. The reflecting glass image (while itself not totally apposite) at least implies that that which is reflected is already illumined. Consciousness is not an illumination. It may not be likened to a searchlight because a searchlight is only the condition of visibility. Consciousness is what sees the illumined. It is the seeingness that in its very existence sees itself. 'The seeingness that sees itself', is still not a wholly accurate means of expression, for consciousness knows itself directly without seeing itself, since 'seeing' is an act which at least linguistically seems to imply a bifurcation between knower and known. The very existence of consciousness is its source of self-knowledge. Its existential nature is its self-transparency. Consciousness is the one perfect case in which ontological status is identical with epistemological function.

What also follows from this is that the knowing subject can possess an immediate awareness of itself. The self does not only know itself as it affects itself, as Kant thought and taught in his first *Critique*. The self, which affects itself, is one and the same self as the subject knower or knowingness. To put it precisely: the subject knower knows itself by becoming aware of itself. There is and cannot be any intermediary. If there were, the entire process would be involved in an infinite regress and self-knowledge would be impossible.

Even the putative knowledge that one knew oneself only as one affected oneself could not be possible. For, if the self were not one and the same self, how could even this alleged indirect knowledge be part of one and the same consciousness? Kant's own arguments for the Transcendental Unity of Apperception in his first *Critique* mitigate against his arguments for self-knowledge as being only affected knowledge. That self knowledge is and only can be direct is the only way to understand the entire consciousness event, or, to make sense of the possibility of its occurrence.[3] Awareness is the primary datum and the sole datum.

The foregoing can now also serve as the model for knowledge. Descartes attributed the certainty of the truth of self-evidence or self-certification to the qualities of clarity and distinctness. The certainty of the truth of self-evidence arises from the inner connectedness that exists between the content of the cognitive experience and the form of its discoveredness, which in the case of the *cogito* are one and the same. The criterion of truth as self-evidence precedes the criteria of clarity and distinctness and is thus more primordial than the criteria of clarity and distinctness. A self-evident truth is clear and distinct but clarity and distinctness are not infallible signs of self-evidence. A self-evident truth is a truth which presents itself as its own evidence in the sense that its truth is inseparable (though distinguishable) from its existence.

It is the same to understand what is necessarily true as true as it is to understand it at all. What is necessarily true or self-evidently true cannot be understood save as true, nor can it be perceived as true without being understood. Mathematics serves as an excellent example of self-evidencing truth. *One cannot understand that 1 + 1 = 2, without seeing this as true. One cannot see this as true without understanding it. Its truth is part of what is understood when it is understood.* This distinction between mathematical truth and empirical, contingent truth is epistemologically evident quite apart from Descartes' concern that a deceiving Deity could arrange it such that one were deluded each time one thought one was aware of a mathematical truth. That problem remains as a separate problem from the issue of distinguishing self-evident truths and truths requiring evidential support. A self-evident truth, that is, a truth that provides the evidence for its truth out of itself, is known as true at the same moment that it is known. It cannot be known without being known as true and it cannot be true without being known. Whether a deceiving Deity could arrange it such that even the distinction between self-evidence and external evidence was a delusion is an issue that belongs to the problem of the existence of the deceiving Deity. Primary examples of mathematical truth cannot be understood in any other way except as seeing them as true; their truth is an inescapable feature of their being understood. Their truth is the condition for the possibility of their intelligibility in the first place.

It is this above criterion that is noticed in mathematical truth that may then be carried over to serve as the criterion of philosophical truth of the first (phenomenological) order. It is not the certainty that attends these truths that makes them certain: it is the inescapable truth that is contained in the very understanding of the *cognoscendum* that carries with it the quality of certainty. These truths are perceived as certain because their very intelligibility derives from the truth of their content. In this sense, they are certain truths. *But, it is not their certainty that makes them true; it is their truth that makes them certain.*[4] Purely definitional truth may also appear to possess this characteristic except that this sort of truth does not seem to tell one anything more outside of itself. In addition, in the case of purely definitional truths, the necessity is arbitrary. *It could be otherwise.* Furthermore, the seeming necessity or the false necessity that attends definitional truths possesses no application to the outside world. In mathematical truth, or in the philosophical truths of space and time, which will be detailed in the sequel, one does learn something more than pure definitions - or - at least one learns some things that do seem to apply to the universe. Knowing something about the subject knower which is not purely definitional serves also as a clue to knowledge about the universe, the truth of which is based upon the fact that the subject knower is a part of that very same universe which is known.

Awareness is the primary datum. It is not legitimate to begin with the observable facts of tables or chairs: that tables or chairs can be data depends upon awareness. Nor is it permissible to begin with the relationship of the subject knower seeing a chair: that is also parasitic upon a previous consciousness. It is very difficult to talk about the primary datum since the primary datum is required in order to talk about anything at all, including itself. As stated above, the knowing consciousness cannot be compared to a kind of illumination or a light of any kind, since, as Plato and Aristotle pointed out, light is that which makes the visible, visible. The subject knower cannot be the illuminator, because that presumes both the prior existence of that which is to be illumined and the one who sees by the light of the illumination - or who sees what is illumined. But, consciousness must be the first existential, and must be that which sees, not that which makes vision possible. If something else is the first existential, then how can consciousness exist? What could cause the existence of consciousness? Awareness cannot be stimulated into existence because awareness must already exist in order that there can be an awareness of the stimulation in the first place.

As argued above, consciousness cannot be likened to a light of any description. The metaphor of a searchlight is an infelicitous metaphor for consciousness. Lights light up something to be seen; lights do not possess a capacity to see. Consciousness can only know itself; how can it know something other than itself? The possibility of awareness itself is only intelligible on the grounds that all awareness is self-awareness; all consciousness is consciousness becoming aware of itself. One is reminded, of course, of Aristotle's brilliant description of the act of thinking of the Divine Unmoved Mover, which is the thinking which is a thinking on thinking.

Aristotle's description of the epistemology of the Unmoved Mover in his *Metaphysics* is in fact a description of all immediate knowledge. In an act of immediate knowledge, there is no separation between the knower and the known. During the moment of knowingness, epistemology and metaphysics merge into a unity. While this may appear to be a bizarre conclusion, its strangeness is not sufficient ground for its falsity. The knowledge or the awareness of the knowing self knows its knowingness.

Consciousness is the primordial datum. That of which one is aware, and what awareness is, is and must be one and the same. It is in this sense that Descartes' discovery was so powerful. Descartes did not make the relatively simpler and untrue point that human beings possess minds. For Descartes, the subject knower *is* mind. The subject knower is not the empirical self, who then possesses a mind. The subject knower is the mind; the status of the empirical self is another question altogether. Cartesian dualism is indeed an unfortunate heritage, and one from which Descartes himself had not fully emerged, though his arguments had made it unnecessary. That the subject knower is a mind or that the subject knower is identical with consciousness, is a fact that cannot be disputed, however far removed such an insight may appear to be from ordinary consciousness. This is the truth of Descartes' discovery.

Summary of the Cartesian Legacy

Descartes is to be heralded not because he discovered the subject, but because he took philosophy's role, announced by Plato, to be a search for knowledge as opposed to opinion, and applied it within the field of consciousness. Descartes has bequeathed to future philosophers the knowledge that so long as one remains within the theater of consciousness that direct knowledge that is certain and universal may be possessed. In addition, Descartes is to be remembered for his systematic use of the evil genius argument, a discovery to be discussed in the present author's, *Space, Time and the Ethical Foundations*.

Did Descartes discover and prove the existence of the subject? No, but Descartes did discover that consciousness was an irreducible fact. In a pre-Husserlian phenomenological reduction, he discovered that while one may be able to eliminate all the contents of consciousness, consciousness itself was ineliminable. Do other truths exist which possess the characteristic of being immediate data of consciousness, the apprehension and the understanding of which are at once attended with necessity and universality? This model of truth, while seemingly more appropriate to geometrical truths, may nonetheless be taken as an analogy for philosophers. In fact, *even knowing why and how geometrical truths are true is to know them as philosophical truths*. In certain cases, the manner in which something is known is equally as important as its content in determining what constitutes a philosophical truth.

Exorcising the Ghost of the Cartesian Circle

It has been alleged by a celebrated cast of philosophers, including among co-temporary philosophers the distinguished example of Thomas Nagel, that Descartes was guilty of having argued in a circle.[5] The accusation is that Descartes first argues that from the clearly and distinctly perceived truth of the *cogito*, the rule can be generalized that whatever is clearly and distinctly perceived is true. Descartes then clearly and distinctly perceives that G-d necessarily exists and that it belongs to the nature of G-d that the Deity is not a deceiver. G-d thus serves as the guarantor of the non-deceptive quality of the truth of Divine existence - hence the circle. The rule of truth both proves and at the same time is dependent upon the existence of a good Deity. However, even if this allegation is well founded, it does not follow that Descartes' legacy of the awareness of consciousness is suspect, because his proof of the existence of consciousness does not depend upon either the clarity and distinctness criteria or the existence of the Deity (despite Descartes' own statement in *Meditation II* that he cannot be certain of anything without the existence of the Deity). Thus, the Cartesian circle does not affect the greatest legacy of Descartes, the *cogito*. To put this in another way, the certainty of the truth of the *cogito* was not a product of its being clear and distinct. This was perhaps a misleading description of Descartes', an afterthought which was in a significant way, a misdescription. The certainty of the truth of the *cogito* arose from its undeniability, not from its qualities of clarity and distinctness. The generation and generalization of false criteria was to lead Descartes and his future readers astray. But regardless of whether Descartes' self-description of his criteria of truth is valid or not, one may assess his argument on phenomenological grounds.

The Cartesian discovery of Self is not a mere psychological episode that lacks logical, physical, and ontological continuity. It is, so to speak, a species of a phenomenological revelation, the truth of which carries with it an epistemic certainty. Every time that Descartes (or anyone for that matter) doubts, that doubt must exist. The question of the existence of consciousness when one is not thinking does not arise for the phenomenologist. There is no epistemologically relevant moment of non-consciousness, as this possibility is a matter of pure speculation, and thus falls outside the realm of phenomenological interest and discovery. (Berkeley commits a similarly unnecessary error, incidentally, when he thinks that he requires a Divine audience to hear the sound of the tree falling in the forest). Whenever one conceives of oneself, one must exist. *When one is not so conceiving, the question does not arise for oneself qua phenomenologist.* The question falls outside of the realm of legitimate inquiry, because it falls outside of the realm of validation. It becomes a matter of mere non-phenomenogically verifiable speculation, and as such, cannot be treated as a question that needs to be addressed by phenomenological methodology.

Descartes himself thinks that the existence of a good G-d is definitely required to guarantee the nature and the existence of the external world. But, for the conditions of pure phenomenological truth, all that is required in *sensu stricto* is the fact of the truth of the moment. From the standpoint of the present work, it is equally irrelevant whether 2 + 2 still = 4, when it is not an object of any consciousness, as the putative possibility of this kind of truth existing in the first place is an hypothesis that is utterly incapable of being entertained as possibly provable. In fact, one could argue that the proper understanding of the truth of the moment is not impugned even by the hypothesis of the evil genius since the evil genius can only call into question the truth status of what one thought to be true. But the machinations of the evil genius cannot affect the fact that at the moment of truth, the knowing subject was conscious of something. In any case, the very hypothesis of the evil genius is a theoretical construction and falls outside of the realm of the data of phenomenology. However, the hypothesis of the evil genius does contain a heuristic significance to be discussed in the sequel.

According to certain commentators, Descartes only needs to appeal to the services of the Deity to guarantee the reliability of his memory that once he really did clearly and distinctly conceive something to be true.[6] However, if one applies the phenomenological criterion, there is no need to guarantee the reliability of memory. All phenomenological truth is the truth of what is present to consciousness. What is not immediately present to consciousness - or what is a remembered content - falls outside of the realm of phenomenological truth.

Exorcising the Ghost of the Hermeneutic Circle

What of the hermeneutic circle? Here, according to Heidegger, before one engages in any kind of truth claims, one is involved in certain prelogical acts such as belonging to a world. This certainly cannot be denied. However, this circle, unlike the circle in the argument of which Descartes is accused, is considered quite a good thing according to Heidegger and to hermeneuticists. But, one may wonder what the significance of the hermeneutic circle is. It seems to be just the sort of truth that, 'a subject knower must have a body before one can write', is, and has the equivalent relevance for philosophy. Yes, it cannot be gainsaid that each person must belong to a world, and must share a common preconceptual and conceptual network, but what has this to do with the validity of the concepts that one can then proceed in any case to establish or disestablish? As far as can be surmised, this level of precondition is of very little direct relevance, and therefore, for all practical purposes, the hermeneutic circle does not exist for the simple reason that it cannot affect any argument that may be advanced since it affects all arguments indifferently.

What do these two circles have in common beside the name? It may be considered that as neither exists, those who seem to think that they do, appear to share a lack of awareness of the nature of philosophical truth. Those who believe in the existence of either circle tend to think that philosophical truth rests upon some extrinsic foundation or does not exist at all. In the one case, if philosophical truth exists, it must rest upon a Divine foundation; in the other, philosophic "truth" is replaced by hermeneutics, the authority of the context of culture or history, the twentieth century replacement for the authority of the Divine. There are differences to be sure. While Descartes' circle requires a certain foundation for its alleged certainty, the hermeneutic circle undermines all claims to certainty. But, both share the same attitude towards philosophical truth: it cannot stand on its own two feet or it does not exist at all. For the Cartesian circle, G-d is the only guarantor; for the hermeneutic circle, there is no guarantor and there should be none.

Neither circle exists in such a wise that philosophical claims to truth are significantly affected. For Descartes, the certainty that attends the discovery of the existence of consciousness does not require, at the moment of its cognition, any further support. Any sincere subject thought experimenter, already in a moment of philosophical reflection, must come to the selfsame awareness. The only audience which philosophical claims to truth address is an audience of philosophical reflecting agents. Any audience outside of this one has no stake in ascertaining the truth claims discovered by the philosopher. *A fortiori*, a state of audiencelessness is one to which no appeal can be made, whether for confirmation or disconfirmation.

For the post-hermeneutic philosopher, the hermeneutic circle has no meaning. Claims to truth must all be assessed on their philosophical merits, as all philosophy, willy nilly, will have developed from some culture or history. There are no circles, Cartesian or hermeneutic. If such circles exist, their existence is irrelevant to the truth claims that are being lodged. If one wishes to allege that a circle does exist, whether or not relevant, what is of importance is whether the circle is a vicious one or an innocuous one. In a *circulus vitiosus*, the argument must intend to prove something, and that which is to be proved must itself be presumed in order that the proof be a valid one. In the cases of the so-called Cartesian and hermeneutic circles, neither argument is viciously circular. Descartes does not need the hypothesis of G-d to prove the existence of the *cogito*. It would fall under Newton's dictum, *hypotheses non fingo*. Whether or not Descartes, by implication, thought he needed it, is beside the point. Whoever doubts cannot doubt the doubt. Does one have to doubt first before she or he exists? This is not the relevant consideration. The only consideration relevant for the phenomenologist is that one must first doubt before she or he can *know* that doubting establishes existence. All that needs to be established is the truth of the *cognoscendum*. This is the legacy that a proper understanding of Descartes has bequeathed. The *cognoscendum* is that consciousness exists, and this cannot be denied by any philosophic subject knower.

In the case of the post-hermeneutic philosopher, the cultural or historical context is irrelevant to the *validity* of any philosophical truth claim that is to be established. It could even be said that Descartes' own proof is a post-hermeneutic one in that it is trans-historical and trans-cultural. Every subject knower is "guilty" of being embedded in an hermeneutic standpoint. In this case, the circle is so wide as to be perfectly neutral and harmless. It is only if one made use of it in establishing the truth or untruth of anything that it would be a problem.[7] It is safe and it is high time that one return to philosophizing again. The ghost of the hermeneutic circle can be exorcised together with the ghost of the Cartesian circle. Today's hermeneutics is the functional equivalent of scholasticism and it has been as influential in keeping one from philosophy as the scholasticism of Descartes' day was in keeping one from appreciating the power and scope of Descartes' discovery. This is not to say that philosophical truth claims have no checkpoint for their veracity at all. Once the ghost of the hermeneutic circle has been exorcised, the proper task of how to establish or disestablish the veracity of philosophical truth claims can be addressed. One will be free to engage in the vitallly important task of establishing philosophical truths and disestablishing philosophical falsities without having the ghost of any circle around to haunt one whether hermeneutic or Cartesian.

Notes

1. *Cf.*, Elizabeth S. Haldane and G. R. T. Ross, *The Philosophical Works of Descartes*, Cambridge: Cambridge University Press, 1967, p. 159. That Descartes himself questioned whether he could be certain of his own existence without first being certain of the existence of a good Deity is emphasized by Robert A. Imlay in his essay, 'Intuition and the Cartesian Circle', in Willis Doney, (ed.), *The Philosophy of Descartes*, New York and London: Garland Publishing Co., 1987, p. 155. How much importance to attribute to this statement of Descartes is another matter. If one were to consider the *textual* Descartes then this statement has great significance in terms of what Descartes thought he was obliged to consider. But in terms of Descartes' argument, he need not have stated that he could not be certain of anything (including his own existence) without the offices of the Divine. For the argument for the existence of consciousness stands on its own. It may well be, however, that one of the reasons why such a division of opinion continues to exist as to whether there is a Cartesian circle or not is a failure to distinguish between the textual Descartes – what hypotheses Descartes thought he needed to assume for his proofs to be correct – and the efficacy of Cartesian argumentation – what the argument of Descartes actually established despite some of Descartes' own thoughts on the subject.

2. For further discussion, *Cf.*, Robert E. Allinson, *CHUANG-TZU For Spiritual Transformation: An Analysis of the Inner Chapters*, Albany: State University of New York Press, 1996, Sixth Impression. Chuang-Tzu's use of the dream argument is different from that of Descartes' since for Chuang-Tzu the main point of the argument is to make one ponder the meaning of life whereas for Descartes the argument possesses epistemological value within a strategic program of doubt. This is not to say that the argument of Chuang-Tzu possesses no epistemological value. But its main epistemological value is to impel the reader to consider the entire project of spiritual self transformation. Descartes' argument is not designed to produce this effect. It should also be noted that Descartes is

not questioning the real empirical locus of consciousness, as is Chuang-Tzu (whether it is man or butterfly). Descartes is only interested in establishing that a thinking thing exists. That Descartes uses the language of 'thinking' implies an activity that possesses duration. However, it may well be the case that all that his argument satisfactorily establishes is the momentary event of consciousness. Nevertheless, this, in and of itself, is something highly significant, whether or not it is, strictly speaking, equivalent to what Descartes thought it was. That Descartes utilizes the language of a 'thing' implies that he thought that consciousness was a thing. Again, this 'thingness' may not be proved by his argument but it does not mean that his argument proves nothing. He may still have provided a proof for consciousness whether or not consciousness is a kind of 'thing'. It should perhaps be mentioned that while Descartes' proof of consciousness as ontologically undeniable is very possibly sound, that such a proof is not required for a pure phenomenology. An ontological proof of consciousness may be utilized as an argument to supply a metaphysical ground for phenomenological claims, but in terms of phenomenology proper, such a proof is not only unnecessary; it is non-phenomenological. This is not to subtract from the greatness of Descartes' contribution since he rightly has placed philosophy on the path of attending to consciousness as a starting point. Even the fascinating argument advanced above that it is only in the unique case of consciousness that an ontological proof can be phenomenological and existential at the same time is not necessary for a strict phenomenology and may very well violate strict phenomenological criteria of proof.

3. There are places in the *Critique* where Kant himself appears to suggest that direct knowledge of consciousness is possible. *Cf.*, 'Its synthesis [understanding], therefore, if the synthesis be viewed by itself alone, is nothing but the unity of the act, of which as an act, it is conscious to itself, even without [the aid of] sensibility' (B 153). *Cf.*, also *Anthropology from a Pragmatic Point of View* (1798), Mary J. Gregor, (trans.), The Hague: Nijhoff, 1974, p. 15 note. The problem for Kant is not simply that this is a self-contradiction with his majority position that one can only know appearances and not things-in-themselves but that his theory of knowledge does not allow for this possibility. What is more is that if such a knowledge of things-in-themselves is possible, then the main thesis of his *Critique*, that knowledge is only of the conditions for the possibility of experiencing appearances is completely invalidated. If this thesis is invalidated, then Kant's main project in the *Critique* is invalidated and one may blithely return to the path of metaphysics.

4. For the view that it is the certainty that provides for the truth status, one may be referred to, Louis E. Loeb, 'The Cartesian Circle', in John Cottingham (ed.), *The Cambridge Companion to Descartes*, Cambridge: Cambridge University Press, 1992, pp. 200-235 for a psychological interpretation of unshakeability.

5. The best-known part of the gifted Arnauld's *Objections* is his classical formulation of 'the circle': 'I have one further worry, namely how the author avoids reasoning in a circle when he says that we are sure that what we clearly and distinctly perceive is true only because G-d exists. But we can be sure that G-d exists only because we clearly and distinctly perceive this. Hence, before we can be sure that G-d exists, we ought to be able to be sure that whatever we perceive clearly and evidently is true.' *Cf.*, Peter A. Schouls, 'Arnauld and the Modern Mind,' in Elmar Kremer (ed.), *Interpreting Arnauld*, Toronto: University of Toronto Press, 1996, p. 41. For evidence that the concept of the Cartesian circle is still alive, one may be referred to, Thomas Nagel, *The View from Nowhere*, New York: Oxford University Press, 1986. Nagel holds that the Cartesian circle consists in using reason to prove the existence of a Deity, and then using the Deity to guarantee the reliability of human reasoning. This is basically the formulation of Arnauld. One can discover distinguished exponents on both sides of the question of the circle. Gewirth argues against the circle on the grounds that Descartes' argument does not use clear and distinct perceptions as true to prove Divine veracity. *Cf.*, Willis Doney (ed.), *ETERNAL TRUTHS AND THE CARTESIAN CIRCLE, A Collection of Studies*, New York & London: Garland Publishing Co. Inc., 1987, pp. 96, 124. Étienne Gilson adopted the sceptical position that the question of the circle could not be definitively answered. *Ibid.*, p. 31.

6. James Van Cleve argues against the memory gambit, which he attributes to Willis Doney in his 'Foundationalism, Epistemic Principles and The Cartesian Circle', in Willis Doney (ed.), *ETERNAL TRUTHS AND THE CARTESIAN CIRCLE, A Collection of Studies*, New York & London: Garland Publishing Co. Inc., 1987, pp. 245-281. For an excellent collection of articles on Descartes and the Cartesian circle, one may be referred to Willis Doney (ed.), *DESCARTES, A Collection of Critical Essays*, Garden City, New York: Doubleday and Co., 1967. For an extended essay on the problem of the Cartesian circle, one may be referred to Georges Dicker, *Descartes, An Analytical and Historical Introduction*, New York: Oxford University Press, 1993, pp. 119-141. Bernard Williams, in his extremely skillful work on Descartes takes the view that it is not the circle that is a cause of difficulty in Descartes - though he does seem to take the position that there is a circle - but that Descartes' arguments for the existence of the Deity are flawed. *Cf.*, Bernard Williams, *DESCARTES, THE PROJECT OF PURE ENQUIRY*, Harmondsworth and New York: Penguin Books, 1986, p. 210.

7. The above argument appears to be similar to that of Fish, who argues that, '... there can be no methodological consequence of being aware of your embeddedness in history.' *Cf.*, Stanley Fish, *Professional Correctness*, Oxford: Clarendon Press, 1995, p. 129. For Fish, following Gadamer's lead, one cannot extricate oneself from history and therefore the awareness of one's historical imprisonment makes no methodological difference.

Everyone is equally ineluctably imprisoned in history. Therefore, so it seems, all viewpoints retain a historical determination despite one's awareness of this determination. From the point of view of the present work, one's historical circumstances do not in relevant cases alter the validity status of the truths one discovers. But this is not because one is a helpless prisoner of history. One must exist in an historical epoch, but it does not follow that one is a prisoner of that epoch. The universal condition of needing to be in some historical epoch becomes irrelevant and its irrelevance is what makes methodological difference and the comparison between methodological differences possible in the first place. For example, since both Plato and Penrose are equally cultural and historical beings in their respective cultures and historical epochs, their cultural and historical conditions are irrelevant to whether their positions concerning the existence of mathematical forms (which happen to be for all practical purposes identical) are correct or incorrect. This is not to say that cultural and historical conditions are wholly irrelevant to understanding how or why a philosopher, for example, has chosen the position that she or he has chosen. Descartes, for instance, was much influenced by Scholasticism in his efforts to show that the Deity was the guarantor of the reliability of thought. But, such cultural and historical influences are irrelevant to the consideration of whether the Deity is the guarantor of the reliability of thought. It may be argued that Kant was much influenced by Newtonian science in his derivation of the idea of causality. Such a cultural and historical genesis of Kant's idea of causality is irrelevant to the issue of whether Kant's application of such an idea was sound. Awareness that historical conditions are irrelevant to the consideration of the validity of one's thoughts may free oneself to inquire into transcendental conditions. Thus, an awareness of the fact that one's embeddedness in history is an irrelevant consideration *can* have a methodological consequence. In a way, Fish, too, must think this way, although for different reasons. When he refers to Gadamer, he states that, 'Gadamer says that true historical thinking must take account of its own historicality'; but this is precisely what true historical thinking (the thinking everyone inevitably engages in) cannot do without ceasing to be historical, without offering itself as a vantage-point from which the pressures of the present historical moment can be surveyed, resisted, and, in a sense, transcended (p. 129). Here, Fish would appear to allow that an awareness of history could permit one to transcend one's history. If this is Fish's position, then he has arrived at the same transcendence as the present work.

Allegretto vivace
Light and cheery

3 Husserl's Red Herrings

While Husserl made great strides in opening up the domain of phenomenology, he also left a trail of red herrings behind him. These red herrings have led those who wished to follow in Husserl's wake further away from phenomenology rather than taking them closer to it. The strides he made lie in the area opened up by the *epoché*. The red herrings lie in what exists outside of the *epoché*.

Husserl's *epoché* has been criticized presumably because there is no presuppositionless consciousness. What is needed here is the explanation, which this book and its sequel, the present author's, *Space, Time and the Ethical Foundations*, will attempt to provide with their emphasis on the certification of truth, for how and why presuppositions are irrelevant to the truths of consciousness. It is hoped that Husserl's *epoché* can be restored to its rightful position of importance for philosophers.

What is of interest, at the moment, are some of Husserl's red herrings. There are four such red herrings that can be analyzed one by one. Such an analysis is important because it is only if one no longer pursues Husserl's red herrings that one may be predisposed to continue Husserl's line of thinking in its most fruitful direction.

Husserl's Red Herring #1: The Intentionality of Consciousness

It is most apposite to begin with that most heralded and cherished of shibboleths of phenomenology, which is, according to Husserl, that all consciousness is intentional, or every consciousness is a consciousness of something.[1] This is a confusion of reflective orders. In a reflective consciousness, one is conscious of a previous consciousness. But this is a *specious* order. Every reflective consciousness is not a consciousness. A consciousness proper, as argued in the sequel, is only of itself, not of any other. The previous consciousness is never that of which one can be aware.

While arguments have been put forward on behalf of the specious present, according to the view advanced in this present work, it is the future and the past that are specious, not the present. With regard to retrospective consciousness (though the same arguments can be adapted to fit prospective consciousness) every memory is present. Every memory (as distinct from the event remembered) is new.

Consciousness is only and always of itself. It can never be of another. The division between an object and consciousness is a conceptual abstraction. A divided consciousness can never be known by an act of phenomenological introspection. Consciousness is like Hydra's heads. Each time there is an attempt to divide consciousness, new acts of consciousness come into being. Consciousness can never be anything but unitary; consciousness is indivisible. Even Hegel's memorable invention of the contrite consciousness is a theoretical construction; from the phenomenological standpoint, a division of consciousness can never be experienced. It only requires a moment's sincere thought experiment to verify this. There are those who may disagree with this position but the important point is that such a disagreement cannot be resolved on a theoretical level. In order to know that consciousness is indivisible, one must perform an act of introspection. And such an act can only be properly performed after one has practised the *epoché*.

It may seem that consciousness is intentional. But, this is a logical deduction, not a phenomenological awareness. Consciousness is never *of*; it only *is*. If, for example, it were said that there could not be a consciousness without an object, one refers to the specious consciousness which masquerades as a real consciousness which is in reality only a tacit deduction about the "structure" of consciousness (what consciousness "must" be like). It must not be assumed that the intentional consciousness is a phenomenological datum. To assert that consciousness is intentional is not to offer a pure description of consciousness. It is to offer a theoretical construction of consciousness. And, it is not only that consciousness is not always of an object: it *never* is. Consciousness is always objectless. Any object of consciousness is a logical construction of a previous consciousness that has already passed. Phenomenological introspection provides the proof that consciousness is always and only undivided.

Red Herring #2: The Reality of Other Minds

Husserl thought that he was committed to acknowledging the existence of other minds. From the point of view of the present author, the recognition of the reality of other minds requires a departure from a strict phenomenological standpoint. The assumption of the existence of other minds reflects the acceptance of a realism in perception which is a variation of Husserl's acceptance of the reality of the external world. But if one considers either Descartes' dream argument or his wicked genius argument, there is no guarantee of the existence of other minds. It does not follow that one is committed to being a solipsist, for the existence of the empirical mind of any subject is a matter which is equally outside of the phenomenological standpoint. Husserl accepts the existence of intersubjectivity but such an acceptance signifies a departure from phenomenology and is not justified.[2] There is no need for Husserl to claim that what holds true for himself also holds true for others. In fact, such a claim deviates from strict philosophical standards of proof. Each individual subject must discover what is true for herself or himself. Thus, it is of no assistance to assert that what holds true for one must hold true for others. It may sound paradoxical to state on the one hand that the hypothesis of other minds is non-phenomenological and to state on the other hand that each consciousness must find the truth for herself or himself as the latter statement seems to imply that other minds do exist. But the statement that each consciousness must discover truths for herself or himself is directed only to the consciousness that is aware of this statement. Each consciousness can and must only be aware of truths for itself.

Red Herring #3: The Transcendental Ego

Here, Husserl has fallen away from phenomenology into a metaphysics of the Self. It is both unnecessary and non-phenomenological to have recourse to a metaphysical condition as a basis (which is different than a ground) for truth discovery. What is more, the existence of any self, transcendental or otherwise, is a theoretical construction, not a phenomenological fact.[3] Any "self" is a construction, whether a necessary construction, an empirical construction, or a construction which is a conclusion from a logical deduction. All constructions fall outside the realm of immediate consciousness, the proper sphere of phenomenological attention, and are as such phenomenologically unverifiable.

Perhaps, Husserl was overly guided by Descartes in this instance, thinking that all discoveries had to be "backed up" by the existence of a self. Otherwise, presumably one is faced with the bogeyman of the free floating or homeless consciousness. However, the Transcendental Ego does not solve that problem, since a Transcendental Ego (unlike an empirical ego) has no privileged claim to association with any particular body, and consequently is just as homeless as a free floating consciousness.

More importantly, however, is that for transcendental introspection or transcendental reflection, all that is necessary is that the putative truth in question be, to use Husserl's language in a sense in which he himself may not have employed it, *noematically* undeniable. Further questions, such as, how can such a truth exist without a consciousness in which it resides, are beside the point. The understanding of the truth and thus its undeniability (the identity of understanding and truth that has been discussed in previous chapters) is all that is necessary for the establishing of the truth in question. The addition of an Ego is neither of assistance in the *noetic* possibility of the truth being known, nor for its *noematic* truth bearing quality. The Ego is, if anything, an epistemological encumbrance and a hindrance, and a metaphysical nuisance since it raises further, unanswerable questions. But, it is not for this reason that it ought not to be entertained as a philosophic hypothesis. It is simply an irrelevant intrusion. As a non-phenomenologically based interloper, it both calls into question the significance of and at the same time the validity of previously established phenomenologically based truths. The Transcendental Ego, along with Intentionality, appear to be metaphysical postulates or metaphysical constructions rather than phenomenologically grounded truths, and as such, are to be jettisoned.

Red Herring #4: The Proof of the External World

The need to prove the existence of the external world is the demand of the rationalist or the empiricist metaphysician; it is not the concern of the phenomenologist. This demand Husserl shared in common with Descartes and Hume. Descartes thought he could prove that an external world existed and supplied a rational proof. Hume thought that the external world demanded an empirical proof, but that it could not be supplied. Husserl thought that the external world demanded a proof, and that he could supply a "phenomenological proof". His proof, such as it is, is flawed in two essential respects.

1. While it may be argued that Husserl is not attempting to provide a "phenomenological proof" of the existence of an external world, it cannot be denied that he provides arguments to establish that one can distinguish between an object of perception and an object which is an object of fancy. The issue of the existence of an external world, thus, is one which is important for Husserl. If the existence of an external world were unimportant for Husserl's epistemology, there would be no need to set forth the distinctions that he endeavors to provide. In this sense, then, perhaps it could be said that Husserl is involved in the attempt to prove the existence of the external world. Husserl's main, "phenomenological" argument, that a perception is introspectively distinct from an object of fancy or an imaginary object, is flawed. From the standpoint within consciousness, if one recalls Descartes' dream, during a dream, one cannot know that what appears even within consciousness as perceptual is something other than an object of one's imagination. During a dream, one can *experience* one's dressing gown as real and a fire as a perceptual (rather than an imaginary) object. But even though, to the dream consciousness, one perceives the fire as real (as opposed to being imagined), the fire possesses no perceptual reality. Experience, or consciousness, provides no reliable test to distinguish what is merely imagined from what is actually perceived. The internal distinction between an imaginary and a perceived object is one which can be made during the dream state and hence is no guarantee that what is phenomenologically distinguished as a perceptible object is indeed a perceptible object. The introspective criterion of Husserl's argument is that if one inspects one's own consciousness, one can internally distinguish between the experience of perception and the experience of imagination.[4] While Husserl's

argument is not easily discernible, it can be found in several places in *Ideas*. For example, he states in Part II, Chapter Four, Paragraph 42 that, '*An experience has no perspectives*', ('*Ein Erlebnis schattet sich nicht ab*') (emphasis his). This is a continuation of his argument in Paragraph 41, 'The Real Nature of Perception and its Transcendent Object'. But in a dream, one can walk around the fire and see it in its various perspectives. A dream experience is certainly an experience. Husserl's distinction (the internal one between an object of fancy and a perception) is one that is easily made during the dream state, and yet has no empirical foundation to it. *Using Husserl's criteria, during a dream one can easily distinguish between a "perceptual state" and an imagined state despite the fact that there is no perceived world that is part of the "perceptual state".*

Or, instead of the dream state, one may call upon the services of Descartes' evil daemon, who may perform the same office of deluding the subject knower in regard to the existence of any objective basis for the distinction between imagination and perception that the subject knower may be introspectively drawing. Husserl's argument, however ingeniously built up, is nevertheless completely susceptible to the evil daemon hypothesis of Descartes and hence is epistemologically flawed.

2. Husserl's presentation of any kind of argument or proof to establish the existence of the external world assumes what he is trying to prove (or what Hume was trying to disprove), namely, the existence of the external world, and hence begs the question. It may be objected that Husserl is not setting out to prove the existence of the external world. However, in stating that there is a distinction between an object of perception and a consciousness or experience that is not a perceptual experience, Husserl is drawing a line between two worlds, one of which is internal and one of which is external. Thus, while the arguments may not be explicitly set forth as proofs of an external world, Husserl is providing what he considers to be definitive ways in which one can establish that one can experience the external world. In order that such arguments be possible in the first place, Husserl must assume the existence of the external world. Since such a belief is one which may be held by someone who is dreaming, and therefore might be a figment of one's imagination, the assumption that this belief cannot be doubted implies the existence of an external world which is not subject to doubt. But if one is more rigorously phenomenological in the first place, in terms of the criteria of the author of this present, respective work, if one were to speak in a very unrefined way, the most that one

may be said to possess as an object of consciousness is the experience of a world, not the experience of an external world. (Strictly speaking, as argued in the course of this work, all that one possesses as a matter of phenomenological awareness is the immediate datum such as red, blue, and so on. The concept of a world is a highly theoretical object which manifestly could not be an object for a phenomenological consciousness if one were to think in a rigorous fashion). By definition, according to the criteria of the work of the present, respective author, an assumption of a world external to one's own consciousness, and the assumption of other minds, would be non-phenomenological. In order to prove the existence of the external world, Husserl is assuming a datum (the external world) which (at least at the outset) exists outside of the phenomenological circle.[5] But, one must consider that such an assumption is pre-phenomenological in a sense analogous to the sense in which Locke's arguments could be labeled pre-Critical from a Kantian standpoint. There is no exit from the phenomenological circle if one is to remain a strict phenomenologist. Once one exits from the phenomenological circle, one becomes a speculative metaphysician, and having taken that step without making reference to special qualifications, any claims made on the behalf of the phenomenological method are rendered invalid or at least without efficacy. If one may become a speculative metaphysician at any turn, then why stay within the phenomenological circle of consciousness at all? Such an unqualified step outside calls the phenomenological project into question, in addition to then raising theses that cannot be validated in any terms, phenomenological or otherwise.

The very idea of trying to prove an external world in the first place assumes a domain outside of phenomenological inspection, and hence posits a realm which is inaccessible given the limits of verifiability of immediate consciousness. What is a critique of Locke, (that one is locked within one's own consciousness, or, that one can never get outside of the ideas of one's mind), is a precise statement of both the scope and the limits of *phenomenological* truth. Husserl's project to prove an "external" world undoes the work of the *epoché*, and raises the problem of two worlds all over again. The phenomenological inspector is now faced with a datum that is part of the non-phenomenological world, and must relate that datum to the data of consciousness. Of course, it can be claimed (as Husserl does) that the data of the external world is part of the phenomenological circle of consciousness. But, this is precisely the mistake that Kant commits both in his "Refutation of Idealism", and also in his Second Analogy of

Experience in the first *Critique*. In both of these arguments Kant grants himself illegitimate (according to his principles) access to the thing as it exists in itself.[6] In Husserl's case, he grants himself illicit post-*epoché* access to the non-phenomenological world. And, the reasons Husserl offers for being able to possess such access are no less liable to the strictures of Descartes' dream argument than those of Kant's. If the philosopher is to step outside the bounds of phenomenological consciousness to refer to data which are not part of immediate awareness then such a step must be taken with great care. The existence of a world outside of consciousness cannot simply be assumed in order to become the subject for a proof.

It should be stressed that it is unnecessary for the philosopher to prove the existence of the external world. While it may become necessary in the course of philosophy to entertain the question of the ontological status of the world, to take on this task gratuitously violates the bounds of common sense. When philosophy takes on this task without first showing very good reason for doing so, it quite rightly arouses the laughter, mockery, wrath and censure of non-philosophers, and plays a large role in creating the reputation for philosophy being the puerile and useless pastime that it is accused of being.

Additional complications are also produced as a result of attempting to prove the existence of an external world. The main complication is that one is left with the problem of the existence of two worlds: the world of philosophy and the world of the empirical scientist. Philosophy either stands as a competitor with empirical science in the contest for *which* world will be taken as the "real" one, a contest which philosophy cannot help but lose; or, it proposes yet another world which stands over against the world of the scientist, and thus creates the compounded problem of relating these two worlds to each other.

There are a variety of options. One option is that the world of the philosopher is reduced to that of the scientist, and the world of the philosopher is superfluous. Another option is that the world of the scientist is reduced to that of the philosopher, and the world of the scientist becomes illusory. Another option is that one can have both worlds existing side by side with no relation possible. Alternatively, it is possible that a third world (or multiple worlds) exists or exist, from which standpoint (or standpoints) both of these previous worlds are illusory. Another possibility is that any and all worlds are illusory.

If it were to be said that at least some world must possess reality, or one could not even have the concept of an illusory world, one can once more call upon the services of Descartes' *Deus Deceptor* who could also perform the office of deluding one into thinking that there must be a reality in order for one to possess the concept of illusion. For, if such an evil genius could make one think that 2 + 2 is 5 every time 2 were to be added to 2, then it should not be beyond the powers of such a malignant being to convince one of a false but seemingly true philosophical argument. But, it must be borne in mind that the concept of deception only makes sense against a background of truth. So, while any particular philosophical argument might be false, all philosophical arguments cannot be false. If all philosophical arguments are false, what is the status of the evil genius argument? This is the reason why, in the present work, the grounds for truth, which are discovered in and based upon the phenomenological "world", provide foundations as well as bridges to the "other worlds". For the evil genius to possess the power to create merely seeming foundations and merely illusory bridges, not one, but all philosophical arguments would have to be false. In that case, there is no reason to place any particular stock in the argument that the evil genius either exists or possesses such power. Nevertheless, if all philosophical arguments cannot be false, it remains true that it is unknown which ones are false and which ones are not. The evil daemon hypothesis may not be one of the false philosophical arguments. The ghost of the evil genius will not be so easily banished and it will be of great interest in the sequel to explore the benefits of regularly contemplating the hypothesis of the evil daemon. After all, the evil genius may choose not to deceive one in every instance and therefore may allow certain moments of genuine cognition to occur. It seems that it is not an easy matter to exorcise the evil genius and therefore, despite the willful transgression of phenomenological limits, for the health of philosophy, it may be useful to keep it around as a philosophical watchdog.

If one raises the question of how the world of the pure phenomenologist relates to the world of the scientist, it must continuously be borne in mind that the phenomenologist, *qua* phenomenologist, has nothing to say about the world of the empirical scientist, any more than the artist or musician, as an artist or musician, makes claims about the empirical world. This position will receive qualification in due course. After all, philosophers cannot or will not leave the question of the external world entirely untouched. But it is to be hoped that with the appropriate qualifications any discussion of the external world will not result in a host of unrestricted metaphysical truth claims that are the wont of speculative metaphysicians.

Notes

1. For Husserl, 'The expression *ego cogito* must be expanded by one term. Every *cogito* contains a meaning: its *cogitatum* ... . *The Essence of consciousness, in which I live as my own self, is the so-called intentionality. Consciousness is always consciousness of something.* Edmund Husserl, *The Paris Lectures*, Peter Koestenbaum, (trans.), The Hague: Martinus Nijhoff, 1970, pp. 12-13 (emphasis his). Even Hegel, despite entitling his great work, *The Phenomenology of Mind*, considers that consciousness in one of its forms can be conscious of an object. 'For consciousness is, on the one hand, consciousness of the object, on the other, consciousness of itself ...' G. W. F. Hegel, *The Phenomenology of Mind*, J. B. Baillie (trans.), New York and Evanston: The Academy Library, 1967, p. 141. On the other hand, in the A edition of his *Critique*, Kant argues that, '... each representation in so far as *it is contained in a single moment* can never be anything but absolute unity (A 99, emphasis his).

2. Edmund Husserl, *Ideas, General Introduction to Pure Phenomenology*, Part II, Chapter Three, Paragraph 29, R. Boyce Gibson (trans.), New York: Macmillan Publishing Co., Inc., 1962, pp. 94-95.

3. *Ibid.*, pp. 114-115. Fink acknowledges the problem of the Transcendental Ego. In the *Sixth Cartesian Meditation*, he writes, '... the subject of phenomenologizing, i.e., the one phenomenologizing, is the *transcendental ego* ... On the other hand, it is quite undeniable that phenomenologizing is a theoretical cognitive practice on the part of a *man* "philosophizing" there' (p. 110). The attempt to phenomenologize about the Transcendental Ego reaches a point of great sophistication in Fink. At the same time, the difficulties with attempting to keep a Transcendental Ego become painfully apparent. In the *Sixth Cartesian Meditation*, Fink argues that, 'The full-sided subject of phenomenologizing is neither the transcendental I (sticking to its transcendentality), nor "man" closed off against the transcendental, this closure being what constitutes the naiveté of the natural attitude, the *full-sided subject* is rather *transcendental subjectivity* "*appearing*" ... the "who" under inquiry is a theorizing subject that must be characterized *both as transcendental and mundane*'. Eugen Fink, *Sixth Cartesian Meditation*, p. 116 (emphasis in the original). Nietzsche, on the other hand, takes a different position: 'We used to believe in the "soul" as we believed in grammar and in the grammatical subject; we used to say that "I" was the condition, "think" the predicate that conditioned, and thinking an activity for which a subject that *had to be thought* of as its cause. But then we tried, with admirable persistence and guile, to see whether the reverse might not perhaps be true. "Think" was now the condition; "I" the thing conditioned, hence "I" only a synthesis which was *created* by thinking ... the possibility of an *illusory existence* of the individual subject (the "soul") may not have been a thought foreign to him [Kant]. It is the

same thought which has already existed as an immense power on earth, in the form of Vedanta philosophy.' *Cf.*, Friedrich Nietzsche, *Beyond Good and Evil*, Walter Kaufman (trans.), New York: Random House, 1966, III, 4 (emphasis his).

4. For another point of view, one may be referred to Sankara, *The Mandukyo Upanisad with Gaudapada's Karika and Sankara's Commentary*, Swami Nikhilananda (trans.), Mysore: Sharada Press, 1968, II., 16.

5. The very concept of transcendence (in Husserl's sense) carries with it the implication that one can perceive something outside of one's imagination, i.e., the external world. *Cf.*, *Ideas*, Part II, Chapter Four, Paragraph 41, 'The Real Nature of Perception and its Transcendent Object'. In terms of the present work, such an implication by its very nature exceeds the phenomenological standpoint. It is true that Husserl may be interpreted as wavering on this fundamental point as when he argues in his English introduction to *Ideas* that, ' ... the real world indeed exists, but ... in such a way that it can have its meaning as existing ... reality only as the intentional meaning-product of transcendental subjectivity' (p. 14). On the other hand, he also says on the same page that, 'That it [the real world] exists - given as it is as a universe out there ... in an experience that is continuous, and held persistently together through a thread of widespread unanimity - that is quite indubitable.' It is not relevant to the arguments presented here to attempt to sort out or even claim that a possible self-contradiction occurs here. It is only to the point that it amply illustrates that for Husserl it is important to treat the problem of the reality of the external world. It is the treating of the reality of the external world (and other minds or intersubjectivity) as an initial problem or a first order question that is, as the argument above alleges, a red herring. Whether or not it is a red herring for Husserl is not the essential question. The point being made above is that it is a red herring that Husserl has left behind for subsequent philosophers. As for what the raising of this question means for Husserl, this is a question for Husserl scholars. One may take note that the same ambiguity appears in Husserl's definition of Phenomenology in the 14th edition of the *Encyclopaedia Britannica* when he states that, 'The world and its property, "in and of itself," exists as it exists, whether I, or we, happen, or not, to be conscious of it. But let once this general world, make its "appearance" in consciousness as "the" world, it is thenceforth related to the subjective, and all its existence and the manner of it, assumes a new dimension, becoming "incompletely intelligible", "questionable" (p. 710). And/or, 'For all objective existence is essentially "relative," and owes its nature to a unity of intention, which being established according to transcendental laws, produces consciousness with its habit of belief and its conviction' (p. 702). Husserl seems to wish to have his cake and eat it, too. It is, to be sure, a most admirable and enviable attempt.

6. In the Proof of his Refutation of Idealism, Kant writes, ' ... the determination of my existence in time is possible only through the

existence of actual things which I *perceive* outside me' (Kemp Smith translation, B276). In a note to his Refutation of Idealism, Kant writes, 'The *immediate consciousness* of the existence of outer things, is, in the preceding thesis, not presupposed, but proved, be the possibility of this consciousness understood by us or not' (emphasis added). In contrast, in his Preface to the Second Edition to his first *Critique*, Kant writes that, 'though we cannot *know* these objects as things in themselves, we must yet be in position at least to *think* them as things in themselves, otherwise we should be landed in the absurd conclusion that there can be appearance without anything that appears'. In his note to this statement, he explains that to think about the thing in itself is to accord it only a logical possibility (emphasis in the original, Kemp Smith translation, Bxxvi-xxvii). There have been various valiant attempts to save Kant's Refutation of Idealism from relying upon knowledge of things in themselves and hence undermining the *Critique*. Adamson argues that Kant does not need to make reference to the thing-in-itself but only to the existence of external phenomena. Thus Adamson argues, 'When, therefore in the Proof he uses the expression *Vorstellung eines Dinges ausser mir* in contradistinction to *Ding ausser mir*, he is aiming solely at the difference between imagination and perception. *Cf.*, Robert Adamson and A. G. Henderson, *On the Philosophy of Kant and A Sketch of Kant's Life and Works*, London: Routledge/Thoemmes Press, 1993, Appendix I., p. 251 (a reprint of the 1879 and 1854 edition). But this is the very question at issue. How does one determine if one is imagining or perceiving? If one claims that one is perceiving because the object is external then one must *ipso facto* possess access to that which is outside of the imagination. The late Lewis White Beck claimed that the argument of the Refutation of Idealism does not require of any particular outer experience that it be veridical. *Cf.*, Lewis White Beck, 'Did the Sage of Königsberg have no Dreams?' in, *Essays on Kant and Hume*, New Haven and London: Yale University Press, 1978, p. 55. But with no access to a particular veridical outer experience, it seems that Kant's argument does not refute subjective idealism. It is analogous to the entire problem of the Analytic of Concepts, Chapter II, Section 1, B#13 over again. In B#13 Kant writes: 'Objects may, therefore, appear to us without their being under the necessity of being related to the functions of understanding ...' and, even more strongly, 'For appearances can certainly be given in intuition independently of functions of the understanding' (B122). While this section has caused astonishment and even indignation among commentators, it appears to this present author that not only did Kant make this statement, he made it knowingly. There must be a "something" to which the categories apply. The categories cannot apply to themselves. But if this something can appear, then categories are not necessary for appearances. This is a fundamental problem for the *Critique*. B#13 is necessary to the argument of the *Critique* while it invalidates it at the same time. Kant does require access to external objects in order to free himself from idealism but if he refutes idealism he allows himself access to an Uncategorized Object or in other words, the thing as it is in itself. His Refutation of Idealism permits him access to the thing in itself to which he is not entitled. A similar problem occurs in the Second Analogy. In Beck's 'Six Short Pieces on the Second Analogy', he argues that in order to distinguish an objective event from an enduring state of affairs, Kant requires that the representation of the event must occur in a fixed position in the order of our representations. *Ibid.*, p. 133. (This he says in spite of his argument that for Kant's Refutation of Idealism, no particular veridical access to an outer experience is necessary). Beck's statement that for Kant the representation of an event must occur in a fixed position is disputed by Adamson: 'Kant's contrasts are never, so far as I am aware, between successions of events which are irreversible and others which are reversible', Adamson, p. 64. Beck does point out that Kant's concept of an object (B236) is the rule which underlies the distinction between substances which are permanent and states which change (Beck, p. 140). But this rule would also distinguish between an enduring state of affairs and a succession that took place within a dream. Thus it would not make sense to say that 'Kant's irreversibility criterion is applied to apprehension, not to imagination,' (p. 137) unless by that Beck means to include apprehension within a dream as distinct from the free play of imagination whether within or outside of a dream. But to include apprehension within a dream will not permit one to distinguish between dream and outer reality. This appears to be the substance of Lovejoy's argument in his 'On Kant's Reply to Hume'. *Cf.*, Moltke S. Gram, *Kant: Disputed Questions*, Chicago: Quadrangle Books, 1967. In 1906 Lovejoy stated that Kant's inference from the definiteness of the order of the temporal position of an event to its irreversibility and to the necessary uniformity of sequence in all like cases was '... one of the most spectacular examples of the *non-sequitur* which are to be found in the history of philosophy' (Gram, p. 303). In 1966 Strawson said that this passage was 'a *non sequitor* of numbing grossness'. *Cf.*, P. F. Strawson, *The Bounds of Sense*, London: Methuen, 1966, p. 137. That one can remain a Kantian under such conditions is a testament to philosophical loyalty.

Andantino con moto
Fairly fast, with rhythmical accent

4 The Bogeyword, 'Intuition'

It may be advisable, given the present climate of opinion, to say a word about the bogeyword, 'intuition'. Since the claims being made within this work do not appear to be buttressed by either a coherence theory of truth, a simple correspondence theory of truth, or arguments from transcendental conditions, in which the putative truths claimed to exist must cohere with other known truths, or wherein the truth claims alleged are checked against the external world of fact, or are justified as being transcendental conditions for the possibility of other known truths, despite whatever has been said to the contrary, it must be the case that some form of rampant intuitionism is being put forward. As intuition is not given much credence as a respectable source of knowledge these days, this should be enough to discredit the various claims made herein. Indeed, since to some extent the approach appears to bear distinct resemblances with the work of Husserl, it must follow that it is being claimed that one possesses a power to "intuit essences" which should give any thinking person sufficient reason onto the day to shake her or his head with dismay and lay this book down with a heavy sigh.

It should be stressed that it is not being claimed that the source of knowledge of philosophical truths is "intuition". The problem with intuitionism as a source of truth is presumably that everyone may lay claim to have different intuitions, and since no one's intuition is privileged and qualifies as an arbiter of truth, intuition is inherently flawed and the matter is once and for all put to rest. Why should any one's claimed intuitions be given any more credence than anyone else's?

On the other hand, it is not a simple matter to do away with intuition altogether. For example, in the simple case of $1 + 1 = 2$, it is the case that even those who consider that this is an analytic truth when severely pressed might tend to admit that the analyticity of the truth equation must still be intuited. Although they would doubtless react with horror to the use of this word 'intuited', it remains difficult to find a substitute word that can describe the cognitive function performed. Though one may attempt to argue that $1 + 1 = 2$ is true by definition, this is an incomplete answer. How is it known to be true by definition? Is it via a deduction that $1 + 1 = 2$ is considered to be true by definition?[1] And, if it were, as they may very well insist, a deductive inference, then how would the deduction known to be valid? Is this a further act of knowledge that is also to be inferred? And, what of the deductive inference itself? Is every instance of inference known to be true by a further inference? Surely not or one's credibility would be stretched to the breaking point. Such a merry-go-round of inferences would have no end and as a consequence one would never know any inference to be true. But this is contrary to fact.

If every act of knowledge were an inference from a premise, then how would it be possible that there would be knowledge of any premise? And, indeed, what is meant by claiming that one knows x via an inference? Is this knowledge also inferred? What kind of act of knowledge is an inference? An inference is a kind of mental activity. One still has to come into contact with the knowledge provided by the inference. One would not even know what an inference was unless one possessed direct knowledge of an inference. The process of the justification of knowledge cannot be infinite or no knowledge of any kind would ever be possessed. Of course, Aristotle knew this some time ago.

It may very well be alleged that one generalizes from previous inferences and judges that a current generalization is comparable to a previous generalization. But, all of this simply pushes the argument back several steps. How does one judge that a generalization is comparable with a previous generalization? There must be a moment of cognition when one knows something. And this moment of knowing must be an instance of direct knowledge.

Nevertheless, it is of no singular advantage to prove that all knowledge requires some intuitive element or direct knowing that is not inferential. Of far greater importance is the need to pay close attention to the nature of the content of the discrete truths that one cognizes. In this work, what is given importance are the particular truths that are discovered and the character of those particular truths, not the successful labelling of one's discovery or certification of them with any particular vocabulary. This was, perhaps, the unfortunate fate of Edmund Husserl. While any particular truths he may have happened upon are not always so well recalled, for some reason the fact that he claimed that one could "intuit essences" is what is remembered.

Notwithstanding Husserl's philosophical misfortune, if one insists upon some label to refer to the cognitive side of the knowledge event, or to use Husserl's fine distinction, the *noetic* side, then 'intuition' could be employed as a term to characterize the cognizing side of the discoveries made in this work, if indeed such a label is really needed. It would be better to avoid the use of the term altogether but it is not likely that future readers will be so obliging. It does not follow that truth is discovered by intuition, or that there are essences that are intuited. And for this reason, it is advisable to handle the label 'intuition' with great care.

It is not accurate in *sensu stricto* to say that truth is discovered by intuition, because this implies that the work of discovering the truth is accomplished by a faculty power. The point made in this work is that the component of truth in a cognition arises from the side of the object (using the word 'object' in the Cartesian sense of an object for consciousness), or, to use Husserl's language, but perhaps not in his sense, from the *noematic* side of the knowledge equation. The truth does not arise from the fact that the appropriation of the knowledge is via an intuitive mode of apprehension; the truth arises from the inherent property residing in what is known, howsoever this property comes to be noticed. If the implication of this concept of truth is that truth is the *noematic* dimension of existent properties, then this implication must be accepted, however frightful to some the notion of resident properties might be.

All that is really necessary to establish or disestablish the validity of the claims that are made herein is to perform the phenomenological introspection that is required in order to understand the claims put forth in the first place. If one wishes to label this act of phenomenological introspection, 'intuition', then so be it. It would be preferable to call the process of cognition a realization of the truth of the discrete truth claims that are being made. However, it is a bit awkward to have to rely upon a whole sentence to refer to one's truth recognizing capacity. In this sense, the term 'intuition', if employed with caution, serves the need of possessing a convenient term of reference.

Apart from isolated cases such as Plato, Husserl and Bergson, most Western philosophers have not been considered to be intuitionists. Despite Descartes' self-descriptions, Descartes has not been known as an intuitionist.[2] To the contrary, it is textbook tedium that Descartes is an arch rationalist. And this despite the fact that his most famous piece of acquired knowledge, the knowledge of his thinking self, was not acquired via an act of deductive reason! Generally speaking, the subsequent history of philosophy does not regard Aristotle as an intuitionist either. He has been labeled an empiricist. This despite the fact that he has asserted that inferential knowledge cannot be infinite and that one must at some juncture possess recourse to immediate knowledge.

There seems to have been a conscious avoidance of the use of the term 'intuition' and earlier in this work reasons have been suggested for why this has been so. While the choice of a proper term remains open, what is of significance to determine is what function the use of some acceptable term would serve. It would appear that the function that such a term would serve is to discriminate individual cases of truth that could be known in and of themselves to be true. More important than the revival of the term 'intuition' is to take note that there are individual self-subsistent truths in philosophy and it is a prime function of philosophy to become aware of such truths.

Earlier in this work, allusions were made to the intriguing, but either much neglected or otherwise interpreted statements of Kant's, that there are two stems or sources of knowledge.[3] Similar to the later Verifiability Principle formulated by A. J. Ayer, Kant's claim that there are two stems or sources of knowledge is not verifiable according to the standards of knowledge of either source. By which source of knowledge is it known that there are two sources of knowledge? Does this imply that there are three (or more?) sources, or that the two sources are only logically, but never existentially distinct? Kant's knowledge that there are two sources of knowledge is not knowledge in the Kantian sense of that which is brought under the categories. It is of extreme interest for epistemology to know how Kant knew that it was true that there were two distinct sources of knowledge. Strict Kantians generally have no reply to this other than the standard one that Kant's system, taken as a whole, possesses a certain explanatory power. In Kantian terms, his system provides a transcendental condition of how other cognitions (such as mathematics and the sciences) are possible. His system srongly rests on the simple claim that it provides the conditions which make other known truths possible. But, for Hegel, such a claim was not enough. However, in no sense was Hegel critical of Kant for not building a system on a secure foundation. For Hegel, one could start philosophizing anywhere, since truth for Hegel, was both a whole and a circle.

In the present work, no so-called truth will be left at the level of being known to be a truth only because it is the condition for the possibility of the existence of other truths. Each truth alleged to be a first order truth must be capable of being known as a truth on its own. This is not because according to the present work that a foundation for truth or for a system of thought must be established. It is because, for the present work, no truth is privileged. Every truth must supply its truth knowing conditions out of itself. No truth can stand as true by borrowing its credentials for truth from another. When every truth, to be a truth, is known as a truth, then foundations for further speculation will willy-nilly have been laid. But the requirement that each truth be self-justifying is not for the sake of providing foundations for any other set of truths. The requirement that each truth be self-justifying is simply a requirement for truth. If the indirect result of the work of truth discovery is the laying down of foundations, then such a result is only indirect and is not and cannot be the rationale for truth discovery.

The danger of positing foundationalism as a rationale for truth discovery is that one may be led by the zeal of finding foundations to allow candidates into the inner circle of truths without sufficient vetting. Truths which may in the end serve as foundations or stepping stones can only serve in this capacity if first they have proven themselves as truths.

In the present, respective approach to foundationalism, foundations are not merely sought as a means by which and from which other otherwise unfounded claims may be inferred. Foundationalism in the sense accorded to it in this present, respective work is a search for foundations as ends in themselves. In this sense, truth is the only foundation and each truth that is discovered is a foundation for itself. While certain examples will be posited in the sequel that appear to be qualifications of this point of view, such examples will be differentiated in terms of being first and second order truths.

With regard to Hegel's system, despite his famous assertions in the *Zusatz* of *Encyclopaedia* 22 cited below, for many of his truth claims, no individual justifications are supplied. One could argue that since for Hegel every truth is partial, one must pay attention to the truth of his system taken as a whole.[4] The problem with the 'system as a whole' approach is that it becomes too vague to be comprehended or cognized as true because the content of a system is too vast to fit into a single cognition. This mode of certification is not, in the philosophical opinion being advanced in this present work, sufficient to qualify truths to be philosophical truths. A truth must be cognizable on its own, not as synoptic of all reality nor as a condition for any other or even all other truths. While Hegel also insists upon the cognizability of individual truth, he does not appear to supply a fully convincing argument on its behalf or always provide completely persuasive examples of such. While in certain instances, his individual examples are quite compelling, it is not always the case. In the end, while this is hardly a criticism, it could be said that the efficacy of his discourse rests more on its overall edifying power rather than on its general explanatory function.

If, in any philosophical system, every truth is supported by even a single inchoate truth, then the entire structure rests upon an unknown and hence potentially faulty foundation. In this respect, any system of knowledge that claims to be foundationalist must rest upon self-supported foundations, and at the same time, every other part of the system (if there is a system of truth), must be capable of some measure of self support as well. The foundation of a system is in no less need of self support than any other part; in fact, it is more in need of self support, not less. Even if the foundation of a system were to explain every other part and yet itself remained inexplicable, this would not be satisfactory. It is in this way that many find the hypothesis of G-d unsatisfactory, for even if G-d were to serve as guarantor (as for Descartes) for knowledge of the rest of the world outside of the self, if the hypothesis of G-d were to be unprovable, then what sort of guarantee would this be?

To the contemporary reader of Hegel, his system possesses charm because of its comprehensiveness. Of course, it does not include evolution and hence is not really all inclusive. It could be argued that Hegel's greatness lies in the explanatory power of his concepts, not in particular truth claims that he has made. For example, the concept of *aufheben* is a powerful and helpful means of explaining diverse forms of progress or development, but the particulars of his dialectical logic are not always convincing. The reason for this, in the opinion of the present author, is that Hegel provided no method for ascertaining the truth-value of discrete truth claims that he made. Perhaps this is why some Hegelians who followed Hegel such as Bradley considered that the criterion of truth was best found in the overall coherence of a system rather than in particular truth claims put forth within a system. Hegelians such as Bradley relied more upon a coherence theory of truth, for example, than Kant, who relies upon his own criterion of his system providing a transcendental condition for "known" truths.

However, the "known" truths of science of Kant's day are now being called into question.

In a similar vein, what made up some of the contents of Hegel's system is open to question these days. As mentioned above, his philosophy of nature which does not seem to take account of evolution would not attract many admirers today. Thus, the coherence of a system as a whole is not a fail-safe criterion if some of the contents which make up the system are false. While Hegel's system does possess an undeniable artistic integrity and grand scope, the ingredients that make up the content of his system are no longer very acceptable as appropriate descriptions of the world. Few today, for example, would accept Hegel's ingenious explanation of *die List der Vernunft* (the cunning of Reason). His system, though for different reasons, appears in retrospect as one of Beethoven's symphonies, to be enjoyed for its immensity and profundity, but without any concise predictive or descriptive applicability to the world as it is known.

It would not be fair to Hegel to depict his criterion for truth as system coherence especially when one considers that he firmly believed that one could know the truth as in his famous passage, 'We said above that, according to the old belief, it was the characteristic right of the mind to know the truth. If this be so, it also implies that everything we know both of outward and inward nature, in one word, the objective world, is in its own self the same as it is in thought, and that to think is to bring out the truth of our object, be it what it may'.[5] Such a trust in the human mind to know the truth is very different from the Cartesian starting point of doubt. The only problem is that, as stated above, some of Hegel's particular truth claims either do not accurately reflect the objective world or represent a fully credible metaphysics.

In the present respective work, human beings must possess necessary knowledge because the necessity that is informed upon is a feature of the reality of the known. That necessity is a feature of reality is discovered in and through the discovery of epistemological truths and the reflection upon the condition of their possibility. There is no other explanation as to why necessary and universal knowledge can be discovered in a finite particular.

Any system of philosophy is only as sound as the individual links in its chain of truths. In the end, it is safer and more informative if one's inspection of truth were restricted to an examination of the individual links. Truth can be certified through the inspection of particular truth claims for their intrinsic truth-value. As a result, no system as a whole is to be constructed at the present time. This is perhaps the legacy of the analytic movement in philosophy. But, unlike analysis, one can and will produce particular, substantive truth claims that can be tested in the crucible of one's inner experience.

This does not open up a philosophical open house to any and all possible intuited truth claims. There is no need and there is possibly a danger in the positing of a general power of "intuition" as a source of truth. The point of departure is not the justification of a source of knowledge, but the particular cognitive claims that are to be made. It is the knowledge claims that are true or false. One should not and need not begin with a general power of intuiting truths. One may begin very simply with the objects of knowledge: particular cognitive claims. If one does not leave this arena, there should be no special problems. All that is required is to apply the test of introspection to the particular truth claims that are made herein. Nothing more and nothing less.

So, no Pandora's box of "Intuitionism" is being opened. There is no reason to have the fear that any and all claims will be admissible. Only those claims that meet the standards of truth discovery that are set down herein are admissible. What is being set forth is a method for certifying particular truth claims such as Kant's claim that there are two sources of knowledge. This is one task that the epistemological side of this work proposes to do. Another task is to set forth some truth claims in particular. It is not proposed that the truth claims set forth herein are exhaustive. More candidates can be added to the list so long as they satisfy the criteria set forth within for introspective truth certification.

There are no truth claims to be made which cannot either be found in or among or between the pure data of consciousness, or which cannot be found in deductions which are derivative from the pure data of consciousness. For example, that there are two (or more) sources of knowledge is not an item to be found among the pure data of consciousness; it is a deduction from the pure data. But it is in no way *justified* because of its status as a transcendental condition for knowledge, although, ironically enough, the existence of a third source of knowledge may be inferred to be a transcendental condition for knowledge. The truth-value of the existence of a third source of knowledge stems from and only from its original discovery in concrete and discrete cognitive acts, and no justification for its truth-value is to be inferred from any source other than the pure data of consciousness. That it happens to be a transcendental condition for philosophical knowledge, (not empirical experience), is a welcome fact, but this fact in no way justifies its truth status as a philosophical claim. That the various truth claims discovered within may in certain cases assist one in understanding physics or psychology or ethics is a welcome discovery of the comprehensiveness and the coherence of the philosophical discoveries made herein, but such consequences cannot suffice as sufficient conditions for the truth value of the philosophical claims themselves.

All philosophical truth claims must meet an individual truth test in their discovery/explication and their claims cannot rest on their explanatory power. What is being attempted within is to supply what Kant did not supply. If one places exclusive reliance upon the justification of transcendental conditions in the manner of Kant, what will be the status of the transcendental conditions if the putative truths the possibility of which they are the conditions are themselves later called into question? On the other hand, if one relies upon a coherence theory of truth or at least does not supply an explanation or a justification for particular truth claims that are made, then the individual parts that make up the whole may prove to be false in the light of future empirical discoveries. Philosophical truth claims must possess their own criteria of certification within themselves and must meet their own truth standards.

Perhaps, therefore, rather than "intuiting essences", the best descriptive mode of reference for the cognitive transaction that is enacted is phenomenological introspection. Or, to put this the other way around, the pure data of consciousness are discovered and can only be discovered in pure introspective acts. Truths are discovered (and known to be true) only in the act of their being discovered. There is no special act of intuition that is performed on them that is separate from their formulation in consciousness. They spring into being as cognitive objects in the same moment that they are discovered to be apodeictically true. Their cognitive being is the other side of the coin of their discoveredness. One can abstractly isolate their truth and their being known as two separate logical moments, but such a separation possesses only a logical and neither an epistemological nor an ontological validity.

There is no separate cognitive power that independently discovers cognitively full and truth empty (but potentially cognitively true) data and endows these (as yet not true) candidates for truth with truth-value. Similarly, there are no truths which are objective truths awaiting an empty power of intuition to recognize them as true, which subsequently endows them with truth value. Their being known to be true and their truth are of one and the same moment. They cannot be known or cognized unless they are true, and they cannot be true unless they are cognized. Their being known and their being known to be true cannot be separated epistemologically, and it is this quality that demarcates them as philosophical truths of the first order.

In the end, this present work may be understood as an attempt to characterize philosophical knowledge by phenomenologizing Aristotle's description of G-d's nature, the thinking which is a thinking on thinking. Aristotle's description of the Divine activity of thought is the truest characterization of philosophical knowledge that has been articulated. It is hoped that this chapter may perform some service in giving a more concrete reference point for this famous phrase.

The intention of this present work is to return philosophy to its proper calling of the discovery and the contemplation of particular truth claims, and it is herein that its value derives, and not in calling one's attention to any particular empty cognitive capacity. What is of main concern throughout this work is to return philosophy to its proper calling, and in order to do so, it must be provided with a more clear account of its own unique body of knowledge that forms its subject matter proper.

What is perhaps most to be noted about the subject matter of philosophy is that the content of its subject matter and the truth of its subject matter are discovered simultaneously, such that what is known is at once known to be true, and what is known to be true is known to be true in its being known. It is in this sense that the proper object of philosophical knowledge is truth in the same sense that the proper object of artistic or musical experience is beauty.

A criterion of what counts as philosophical knowledge is that a cognitive object, which is an object of philosophical understanding, must be *known* as true in its being known and must *be* true in its being known. It is difficult to improve upon Aristotle's description of Divine thinking (*Metaphysics*, 1072b19-24). It is in the act of thinking of the Divine thinker, that the thinker, the object of thinking and the act of thinking are one. What is the proper object of philosophical knowledge is the knowledge that knows itself as its own object. Such a description obviates one from having to posit a separate cognitive agent apart from what is to be known, a separate truth to be known, and a separate act of knowing which brings together agent with knowledge. The knowing act is nothing other than that which is to be known, and this is how and why what is known is known to be true, and what is known to be true is what is known. With due apologies to Keats, truth is knowledge and knowledge is truth and this is all that ye know and all that ye need to know.

Notes

1. It will be immediately objected that what is an apparent truth in such an elementary case that is being given is not an apparent truth in cases of higher mathematics where a truth in question is not known to the mathematician outside of resorting to a complex mathematical operation. For example, Frege argues that, '... it is possible for a mathematician to perform quite lengthy calculations without understanding by his symbols anything intuitive ...' *Cf.*, Gottlob Frege, *The Foundations of Arithmetic*, J. L. Austin (trans.), Evanston: Northwestern University Press, 1980, p. 22. Such an objection may be answered in two ways. First of all, one may be limited here by the empirical psychology of the mathematician in question. While the majority of mathematicians may indeed require complex and thus indirect proofs, it does not follow that it is not in principle possible to know a mathematical truth directly. The case of the *idiot savant* discussed in Part II., Chapter 1, is an example of the truth knower knowing amazingly complex truths without psychological limitations. Einstein claimed that the truth of relativity was not the result of any logical inference on his part. Secondly, it may also be said that it is not necessary that every mathematical truth be known directly. It is only necessary that every mathematical truth is based upon and logically dependent upon some previous mathematical truth that is known directly. Brouwer, the leader of the intuitionist school of mathematics, whose first writings date from 1908, stated in a course taught at the Sorbonne (December 13, 1949): 'Intuitionist mathematics constitutes an activity of the human mind which finds its origin in the perception of time. This perception of time can be described as the decomposition of an event into two distinct and qualitatively different things, one of which disappears before the other. When the bi-unity born from this is emptied of all qualitative character, a bare form remains, a substratum: this is the "basal" intuition of mathematics'. (Quoted from Suzanne Bachelard, *A Study of Husserl's Formal and Transcendental Logic*, Evanston: Northwestern University Press, 1968, pp. 122-3). What is relevant in Brouwer's account is not so much his claim that the basal intuition is the experience of succession, but that mathematics is based on a non-conceptual or preconceptual experience. While the word 'intuition' seems to carry with it a host of undesirable connotations, it is not an easy matter to find a neutral replacement that connotes a cognitive activity that is prelogical. While time is perceived prelogically, (which may be why Augustine both knew it and did not know it), it does not follow that the perception of time is the substratum of mathematics. Numerical distinction is not a privileged or a special case of preconceptual distinction; it is a non-conceptually based modality of labelling and demarcating preconceptual distinctions.

2. *Cf.*, *Disc.* IV; VI, 38; *Reg.* V; X, 379.

3. *Critique of Pure Reason*, B29, B55. Kant does not intend the same meaning in these two different passages but they possess similar implications for the present, respective work. In one passage, Kant distinguishes between sensibility and understanding as two stems of knowledge. In the other, he marks out space and time as two sources of knowledge. The present, respective author emphasizes the English translated term 'source' because it more clearly demarcates a path for future philosophical inquiry and development.

4. Since Hegel avers that *das Wahre ist das Ganze*, it may be that Hegel considered that the truth of his system resided in the system taken as a whole. In one passage, Hegel states, 'That the truth is only realized in the form of system, that substance is essentially subject, is expressed in the idea which represents the Absolute as Spirit', *Phenomenology*, p. 85. For Mure, 'Truth to Hegel is one coherence, or self-accordance, only because spirit is one in the diversity of all of its phases'. G. R. G. Mure, 'Hegel's Conception of Truth', *An Introduction to Hegel*, Oxford: Clarendon Press, 1959, pp. 169-170. A concise exposition of Hegel's concept of truth can be found in Frederick G. Weiss, *HEGEL, The Essential Writings*, New York: Harper and Row, 1974, pp. 6-7.

5. *Encyclopaedia*, 22, *Zusatz*. Such a belief in the capacity of the mind to know the truth, indeed the objective truth of the world, sets Hegel over against Cartesian doubt in a radical opposition. In the end, with respect to the present author's standpoint, Hegel's viewpoint must be justified or even Descartes' beliefs in the validity of doubt would not be valid. The question only is, at which point in one's investigation can one be satisfied that one is in possession of the truth? While it must be true, with Hegel, that the mind can, nay, must know the truth, the question is, how or when or why does the mind know this? In the present work, an attempt is put forth to offer criteria for demarcating moments of truth and, what may be most revolutionary, in the present author's, *Space, Time and the Ethical Foundations*, utilizing these truth contents and only these truth contents as stepping stones for speculations concerning the world as a whole. Therein, the putative ontological objectivity of the contents of individual truths seems to be analogically linked for the first time in the history of philosophy with individual cases of epistemological certitude.

Allegro giusto
Animated, the rhythm well marked

5 The Laws of the Mind and the Laws of the Universe

If, one were able to discover some truth about oneself, and if it were to be the sort of truth that is of the kind being discussed in this work, that truth would be reflective of the human condition, *per se*. While this appears to be a very far reaching claim, it is crucial to this entire truth project. The first claim that appears to have been advanced is that certain subjective truths are universal. While this claim *per se* may not be testable, the classes of truths that fall within its scope are.

What has been alleged so far is that all human beings possess the capacity for recognizing what is true in each truth claim in a philosophical discourse. This is a reflected transcendental truth, or a second order philosophical truth. The groundwork for this is that any human being, speaking from the phenomenological depths of experience, is speaking as all human beings, since human nature is universal. That some claim or another happens to come forth first in the speech of any one human being is immaterial and accidental. That human being simply speaks on behalf of all human beings. What may appear as a "philosophical claim" is in fact a description of human experience in the private experience of one subject knower, which, in fact, is a revelation about human nature, which is accessible to every subject knower. Another way of putting the above point is that human beings are truth bearing and truth validating animals. Certain classes of subjective truths are reflections of the universal human condition itself.

As an example, the elementary arithmetic proposition, $1 + 1 = 2$, may be adduced to be a universal and necessary truth. It may be maintained, that this is but an empty definition, and that such a "truth" as the one chosen is entirely uninformative and hence unimportant. But, it must be acknowledged at the very least that agreement has been established that in this one case human beings can discover a truth within themselves (however empty it is presumed to be) which is one which is both necessarily true and universally true.

At once, an outcry of protests will ensue that too much has been made out of too little. Objections shall be raised that the truth of such an arithmetic proposition as $1 + 1 = 2$ is simply based upon a universal acceptance of the meaning of the symbols that are being used.[1] This is an undeniable component of why what is held to be true is acknowledged as true. But, the point remains that once the meaning of the symbols has been established and agreed upon, human beings do possess the capacity for recognizing and in fact are *compelled* to recognize this claim as being true.[2] Despite the efforts to attempt to derogate the importance of the above discovery by referring to the truth claim as an analytic or empty truth, one inescapable fact cannot be gainsaid, which is that every human being (with the requisite intelligence quotient) seems to possess the capacity for recognizing and thus certifying the truth claim that has been lodged. That there is a universal truth recognizing ability that belongs to human beings cannot be denied.[3]

From the foregoing, it can be argued that an additional truth has been gained. *The meta-statement that with respect to at least one truth claim, (that $1 + 1 = 2$), that all human beings have a truth recognizing capacity, can now count as an additional truth.* The second truth claim is an inference from the first, and therefore does not come under the class of first order phenomenological truths. It is not thereby either unimportant or untrue.

As to whether the arithmetic statement is analytically true or synthetically true, it must be that it is both. It is analytically true in virtue of the meaning of the symbols used. However, it is a metaphysical condition that provides the reason why the symbols in use prove to possess analytically true relationships for the human being. In a preliminary sense, the arithmetical statement may be said to be synthetically true in the sense that one must act to put the symbols together and to perform the operation of addition. All analytic truths are synthetic in this sense. It is also synthetically true in the sense that at the moment of seeing the truth of the relationship of the symbols (and not merely accepting on the basis of some authority that this is a true equation), one knows something that one did not know before. But, this dual nature of the analytic and the synthetic character of truths in arithmetic represents only one side of the epistemological story. It is one side of the story in that the explanation of the synthetic in terms of additional action or additional recognition on the part of the subject knower is only a provisional and partial explanation. Even to explain the synthetic in terms of new knowledge that is gained by the knowing agent or required by the knowing agent is still only a provisional and partial explanation.

There is another and for the present purposes more important reason why the above explanation of the dual presence of analysis and synthesis in all recognition of truth represents only one side of the epistemological story. The rather more crucial question, which is prompted by the simple arithmetical example above, is, from which side, the side of analysis, or the side of synthesis, does the truth derive? And, in the end, the truth of mathematics must stem from its being part of the structure of the world, and not from its being part of a universally agreed upon set of symbol making operations. For, that it is a part of some universally agreed upon set of symbol making operations is arbitrary. That some such a set of symbol making operations must be employed and cannot not be employed, and, when employed, applies to the world, is not arbitrary. It is these latter attributes that mark mathematical truths as not merely definitional, but as metaphysical truths, which also happen to be definitionally true. In this sense, in the most profound sense, the truths of mathematics are synthetic, not analytic, in that they are primarily derived from the nature of the universe, not from the nature of language. That they cannot but be definitional truths as well stems from the fact that human beings, in their symbol making abilities, reflect, as it were, consciously, intellectually, conceptually and linguistically, the structure of the universe. This could not be other than it is since human beings are part of the universe. For Spinoza, perhaps it could be said that human beings know more than what they can seemingly empirically know because in the act of knowledge the knowing of human beings is G-d knowing what is known (*Ethics*, Book I, Prop. XI, Corollary). In the description offered in this present, respective work, human beings cannot help but knowing necessity because human beings are the intellectual reflection of the necessity that resides in the structure of the universe. Indeed, from the standpoint of the present work, it is the unique function of the human animal to cognize the laws of nature. In the present, respective work it is the role of human beings in nature that provides the means by which each human being knows what she or he knows and it is the necessary structure of the universe that provides the universality of the knowledge that is known.

The direction of this present work is that if greater truths are evolved, of more substantive value than the truth that $1 + 1 = 2$, that they will come to be recognized as being universally true. The first of these greater truths that seems to have been discovered is that human beings possess a truth recognizing capacity. Earlier, the fact that there is knowledge that one can arrive at universal truths was described as an inference from the fact that one does. While it is an inference, it is at the same time not merely an inference. It is an inference about one's personal, subjective experience and at the same time, it is a discovery about human nature.

One begins with the discovery of a truth (in this case one of an arithmetical relationship). One then proceeds to discover that this is a universal and necessary truth. One deduces from this discovery that human beings are able to discover that they possess the capacity for discovering and recognizing universal truth. The truth from which the discovery was originally made was a simple arithmetical truth. But, what was discovered about human beings from this was something that went beyond the truth of the mathematical relationship. One discovered at once that one possessed truth recognizing capacities. This (even if limited to mathematics), is a truth, not about mathematics, but about human beings.

If other human beings had been required to confirm the truth of what was discovered, the truth of what was perceived as true would not have appeared in the first place! The so-called truth in question would have appeared as a neutral (truth free) datum. But, the truth in question did not initially appear as a neutral datum. In the case of $1 + 1 = 2$, it is not merely that one knows (in the sense of being conscious of) that $1 + 1 = 2$. One knows that it is *true* that $1 + 1 = 2$. One cannot know that $1 + 1 = 2$ without being aware that it is true that $1 + 1 = 2$. That other human beings can and in fact *must* make the same discovery as the subject knower who is enacting the truth discovery is not the proof of the truth of the discovery. It is an illustration of it. Each subjective act is not merely a subjective act, but is at the same time a revelation of the universal human nature that lies within human beings. If this were not the case, there would be no way that any human could have known the truth claim to be apodeictically and universally true upon discovering it within the privacy of her or his own consciousness. This differs from Plato's brilliant explanation of knowledge of the necessity of mathematics as being due to the remembrance of the knowledge of the Forms in a previous existence. The problem with Plato's explanation in the *Meno* is that it does not account for how one knows the Form in the first instance that is later to be remembered. In the present, respective work the explanation is provided that one must know the necessity of truth in the first instance and in each subsequent instance for the very same set of reasons. One knows the necessity of the truth because a constitutive universality informs the knowledge content. Epistemic certainty in cognition is the subjective awareness of universality and necessity in the known. One could not know the necessity in any instance unless the necessity were already there as part of the ontological fabric of what is known. It is the ontological existence of the necessity as part of the structure of the *cognoscendum* that makes it possible that what is known is known with necessity.

That mathematical truth was a universal and metaphysical truth to begin with is what made its truth quality possible in the first place. But, this cannot simply be announced as a theoretical assumption that accounts for the truth-value of individual truth claims. It is itself the product of a philosophical discovery. What accounts for the apodeictic truth quality of the truth bearing statement in question is that it is a universal truth, which possesses its certainty in virtue of the fact that it *is* universal. It is the universal (true both of human nature and of the universe that is known) quality of the truth bearing statement which is responsible for its appearance as psychologically, phenomenologically and metaphysically true.

In the case of analytic truths such as, 'All bachelors are unmarried males', there is no apodeicticity because there is no necessity in the idea of a 'bachelor'. It is a pure convention of culture. The felt certainty that attends the recognition of this analytic truth is purely definitionally based. But, in the case of $1 + 1 = 2$, the relationship between the terms which is signified is trans-cultural; it is not "made up"; it is discovered. It is impossible not to discover the truth of this relationship.

What has been discovered by rediscovering the humble truth of $1 + 1 = 2$? It has been discovered that human nature is universal. It has also been discovered that necessity is part of the structure of the universe. It has also been discovered that human nature is such that it must be constituted so as to be a necessary feature of the structure of the universe such that it can apprehend the logic of the universe. It is not fashionable, at the *commencement-de-siècle* of the twenty–first century, held as it were in the grips of empirical science, to speak about the universality or necessity of human nature. It is certainly not in vogue to speak of the capacity of human nature to know necessity. It is not fashionable as the twenty-first century commences to speak about the universe itself possessing a necessary structure. Cultural relativism is the norm. Such talk about universality and necessity is retrograde

Medievalism. It will be said that to claim that human nature is universal is to make a metaphysical assumption. It will be said that what has been inferred regarding the structure of the universe is a pure metaphysical flight of fancy.

The universality of human nature is the epistemological discovery place for further metaphysical explanations. If the arguments for the universality of human nature are persuasive, then further metaphysical explanations are necessary to understand how it is possible that universal human nature can know necessary truths. An attempt has been made by the foregoing exposition to show why and how the truth that human nature is universal is not a metaphysical assumption. An attempt also has been made to show that the truth that human nature is universal is not merely an inference (although it is also an inference). It may be important to mention that it is not merely a transcendental condition (although it is also a transcendental condition). It is not merely a transcendental condition, because its truth-value lies in the condition of its phenomenological discoveredness, not in its being a condition for other truths. To put it another way, its truth-value is revealed in the very act of understanding its being true. *One certifies what is true in philosophical discourse within philosophical discourse.* At the same time that something which is true about the human condition as such is discovered, a discovery is made about how that truth and subsequently, how all truth is discovered. Metaphysical truth always appears after an epistemological search warrant for it as the condition of its own possibility as being known has been issued. What is remarkable is that philosophy, or pure phenomenology, in the sense, which is given herein, carries its truth certifying criteria within itself. One could not *know* something to be true unless it were already a universal truth in the sense of being metaphysically true of human nature, which is to say, of the structure of the universe, as such. Metaphysical truth is the condition for anyone being able to apprehend a certain class of so called subjective truths. This cannot be "proved" by some other means, but there is no other way of accounting for how it is possible that what appears to be a mere subjective condition is in fact a universalizable truth certifying condition. That one can, *only* on an individual basis, discover and subjectively verify a universal truth condition, entails that the truth condition is a universal one. Otherwise, a universal truth would not be discoverable by and comprehensible to an individual subject knower. It would be impossible how, on an individually distributed basis, one could subjectively become aware of any universal truth. When one knows what one knows to be necessarily true, one knows that it must be universally true. But, this can only be possible if it *is* universally true. Human nature must be universal in order to comprehend any universal truth. Human nature, though distributed individually, is universal. A metaphysical condition or a metaphysical truth is the condition for the certification of truth in philosophical discourse. This metaphysical truth is the springboard for the understanding that not only is human nature universal but that its universality is part of the very structure of the universe and its knowledge of necessity must therefore be   part of the necessary structure of what is known. The foregoing may differ from the concept of Innate Ideas because it does not seem evident from the notion of Innate Ideas why Innate Ideas should be universal and why Innate Ideas should correspond to the nature of the universe. The concept of Innate Ideas appears in some respects to be an arbitrary solution. Why should the Deity implant certain Innate Ideas in human beings? What then is the connection between these Innate Ideas and the world? When Innate Ideas are better understood as the necessary consciousness of a universal human nature understanding the universal and necessary laws of the universe, an explanation will have been furnished for why necessity can be known in the first place.

Notes

1.   The formalist approach would argue that all the true propositions of arithmetic could be established by a formal system of sound mathematical rules. But, this argument does not address the phenomenological fact of the epistemic experience of the truth of some individual propositions. Further, according to the Oxford mathematician Sir Roger Penrose, '... Gödel indisputably established ... that no *formal system* of sound mathematical rules of proof can ever suffice, even in principle, to establish all the true propositions of ordinary arithmetic'. *Cf.*, Roger Penrose, *Shadows of the Mind, A Search for the Missing Science of Consciousness*, Oxford: Oxford University Press, 1994, pp. 64-65 (emphasis his). For Sir Roger, Gödel's theorem is '... the most important theorem in mathematical logic of all time'. *Ibid.*, p. 64. According to Penrose, Gödel's theorem '... argues powerfully for the very existence of the Platonic mathematical world. Mathematical truth is not determined arbitrarily by the rules of some 'man-made' formal system but has an absolute nature, and lies beyond any such system of specifiable rules'. *Ibid.*, p. 65. In the terms presented in this work, that it is possible, or to speak more precisely, that one possesses no choice but to apprehend some truths of arithmetic forms part of the evidence that such truths are not conventional or man-made. The other part

of the evidence is supplied by the fact that some mathematical truths apply accurately and in detail to the universe. If they were purely definitional, why would such applications obtain? In Penrose's words, '... why do physical laws seem so accurately to follow ... precise and subtle mathematical descriptions?' *Ibid.*, p. 208. It perhaps should be noted that the true propositions are not, strictly speaking, truths of their particular examples, but of eternal truths of which the examples are but illustrations or reminders. In Leibniz's words, 'If in geometry we can accept what we learn from the images ... we would be deprived of what, relating to contemplation, I most admire in geometry, which is to let the true source of eternal truth be seen'. *Cf.*, *Nouveaux Essais*, Bk. IV, Chap. 12, #6, pp. 479-480.

2. As noted above, Penrose does not consider that the truths of mathematics are empty, analytic truths. For Penrose, 'Real mathematical truth goes beyond man-made constructions'. Roger Penrose, *The Emperor's New Mind*, New York: Oxford University Press, 1989, 1990, p. 112. In fact, for Penrose, far from being a construction, mathematical truths are discoveries of what is already present in the mind. Sir Roger compares the discovery of mathematical truths to Plato's theory of knowledge as remembrance and considers that, far from being arbitrary inventions, that mathematical ideas have an existence of their own. *Ibid.*, pp. 428-429. Perhaps, it is not quite accurate to say for Sir Roger that mathematical truths are already present in the mind but he think that they are part of the Platonic world with which one, when knowing mathematical truths, makes direct [mental] contact. *Cf.*, Roger Penrose, Abner Shimony, Nancy Cartwright and Stephen Hawking, *The Large, The Small and The Human Mind*, Cambridge: Cambridge University Press, 1999, pp. 96-7, 116. The main point is that for Penrose, Plato, and the present respective author, mathematical truths are not produced by the mind but are discovered.

3. While it is possible that the possession of such a capacity would appear to be a defining characteristic of all rational beings and not only human beings, the question arises as to whether computers share the possession of such a capacity. If such a capacity is not possessed by computers, does this not indicate that it is not correct to describe computers as being capable of thinking? The possession of consciousness, in this instance, of truth consciousness, would seem to differentiate the human appropriation of mathematics from that of the computer. For Penrose, Gödel established that '... human understanding and insight cannot be reduced to any set of computational rules ...' (*Cf.*, *op. cit.* p. 65) and human insight lies beyond formal argument (*Op. cit.*, p. 418). In a seminar held at the Niels Bohr Institute in Copenhagen on August 19, 1998, that the present author was pleased to attend, Penrose stated that, 'The perception of mathematical truth cannot be reduced to a set of mechanical rules'. Searle attempts to refute Penrose's interpretation of the significance of Gödel's proof by advancing the argument that, '... it is not a requirement of computational

cognitive science that people be able to understand the programs they are supposed to be using to solve cognitive problems' which he presents as representing the objection Hilary Putnam raised in a review of Penrose in *The New York Times*. *Cf*, John Searle, 'The Mystery of Consciousness', *The New York Review of Books*, Volume XLII, Number 17, November 2, 1995, p. 64. In this "refutation", Searle hoists himself on his own petard since the substance of his famous Chinese room argument is that human beings are differentiated from computers precisely because they are conscious of and understand the meaning of the symbols that they use. Deep Blue which beat the Russian grandmaster Kasparov in chess was not aware that it had won a victory over the world champion chess master or that it had even been playing a game of chess. Searle seems to raise other objections to Penrose which appear to concentrate on the point that Penrose has not eliminated the possibility that computers can simulate human cognitive processes and that therefore, *'Nothing whatever in Penrose's arguments militates against a computational model of the brain, so construed.' Ibid.*, p. 65 (emphasis his) But this objection also seems to miss the same point. Whether or not computers can simulate the sequence of thoughts via presumably an annotated system, it does not follow that computers would thereby understand the sequence. If the simulation were provided, it would simply be a symbolic representation of neurobiological functioning. In Searle's own terms, what would this have to do with thinking? How can qualia or insight be simulated? In Searle's own words, '... the problem of qualia is not just an aspect of the problem of consciousness, it *is* the problem of consciousness'. *Ibid.*, p. 63 (emphasis his) But if computer programs cannot simulate qualia, then how can a computer program be a model for consciousness? As Searle himself argues, a computer program must be interpreted (pp. 61-2). But this is the substance of Sir Roger's argument as well. The philosopher of science, Mario Bunge addresses the problem of qualia in his work, *The Mind-Body Problem, A Psychobiological Approach*. While Professor Bunge does not label qualia, 'qualia', in an illuminating passage he remarks that 'While all phenomenal predicates (e.g. "blue"...) belong to ordinary knowledge ... scientific predicates are nonphenomenal. Asserting that the gap between them will never be closed is begging the question ... Indeed, one of the goals of ... [physiological psychology] ... is to explain phenomena in deep (nonphenomenal terms) - just as physics and chemistry explain surface and bulk properties in terms of atomic and molecular ones' (p. 13). This passage well indicates the difference between the phenomenal (sensed quality) and the theoretical explanation or cause of the sensed quality. But the question for the phenomenologist is, how can the sensed quality be reduced to the form of its explanation? While the drive to attempt such a reduction must indeed form a regulative norm for the physiological psychologist and as Bunge states, a rationale of the discipline of physiological psychology itself, it seems that, as with Kant's regulative

Ideas of Reason, it cannot be completely achieved so long as it is possible to subjectively experience a quality. Such a subjective experience will possess a sensed or felt difference, which will not form a part of the explanation of its existence. It does not follow from this that qualia exist as a separate ontological item as Bunge notes: 'To be sure there is a great difference between the two processes ... However, this does not establish the existence of a separate mental entity' (p. 13). From the phenomenological and not the ontological point of view, if the felt sense of the qualia cannot be eliminated, then qualia would remain different *as experienced* from neurological processes even if it were to be claimed that they were ontologically identical. To say that one day it may become possible to conclude that a particular pleasure will always be felt whenever a particular stimulus occurs (as Bunge goes on to argue) may well answer the question *that this relationship exists* but may not answer the question *why* or *how* the relationship exists. From the phenomenological standpoint, the scientific explanation does not successfully epistemologically translate one experience without remainder (the felt sense of the pleasure remains) into the described behavior of the neural system any more than Thomas' *Summa Theologica* successfully translates Dante's *Divina Commedia* without remainder. (The point of this analogy is not affected by the fact that Thomas' work, of course, preceded that of Dante). Dennett's argument that consciousness is a direct manifestation of nerve cell activity in the brain does not *explain* consciousness as in the title of his book but *states* the problem of consciousness. This is to be sure an interminable debate and one which one only hopes is not *un dialogue des sourds* (a dialogue of the deaf). The point emphasized here is that the recognition and realization of truth, is, no less than the experience of a sensed phenomena, a capacity and an experience which is one which is a defining and an explaining feature of what is meant by the term 'consciousness'. From this understanding of what is meant by the use of the term 'consciousness', unless the computer does understand in this sense, the computer cannot think.

Allegro giusto
Quite fast, but easily

6 The Distinction Between Empirical Psychology and Phenomenological Epistemology

The position of asymmetrical causal dualism with its attendant corollary of representationalism has been revived by Searle in an article entitled, 'The Mystery of Consciousness', referred to in the previous chapter, which was published in *The New York Review of Books* in November of 1995. While Searle's position would appear to be well described by this label, Searle himself would probably resist it. As far as can be detected by this reader, after reading this article, consciousness remains a mystery. Perhaps that was Searle's intention. With regard to the one way causal interactionism portion of his thesis, which is explored by reviewing co-temporary books on the subject, including Sir Roger Penrose's, *Shadows of the Mind: A Search for the Missing Science of Consciousness*, it seems to be that neurobiological processes in the brain cause consciousness and that consciousness begins when one awakens from a dreamless sleep and 'switches on and off'. The problem with this view is twofold. First of all, if consciousness arises after one has awakened, then what occasions one's awakening? To put the point prosaically, if consciousness only comes into being upon awakening, how does one hear the alarm clock? Secondly, is there really such a state as dreamless sleep? According to current research, which bases its conclusions on evidence such as REM movements, one has many dreams during sleep though they may not be remembered. In any event, what would the status of a dream be? Is a dream also occasioned by neurobiological processes? If so, then consciousness would not come into being after awakening since a dream would also be a form of consciousness.

Thirdly, how can neurobiological processes cause something that is not neurobiological? To assert that neurobiological processes are the cause of consciousness is another way of asserting that matter causes mind. But this is not a solution; it is a restatement of the problem in fancier and more obfuscating terminology.[1]

Fourthly, how can it be that 'Lower-level processes in the brain cause my present state of consciousness, but ... consciousness itself is itself a feature of the brain [which] provides us with a solution to the traditional mind-body problem, a solution which avoids both dualism and materialism, at least as these are traditionally conceived'.[2] How can that which is the effect of something be at the same time one of its features? Perhaps this is one of the mysteries of consciousness, which is alluded to by the title of Searle's article. But there is a difference between a mystery and an impossibility. To label something a mystery is not a sufficient justification for putting forth a theory concerning its status when its theoretical status would be incoherent with the function it is designed to serve. At another juncture, Searle refers to consciousness as an emergent property of the brain. Again, a sophisticated label does not constitute an explanation. The word "emergent" does not solve the problem; it only propounds it. How can that which is a property or a feature of something come into being, that is, emerge from that of which it is already a part? A feature is presumably a part of something as my features are a part of my body and not an effect of my body. If consciousness is already a feature of the brain, it cannot at the same time emerge *from* the brain. In other words, its existence cannot simply be as an emergent property if it is already a part of that which exists prior to its existence (emergence). In addition, its existence as a property or a feature of the brain would be different from its existence outside of the brain or else it could not be perceived as emerging from the brain. If its existence as outside of the brain (if it emerges from the brain presumably it is now no longer inside of the brain) is different from its existence inside of the brain, then presumably its existence outside of the brain is a kind of non-physical existence. The problem of how matter causes mind is not solved through the use of the language of "emergent properties". To be fair, Searle does say that '... we do not know how brain processes causes consciousness ...', but it is not clear why one should put forth a theory when one is ignorant of how it is possible.[3] Ignorance cannot form part of the justification of the basis of a theory. Searle does not discuss how consciousness may in turn cause brain processes (such as how the author's thought of the author's beloved may cause his cerebral blood pressure to rise). If he did, the paradox might become even more egregious for an emergent property would then be the cause of that from which it had already emerged.

It is indeed difficult to understand how consciousness is an emergent property when one considers the process of decision making which precedes action. When the present author decides to move his hand to wave good-bye, he can then perform the action. If a mental decision cannot be the cause of physical action, then no action is freely chosen and life as understood is a mockery. But if the mental decision is only an emergent property, then it is not a freely chosen act and is not the real cause of the consequent action. If it were to be argued that mind is independent of body after it emerges, the problem would still remain of how that which is non-physical can causally interact with that which is physical. Indeed, how did it emerge (transcend?) from the physical in the first place? The physical level would have been responsible for the causation of the non-physical (if the mind were still physical, then it could not be said to have "emerged").

The representationalism of Searle's thesis fares no better although this is not Searle's unique problem as it has been with Western philosophy ever since John Locke. (Descartes is granted an exemption because of his Divine guarantee). It is just not clear why Searle has chosen to revive it. According to Searle, '... when I look at my watch, I really see the real watch .... . From the fact that our perceptual experiences are always mediated by brain processes ... it does not follow that we never see the real world'.[4] It also does not follow that it is possible to see the real world, or, what is most relevant, that it is possible to know that the world that is seen is the "real world" since no world in itself is ever presented to the subject knower. This was the problem with Lockean representationalism, and one to which Searle's version is equally vulnerable.

One could go further and attempt to reduce all mental processes to physical processes. The reduction of all mental processes to physical processes seems unsatisfactory from the point of view of idealists or those who cannot believe that certain higher emotions or states of mind such as love can be reduced to or are equivalent to physiological states of the brain. On the other hand, the reduction of all physical processes to some kind of mental existences seems unsatisfactory from the point of view of common sense and empirical science, both of which call attention to the demands of the realms of fact. To leave the two (mental and physical) in different realms brings with it the cries of dualism, as one is then left with the unhappy problem of being forced to explain the relationship between two types of entities, neither of which has any common concourse with the other. If the mental and the physical occupy two different realms, and have neither common territory, jurisdiction nor even a common boundary, how can the mental impinge on the physical and vice-versa?

Metaphysical solutions, such as the ingenious one of psycho-physical parallelism proposed by Leibniz (in which the mental and physical are two entirely separate ontological existences which seem to coincide in their operations only because of an artful arrangement by G-d acting as a Divine director of events), seem ridiculous in the eyes of modern man as they fly in the face of common experience and make a mockery out of life. If there is no true connection between the two realms at all as Leibniz suggested, but only a concomitant variation (that mental life is a epiphenomenon that happens to occur at the same time as the physical thanks to the timely intervention of the Divine), the lives of men seem a shamble of meaningless events. Any metaphysical solution that reduces one of the terms to some form of an illusion makes a mockery either out of science on the one hand or the demands of the spirit on the other. If both are reduced to forms of an illusion, then both scientific needs and spiritual needs are again mocked and the problems that beset everyday life have been offered no form of a solution.

Another basic type of a solution has been proposed, which is to suggest that one must avoid attempting to relate the two realms altogether. This is, in effect, the form of solution proposed by Kant, who argues, at least from an epistemological point of view, that attention should be restricted to sense experience or the concepts that relate strictly to sense experience. This legislates the problem out of existence, but again does not satisfy the spiritual needs of mankind. While Kant may have thought that mankind's spiritual problems could be given over to the care of religion or faith, if one considers this possibility without taking into account Kant's conditions for religions that he sets forth in the preface to the second edition of his *Religion Within the Limits of Reason Alone*, and simply interprets Kant's famous statement that he is denying reason to make room for faith in the first *Critique* (Bxxx) to mean that spiritual problems should fall under the province of organized religion, this solution is unsatisfactory since there is no universal way of thinking which can then keep people of different faiths or different religions from quarreling with each other, alienating themselves from each other, and ultimately raising the possibility of exterminating each other. The latter possibility need not be confined to the divisiveness of different religions. Even members of the same religious group can be exposed to the dangers of extermination by a demagogic leader when the realm of faith is separated from the realm of reason.

Kant's epistemological type of solution possessed some twentieth century parallels as with Collingwood's ingenious proposal that the two realms may be considered to be two separate linguistic systems and not two existential domains. When the language of science is employed, one's attention is restricted to matters which are taken to belong to the realm of fact; when the language of mental events is employed, one's attention is restricted to non-factually based values. There is no problem of the interaction of the two realms, since one only needs to switch languages whenever any seeming problem arises.

This solution, however ingenious, leaves unanswered questions in both realms. For example, why should there be any correlation between the stimulation of the cerebral cortex and a certain felt sensation? This is not simply a matter of the choice of the language of description. Again, the subject knower can decide to do something and then physically carry it out. The subject knower is not merely utilizing two different language systems. The subject knower may transfer the experience of one realm into the other. No amount of language jugglery can cover up the fact that in some sense the subject knower appears to be relating to two different ontological levels.

Husserl's proposal that one bracket the natural standpoint altogether and relate only to the phenomenological realm at first seems to hold some attraction. It seems to borrow from the solution of Kant the arbitrariness of selecting a certain realm of experience for description and banning questions outside of that realm, but the scope of the permitted realm is, at least, much wider. One is not limited to sense experience or the investigation of the concepts that make sense experience possible. On the other hand, Husserl, like Kant, wants to claim some realism for his philosophy, and attempts to bring the natural world in through the back door. Like Kant's overly brief and ultimately self-contradictory, 'Refutation of Idealism', Husserl's attempt to prove the existence of the external world undermines the brilliance of his initial starting point of concentrating only on the phenomenological world.

But, it may be that Husserl's starting point possesses some value as a model for philosophical methodology with respect to the attempts made herein in addressing the issues at hand. In philosophy, one is not attempting to reduplicate the work of the empirical scientist. Neither is one simply setting out the methodology (real or imagined) by which empirical scientists work. Fleming's discovery of penicillin, one of the very greatest scientific discoveries made, was not the result of following the hypothetico-deductive method. (It may be that Fleming's subsequent testing of his discovery did approximate the hypothetico-deductive method. But the hypothetico-deductive method would not be a complete description of Fleming's process of discovery.)

To begin with, as with Husserl, one need make no claims whatsoever about the empirical realm or the realm in which one takes for granted either the separate and unchallenged existence of subject and object, or the claims and/or conclusions of the natural sciences. This starting point establishes philosophy as a separate and distinct discipline from that of the natural sciences and as in possession of its own independent and separate realm of data. If these data overlap with those of the sciences, the overlapping is accidental, and has nothing to do with the essence of the approach being utilized. From this standpoint then, philosophy is not in any sense the handmaiden of the sciences. Philosophy is not interested in discovering the absolute presuppositions which govern the work of scientists. Neither is philosophy interested in tracing the methods employed by scientists, nor is philosophy interested in rooting out linguistic puzzles so that one can get back to the sciences where the demands of real work are to be found. Philosophy possesses a body of knowledge all of its own and while it can also be an activity at a deep level in every special science, its work is by no means reducible to that specific application of its method of inquiry.

How does this proposed standpoint differ in some important sense from idealism? If it were suggested that philosophical attention and philosophical claims be restricted to either the pure data of consciousness, or the implications that obtain among concepts which are employed to describe the pure data of consciousness, then would this not be just another form of transcendental idealism? Is this not, in fact, the worst sort of transcendental idealism, the sort that Husserl occasionally fell into, was accused of, and "in his better moments", from which he attempted to extricate himself?

What is being suggested here differs from transcendental idealism in three important senses. First of all, no claim is being made that the realm of matter or the subject matter of the empirical sciences either does not exist or is in some sense an illusion. In fact, no claims whatsoever are being made about the realm of so-called scientific fact. From the philosopher's point of view, no first order truth claims, in terms of matters of empirical fact, can be advanced *vis-à-vis* the realm of the physical sciences. Why should the philosopher's discourse impinge upon the work of the scientist? There is no need to take over the work of the physicist. The physicist is competent to handle her or his own sphere of inquiry. The philosopher has no special competence to pronounce over the methods or the conclusions reached by the physical scientist. She or he is not some sort of theological overlady or overlord of the empirical sciences.

Secondly, and this is a sense that it will require some space to elaborate, such connections that do obtain between the specialized conclusions of philosophy and the realms of science are of a very special kind and the matter of their connection will take the subject reader into another dimension of philosophical inquiry altogether. What is required for the present moment, which is far more than can be handled satisfactorily in this work, is to acknowledge that the philosopher is not interested in or concerned with the realm treated by the empirical scientist. While it may appear that one has already trod on the ground of the empirical sciences, such incursions have not taken the form of legislating particular truth claims but only the form of elaborating general metaphysical statements concerning the necessary structure of the universe.

Thirdly, if by transcendental idealism one has in mind the ultimate positing of some metaphysical subject, then in the approach which is being suggested here, no such positing of a metaphysical subject is proposed. For these three reasons, the label of transcendental idealism is inappropriate. Phenomenological epistemology is a level of inquiry that treats only the pure data of consciousness, and the concepts which are employed to describe the relations that obtain among these data. It makes no claim whatsoever concerning the existence of a mind, or a Transcendental Ego. In this sense, phenomenological epistemology may be called a pure psychology except that it does not have anything to do with what are commonly conceived to be empirical, psychological processes.

While both Kant and Husserl, in their respective ways, attempted to lift philosophy above the realm of another empirical science, they nonetheless seemed to involve themselves in ways of speaking which created the impression that they were creating a super-empirical science. For example, in Kant's transcendental deductions in his first *Critique*, especially in A but also implicit in B, a very problematic issue appears, which is, how can an act of synthesis be required to in some vital sense constitute (though not create) a world of data, when that synthetic act must take place within that world of data? The act of synthesis cannot at the same time constitute something, and require that something as a medium through which and in which it appears. This is, of course, the reason that Kant labels this a transcendental rather than an empirical synthesis.[5] But, the choice of a label does not remove the problem. Kant, as his most sophisticated interpreters would like to aver, could answer that he is only addressing the issue of constitution (not creation), and the logic of the categories involved in the *constitution* and not in the *production* of the world. But what, after all, is in a word? What evils lie inside the Pandora's box of 'constitution'? It is known and it can be accepted that Kant wished to restrict his and his readers' attention to the logic behind the presuppositions which govern empirical sense experience in some sense. But, that Kant's presuppositions are logically implied is quite different from employing the term 'synthesis', transcendental or otherwise. And, to avoid the usage of such a term and still rely upon 'constitution' (a terminological choice Kant did not make) is not a solution to the problem either. 'Constitution' refers to that which has already been 'constituted' and thus leaves the same question unanswered. That something is constituted implies a production and a process of production. In short, if process words are used and a process of some sort is thereby indicated to take place, Kant's synthesis of the imagination, whether it were intended to be transcendental or empirical, must take place in the world as it is known. If no process were to take place, then what sense would it make to speak of a synthesis that never occurred? If a synthesis is a completely fictitious process, why would one refer to the idea of a synthesis in the first place? But, if a synthesis were to take place within the world, such a process could in no sense be responsible for somehow making the world an empirically accessible *cognoscendum*.

It cannot be that such "processes" simply make the world intelligible, since Kant's arguments make use of the reference to the manifold and space and time, which in turn can only be apprehended by the subject knower *after* they have been in some sense brought under the categories. The "world" in short (for Kant), does not exist, prior to the categorial application. It is not simply that the concept of a world is unintelligible prior to the application of the categories. There is the deeper problem that something must be made available to the subject knower in a form in which it can both be apprehended and understood. This is the problem of apprehension of the manifold. A raw manifold cannot be apprehended without the employment of the categories. The very notion of a manifold manifestly already implies an application of the categories. But it cannot or otherwise there is no raw material to synthesize. In order to make full sense of the theory of the subject knower as being intimately involved in the process of apprehension, a special process is required in order to synthesize the manifold. But such a process must take time (however brief). This special process cannot make use of the time of the world, for that would imply that time exists outside of the subject knower, which Kant would deny. In one sense, Kant need not strictly speaking "deny" this, since he could simply say that one could not speak of it (since speaking of it would be to speak about the thing-in-itself). Nevertheless, in some passages Kant does explicitly deny that time can exist in the world apart from the subject knower.[6] The transcendental synthesis cannot take place in the world, if, by the world, one understands the orderly system of appearances that are considered to be the world, since the synthesis (for Kant) is responsible for making up this order in the first place (although not for creating it). Kant is mixing up the realms of ontology and epistemology which he cannot help but doing, since he was not self-consciously doing pure phenomenological epistemology.

One could attempt, as was proposed earlier, to say that the process for Kant does not take place at all, but this too, is something of which no sense can be made, since the very idea of a process requires that it must in some sense happen, or else the word 'process' is to be totally devoid of meaning. A process cannot be a pure myth or else its total explanatory function falls to the wayside. A process that never takes place is equivalent to no process at all. A transcendental synthesis that never occurs cannot be responsible for the ordering of appearances. A transcendental synthesis possesses just as much claim to existence as, in the words of Einstein's description of Kant's *a priori*, the Emperor's new clothes.

What is needed is to become even more Critical than Kant. Kant created trouble for himself by inadvertently referring to the thing-in-itself. He misapplied his categories transcendentally (according to his own criterion) in his very efforts to prove their necessity as a condition for the existence of the world as it is known. In contradistinction, in the approach taken here, there is no need to prove the necessity of the application of the experiences of pure consciousness or the concepts involved in its description to yet another world. Kant wanted to restrict the scope of philosophical application to appearances, but could not help but illicitly discuss the thing-in-itself. A pure phenomenology is the counterpart to a more Critical Kant. One need no longer be interested or involved in the Lockean and Kantian enterprise of presenting or defending philosophy as offering arguments which demonstrate how it is that one is capable of experiencing the world of appearances or presenting arguments which demonstrate what is the condition or conditions which makes it possible for there to be a world of *appearances* in the first place.

In the case of Husserl, a similar problem emerges, despite his explicit statements of the province of philosophy as belonging to pure phenomenology. According to one way of understanding Husserl, it could be said that, if *noema* is defined a certain way, his discussion of the *noetic* synthesis of sensory materials in the production of *noema* falls into the Kantian problematic. Such a discussion, similar to the discussion in Kant, is due to his interest in making his concepts apply to the empirical world which may perhaps be understood, in some sense, to reflect an interest in proving the existence of the empirical world, or, which is the same thing, in connecting his philosophy with realism. Husserl's synthesis, as with Kant's, cannot be productive of the empirical order without appearing in it, as otherwise one cannot know what is meant by a production that does not take place in time.

If Husserl's synthesis were to appear within the world, it could not be productive of that world. On the other hand, if it were to occur at all, it must appear within the world. Either it does not occur, in which case it cannot produce the world, or it occurs and also cannot produce the world. (Since, if it were to occur, it must have already taken place within the world it is supposed to have produced.)

Husserl, like Kant, did not carry his pure phenomenology far enough. One may freely discuss the pure data of consciousness, and the relations that obtain among the concepts which are employed in the description of the realm of pure consciousness, without making any direct reference to the concrete data of the empirical world. One need not say that the empirical world does not exist. In fact, one should not say this for this is to make a non-phenomenologically based reference to the world. However, if there were to be some discussion of the empirical world, this would be the task of the scientist. It is not that the philosopher has something special to say about the empirical world; it is that she or he has something special to say about the world of pure experience which may then and only then possess both a general and a special application to the structure of the universe. Up until now only a reference has been made to a *general* application to the structure of the universe. In the sequel, the present author's, *Space, Time and the Ethical Foundations*, a reference will be made to a *special* application to the structure of the universe. Such references may be divided up into two types: a general theory of metaphysics and a special theory of metaphysics.

It is important to distinguish the concerns of application from the general description of the methodology and domain of first order philosophy. Such applications in no way detract from the description of the proper province of the philosopher to be the domain of pure phenomenology. There are two separate fields of inquiry which overlap in crucial ways but nonetheless must first be distinguished such that the primary truths of philosophy can be understood as being known in accordance with the unique forms of verification peculiar to the discipline of first order philosophy.

If someone were to ask if the pure experience of the phenomenological epistemologist or the phenomenologist proper were to exist in the physical sense, the answer is that of course there is a physical correlate in the sense that there is some physiological occurrence. But the phenomenologist proper steps outside of phenomenology when she or he answers that question. The answer is not simply that there are two separate languages of description. There are in fact two realms. It is only that the phenomenologist proper makes no claims about the realm of the empirical scientist. In this sense pure phenomenology is a stricter version of Kant in that the pure phenomenologist (unlike Husserl, who strayed from the limits of pure phenomenology) does not even say that the thing-in-itself exists. When the pure phenomenologist says that there is a physical correlate, what she or he means is that if she or he were to approach the issue from the standpoint of the physical scientist, then she or he would speak from that framework and would no longer be speaking as a pure phenomenologist. Pure phenomenology has no obligation to speak about the empirical world, if one were to mean by that world a world that exists outside of pure consciousness. It does not mean that the world of empirical science is a realm of illusion or a lesser world in any sense. It only means that it falls outside of the realm of the pure phenomenologist's special claims to knowledge. One does not chastise the artist for concerning herself or himself with the realm of art. Why should the phenomenologist proper be under any obligation to account for or explain the empirical data of the world of the empirical scientist?

This standpoint, however, must be sharply distinguished from the standpoint of the two languages of Collingwood, although it might seem to be another version of his standpoint. The main difference is that the realm of pure phenomenology is a realm of existence, and not simply a language preference, or a conceptual scheme, or a language system. When the pure phenomenologist says that the world of experience exists, she or he does not mean existence in the sense in which the empirical world exists in accordance with the criteria of existence set forth by empirical science. She or he means that the world of experience exists from the standpoint of pure experience, and this is a realm that is never left by the pure phenomenologist in the primary stages of her or his investigation. She or he simply does not refer to the realm of the empirical scientist at all except as a correlate to explain connecting knowledge, but not as a primary cognitive datum. The two realms, then, are not simply two realms of equivalent philosophical concern. The realm of pure experience is the only realm for the proper application of pure phenomenology. The pure phenomenologist *qua* phenomenological epistemologist is not at all interested in proving the existence of the external world or the existence of other minds. This does not imply solipsism as solipsism makes the claim that only the mind of the subject knower (and not those others to whom one is already making reference) exists. Indeed, even to make reference to the mind of the subject knower is already to transgress phenomenological limits.

Whenever psychological processes are discussed, one operates within the confines of the admissible structures of the empirical sciences. If the pure phenomenologist discusses consciousness, she or he is not discussing psychological processes. She or he is not discussing processes that in any way make the empirical world possible or make any reference to the empirical world. If the empirical scientist were to wish to claim that this is a realm of illusion or hallucination, then she or he has leave to do so. But, in this respect, philosophy does not differ from the standpoint of pure art or pure mathematics. This is no more and no less than to say that philosophy is not an empirical science.

Another way of presenting the framework of this sort of inquiry is to explain that one adopts a perspective that is not either subject or object biased. This formulation is the equivalent of beginning with a presuppositionless consciousness, or with a phenomenological starting point. Instead of beginning with a fact or facts of knowledge, as above, one can begin from the minimum starting conditions. The minimum condition, or the most primitive starting point, is bare consciousness. Bare consciousness is the most primordial datum.

In bare consciousness, which can also be referred to as the theater of consciousness, one cannot presuppose subject or object. It can be argued, from the standpoint of empirical science, that one cannot have a consciousness without a subject knower or a brain. But, to begin with a subject knower or a brain is already to have stepped outside of the phenomenological standpoint. The existential status of the subject knower or the brain is an inference from an empirical experience that has not yet been criticized and is therefore still suspect or neutral from the phenomenological standpoint. What one cannot suspect is the existence of pure consciousness. This alone is above suspicion. Whether it is incredible that a pure consciousness can exist apart from a subject knower or that such a supposition can even be stated without a language is beside the point. The starting point of consciousness is subjectless and objectless.

Every notion of a subject or object (and the existence of language is an object for consciousness just like any other) is a datum of consciousness. The putative reality of the data of consciousness is an additional issue. At the outset, all that one needs to be concerned about is the undeniable existence of consciousness apart from the issues of the existence or non-existence of its objects. Within this standpoint, which may be called the phenomenological standpoint, all philosophical truths take root. It is not that all philosophical truths are in every sense restricted to the domain of consciousness, but it is in consciousness that every philosophical truth has its beginnings.

Again, this is not psychologism, for the concern here is not with the fact that every consciousness is some manifestation or epiphenomenon of a brain wave. The concern here is with the specification of the region of philosophical inquiry and the range of validity of philosophical claims to truth. It cannot be said that this is to restrict philosophy to a kind of solipsistic inquiry into an individual's consciousness for that would be to assume that consciousness is individual. The putative individuality of consciousness is a theoretical construct or a metaphysical assertion; it is not a phenomenological datum.

Once one has made the transition to the phenomenological standpoint, no claim whatsoever about the relationship of consciousness to what is normally considered to be the "world" is to be entertained as part of first order phenomenological epistemology. The inquiry is to be focused in the first place purely on the fact and contents of pure consciousness. The first fact of consciousness is that consciousness is both subjectless and objectless. Subjecthood and objecthood are inferences which are drawn from the experiences of an empirical self in a world. From within the phenomenological starting point all that exists is the fact of consciousness. The notion that there is an empirical self, or a world, or that a brain is a necessary condition for consciousness, are one and all everyday empirical inferences with which the phenomenological starting point has nothing to do. All that is available for a pure phenomenological inquiry is pure consciousness and its data.

It will be argued, of course, that such a starting point of pure consciousness is illicit, and that it cannot even be posited without the use of a language, which obviously is based on an empirically learned system. But, such an objection entirely misses the point. The use of language and its dependence upon prior learning are both items for the pure consciousness to entertain. Neither language usage nor its origin have privileged existence despite their being seemingly empirically requisitioned and used without having been accredited. For, their existence and usage are both perceived from within the phenomenological standpoint. This is not to deny the kind of reality the existence and usage of language possesses when perceived from outside of the phenomenological standpoint. But, such a perception has nothing to do with phenomenologically based philosophy proper.

In the attempt to establish the conditions for proper philosophical inquiry and the validation of philosophical truth, it is necessary to begin from a standpoint that is outside of the empirical standpoint and its various presuppositions and beliefs. There is nothing wrong in doing this. It merely means that when one is doing philosophy, one abstracts from empirical reality. It does not mean that one therefore considers that empirical reality is a stream of falsehoods. It only means that the concerns and interests of primary philosophy are of a different order. A later question may then be how to relate these two realms. But, in the beginning, it is necessary to establish the existence and nature of the philosophical realm before any further progress can be made. No claims about the nature or the existence of the empirical world are being made during the primary phase of the inquiry. It is not that the world of the philosopher is better or truer than the empirical world; it is only being established that they are different and that different criteria of truth apply to each realm.

In fact, it is not even being said that there are "two worlds". Such a description can only occur when one stands outside of the phenomenological standpoint. Although it is not strictly legitimate to speak this way, one could say that when one stands inside the phenomenological standpoint, there is neither one world nor two. There is only the omnipresent, ubiquitous and "exclusive" existence of consciousness. From the perspective of this perspective, nothing else exists or can exist except this perspective.

That such a realm of pure consciousness exists, and that it is not uncommon that many inferences are drawn from such a standpoint may be inferred from the fact that translation between different languages is possible. In order to be able to pass from the understanding of water to the understanding of *l'eau* it is necessary that one possesses an understanding of the item under consideration which is not limited to the use of the word in either language.[7] Indeed, even in the act of learning a single language in the first place, when one learns that the verbal or written word 'water' stands for a liquidy, sometimes drinkable substance, one possesses an understanding that already surpasses a linguistic understanding. The understanding that a linguistic symbol stands for a non-linguistic thing is a trans-linguistic understanding.[8]

As argued above, the capacity for being able to know that a word stands for a thing is a capacity that is trans-linguistic. If every relationship that could be known were linguistic, one could never pass from a word to a thing. One's knowledge would be limited solely to words. Trans-linguistic understanding is the condition for the possibility of the existence of linguistic understanding. That it may require words to discuss or communicate the possibility of a trans-linguistic understanding does not demonstrate that there is no such thing as a trans-linguistic understanding. If a trans-linguistic understanding is possible, and, in fact, a necessary condition for learning a language, this is a further argument for the existence of a pure consciousness. For a consciousness which is not limited to, or circumscribed by, or describable by language, is clearly a pure consciousness.

What has been established, then, is not only that a pure consciousness is possible; it is a necessary condition for any and all knowledge. Such an establishment of consciousness may be called the foundation for any and all further knowledge. In this sense, the label 'foundationalist' may be accepted by the present, respective author. The important qualification which must be borne in mind is that every subsequent truth to be discovered must either present itself with its own foundation or it must be shown to be an implication of or a condition for a previously established foundational truth. While post-Modernists have questioned the idea of foundationalism, what they have in mind is no doubt the foundationalism of the enlightenment, that is, assumed premises, deductive reason and deduced conclusions. There is nothing wrong with foundationalism itself. It is only that the previous foundationalists may have begun with the wrong foundation. All genuine and basic philosophical problems are foundational problems. By dispensing with the need for any and all foundations, the post-Modernists have dealt a fatal blow to philosophy since the motive for philosophy must not only lie in the finding of foundations; it must include the ever seeking of new foundations, the construction of additional foundations for further explorations, and the correction and refinement of those previously found. The primary work of philosophy must be perceived as directed toward foundational issues as such. Foundationalism cannot be construed as finding this or that foundation to be the ultimate foundation and thereafter to consider that its work has been carried out. In this present, respective work, an argument is offered on behalf of pure consciousness as the first foundation. All further foundations must take place in pure consciousness and thus pure consciousness is, as it were, the foundation of the edifice of philosophy. Any further floors that are to be added must provide their own foundations from their own materials. Further floors cannot rest solely on the strength of the first foundation.

What is established here as a *starting point* is the fact and the existence of pure consciousness. This may be perceived as an *a priori* truth, if such a label is co-temporally in favour. The starting point of pure consciousness is not a starting point in a genetic sense although the description above may have engendered this interpretation. (Such a description was meant to be understood only in a pedagogical sense). Even the descriptive term itself, 'pure consciousness', is a logical abstraction. Pure consciousness is available as pure consciousness only *in medias res*. When abstracting from all empirical experience, one arrives at the standpoint of pure consciousness. This is the transcendental starting point. All philosophy begins with this starting point. One may make use of this starting point even when one is standing outside of it. For example, in the argument that one must possess a trans-linguistic understanding in order to understand language, one refers to the existence of a pure consciousness as a presupposition. Once inside the phenomenological standpoint, the empirical character of language is disregarded and linguistic forms themselves can become objects of pure consciousness. Inside the phenomenological standpoint, one does not argue that one must presuppose a phenomenological standpoint (although one could). Inside the phenomenological standpoint, one simply focuses upon the pure objects of consciousness whatever they may be. For example, in the present author's, *Space, Time and the Ethical Foundations*, much attention will be given to the understanding of the nature of time or space as pure phenomenological objects. Even the object of perception can be a pure phenomenological object; in fact, it can be nought else. The sense data or the "thing" perceived are both logical abstractions from the pure phenomenological object of perception.

The *a priori* character of pure consciousness is not a supposition. It is not the conclusion of a logical proof. It is not an inference of any kind. It is not an argument from transcendental conditions in a Kantian sense. It is not an empirical claim. It is manifestly not a theoretical construction. It is simply a demarcation of the field of the starting point of phenomenology.

Pure consciousness is thus not an 'innate idea'. An 'innate idea' obviously would belong to a subject knower who possessed 'innate ideas'. But, within pure consciousness there is no subject knower. The 'subject knower' is simply another *cognoscendum* of consciousness.

Pure consciousness is not a Platonic Form. Platonic Forms would exist in a realm (for those who think that Plato's mythical explanation offered in the *Phaedrus* was meant to be taken literally) above the empirical world. But, pure consciousness admits the existence of neither an empirical nor a trans-empirical world. Pure consciousness simply is. It is the initial and original field of investigation.

Pure consciousness is not an essence, nor is it a state in which one investigates pure essences. The notion that it itself were an essence would imply that there were other existences which were not essences. Such a viewpoint could not be a viewpoint of pure consciousness, for it would then be a viewpoint which would admit of varying kinds of existences.

The notion that within pure consciousness one investigates essences is a notion that there are such things as essences (similar, presumably to Platonic Forms). But, such an assumption is similar to the assumption that there is an empirical world outside of consciousness. That there is either an empirical world outside of consciousness, or that there are Essences which pure consciousness investigates, are both claims or assumptions with which pure consciousness has not the slightest interest or concern.

That the work of inspecting Essences within pure consciousness is the work performed by a Transcendental Ego is an additional existential claim with which pure consciousness has nothing to do. The existence of a Transcendental Ego presumes a world outside of that Ego from which the Transcendental Ego is transcendent. But, the positing of such a duality of possible existences is only possible from within a standpoint that is outside the standpoint of pure consciousness proper.

Is this standpoint of pure consciousness, solipsism? To consider it solipsistic is to assume that only a pure consciousness exists, that it is individual, and that the rest of the world does not exist. But, from within the standpoint of pure consciousness, pure consciousness does not exist by itself. The notion of "existing by itself" is parasitic upon a consciousness of a world outside of it and parasitic upon the negation of that world. But such a viewpoint, that the outside world does not exist, is a viewpoint which is already outside the domain of pure consciousness.

Is this standpoint of pure consciousness, scepticism? Scepticism either denies or questions the existence of an outside world. The notion of there being an "outside" world in the first place is already a notion which can only take place outside of pure consciousness. Whether such a second world exists, or does not exist, or how it exists, is of no interest or significance from the standpoint of pure consciousness, and the expression of such an interest immediately signifies a departure from the realm of pure consciousness.

What then is this pure consciousness? Is it a form of idealism? If it were to be a form of idealism, it could not be subjective idealism, since the existence of a subject mind has not been presupposed. It is not objective idealism, since no claim is made that only pure consciousness exists, or that pure consciousness exists in the world. Such existential claims already go beyond pure consciousness into the realm of speculative conjecture, claim and assertion.

Is this pure consciousness a theoretical starting point? It is not a theoretical starting point since no theory of a pure consciousness is being presented herein. Any theory of a pure consciousness must take place outside of a pure consciousness since a theory of pure consciousness would be an hypothesis, and all hypotheses would be conjectural. But pure consciousness is a fact and an initial datum. That up until now the field of pure consciousness has not been sufficiently or properly appropriated as a pure datum is of no concern and possesses only historical or anthropological interest and in no way forms a part of the problematic of this standpoint.

That it will be immediately objected that a pure datum must be a datum for someone is also a claim that holds no significance for pure consciousness. For, that data must be known by subject knowers is simply an idea that is generalized from the world of empirical experience: a starting point that is of no interest to the philosopher at this level, and inferential facts from which hold just as little relevance. One simply begins from the starting point of pure consciousness. *Pure consciousness is not to be accepted or assumed as a presupposition; it is experienced as a datum.* Once pure consciousness is experienced as a datum, it can then be described as a fact. But, it is not a fact in the scientific sense of meeting certain empirical rules for facticity or factuality. In order to avoid such confusions, one may choose not to refer to the fact of consciousness, but may choose to refer instead to the pure datum of consciousness. Strictly speaking, pure consciousness does not exist. Only consciousness exists, for *pure consciousness* implies that there is a less than pure consciousness. However, from a pedagogical standpoint, initially, the language of pure consciousness is preferable to the language of consciousness *simpliciter.*

In a strict sense, there is no phenomenological standpoint, for every standpoint assumes both itself and that of which it is not a standpoint - or, in other words, acknowledges standpoints outside of itself. But within the phenomenological standpoint, there are no other standpoints. There is only pure consciousness. There can be no other kind of consciousness other than pure consciousness. Even an empirical consciousness is in reality pure consciousness. In fact, as is mentioned above, pure consciousness does not exist, because the notion of a pure consciousness implies another (impure) world from which one has dirempted oneself. However, one can speak of pure consciousness while within pure consciousness, because transcendental introspection makes it possible to experience pure consciousness, while being aware that the notion of presuppositions for consciousness, or the "world", are inferences.

The notion of the existence of a phenomenological standpoint is a notion that only arises outside of the phenomenological standpoint, proper. The phenomenological standpoint does not refer to itself as a standpoint. When outside of the phenomenological standpoint, one may refer to it as a standpoint, which is not concerned with claims to reality, whether scientific or metaphysical. Once within the phenomenological standpoint, one simply examines the data of pure consciousness. Pure consciousness does not call itself pure consciousness. One can, as in this discussion, refer to the notion of pure consciousness. In this case, pure consciousness can become a theoretical object of inquiry. But this object is not to be confused with pure consciousness itself. It is only if one adopts the standpoint of consciousness that there can be a pure consciousness. From the standpoint of pure consciousness there is no such thing as pure consciousness.

From the standpoint of pure consciousness, the notion of different kinds of consciousness (pure consciousness and empirical consciousness) is a specious notion. In reality, there is and can only be pure consciousness. Properly understood, there is no need to make reference to pure consciousness since such a label implies the existence of another. Consciousness would be label enough. But, it is difficult for reflection to take rise unless some distinction is made. Pure consciousness is thus a more useful label than consciousness.

Is this metaphysical? It resembles speculative metaphysics except that one is not beginning with a claim of the form, 'Only pure consciousness exists'. Such an existential claim would place this entire discussion within the framework of conjectural metaphysics. Pure phenomenology is simply descriptive of what is experienced; it is not a theoretical claim about that experience. Every claim *about* experience is conjectural. Within pure consciousness one attempts to avoid making any claims whatsoever including the claim that 'only pure consciousness exists'. *It is only when one is within pure consciousness that one finds that only pure consciousness exists. This is a discovery; not an assertion.* When it is said that only pure consciousness exists, this is not an existential claim. It is a description of phenomenological experience. All that appears to one are the pure data of consciousness. Anything that is not a pure datum can be easily recognized and discarded as an empirical theory or an inference from an empirical theory. The remainder is pure consciousness.

What remains is not the "blank mind". The notion of a "blank mind" is the notion of a solipsist with an empty data bank or a computer that has not yet been programmed. Pure consciousness is not pure in the sense of being empty of objects. Pure consciousness is pure in the sense of not being connected to any of its objects except what phenomenologically appears to it. Pure consciousness is only interested in the phenomenological character of an object, not its existential status, whether worldly, imaginary, real or transcendent. Pure consciousness simply abstracts from the empirical characteristics of objects. It does not therefore see "essences" or the "essences of objects". It simply sees what is there to be seen without any existential qualifiers.

In contrast to Husserl, pure phenomenology is interested only in transcendental reflection, not in the character or the limits of the empirical properties of objects, e.g., that one cannot see all the sides of an empirical object. For example, in the pure consciousness of transcendental reflection, one can become aware of the nature of space and time. Such a nature of space-time, of which one may become aware, is a pure phenomenological awareness. *It is not an awareness that makes any claim about the nature of physical space and time.* It is simply an awareness that space and time must have the character that they are discovered to possess, a character that will be elucidated in the sequel.

One does not first start with pure consciousness and in the state of pure consciousness attempt to discover the nature of space and time. *One discovers pure consciousness in, for example, the discovery of the nature of space and time.* When one becomes aware of the phenomenological nature of space and time, one realizes that such an awareness can only have taken place in a state of pure consciousness.[9]

The phenomenological nature of space-time is not a study of perspectives, or of different sides of objects; it is, for example, an awareness of that character of space or time which can never be other than it is. Any other sort of awareness is empirical and may change as its empirical object changes. In the state of pure consciousness, the objects of which one becomes aware are unalterable: they cannot be other than they are. The pure objects of consciousness are necessary objects. They are experienced in their necessity.

If, for example, one were to become aware that during the waking state, one could never become aware of more than one object (whether a transcendental or an empirical object) of consciousness at a time, such an awareness would be a necessary awareness. It is a necessary awareness not because it is simply true by definition; it is a necessary awareness because it is discovered as a necessary feature of experience. It is discovered to be true and in its discovery it is discovered as not being able to be other than it is. It is not defined to be that way (or any way). Its necessity is discovered in the very discovery of its actual character. An example of a phenomenological truth is: *every awareness is always a new awareness.* This is not an assertion. It is a pure description of phenomenological experience or a description of pure phenomenological awareness.

It may be argued that no knowledge would ever be possible if it were to be the case that every experience were new. But within the phenomenological standpoint, every experience is new. What implications this has for knowledge is a question which takes place outside of the phenomenological standpoint, as it concerns a field of knowledge which is relevant only outside of the phenomenological standpoint. The phenomenological fact, or the phenomenological datum, is simply that every experience is new. Any qualification of this truth is a qualification that takes place outside of the phenomenological standpoint (that is, it makes use of theory, arguments from empirical experience, and so on). But if one transcends from other standpoints, and from the limitations of language, one is capable of discovering with absolute certainty and universality the phenomenological fact that 'every experience is new'. This is only another way of saying that only one experience is possible at a time.

Can it be argued that what is being said here is only trivial? Triviality as a description requires a standpoint of evaluation. Within the phenomenological standpoint, the newness of experience is not trivial, for there is no other experience to compare it against. As every experience is new, only the new experience is experienced at the time. And the capacity and the reality of experiencing a new experience is and can in no sense be trivial. To be truly open to a new experience - indeed - to experience it as new - is to open the door of wonder of philosophy itself. To truly experience anything at all as new is to see the world from the eyes of the infant, to experience the wonder and terror of reality. Such an experience would be the most wondrous and terrible realism and mysticism at once although neither label really applies since both refer to other realms.

It is innocence, not experience, which is experienced in the experience of the new. New experience does not call itself innocence, since that already entails another perspective to contrast with its present one. *Innocence is innocent of its innocence.* Innocence does not call itself innocence, for if it were capable of that, it would no longer be innocent. With no perspective to contrast with its present one, reality may be experienced in all of its rich detail and awesome meaning. Even the most ordinary experience becomes divine. It is in this sense that it may be said that to experience everything always anew would be to live like a god among men. Such an accomplishment would hardly be trivial. The description of pure phenomenology as living each moment as if it never happened before and never will again is a description of reality, truth and necessity all at once and a description that itself disappears as it utters itself and dissolves into the wonder that is the birthright of mankind. Such is the dare to existence that pure phenomenology hurls out for all of those who are bold enough to carry such a banner into the fray of life. It is in attempting to live such a challenge that phenomenological knowledge and truth become one.

Defining the Realm of Pure Phenomenology

In pure phenomenology one attempts to do what Husserl set out to do, that is, to demarcate a realm of description for philosophy. It is better to avoid making reference to this realm as a realm of essences, since to do so would be to adopt a conceptual standpoint and to treat philosophy as a theory, which is exactly what is to be avoided. In fact, even to make such a claim, as Husserl did, that every consciousness is a consciousness of an object, is already to subscribe to a conceptual standpoint. The so-called intentional structure of consciousness is not a phenomenological datum; it is a mental construct. In any moment of phenomenological introspection, or, to put this in another way, in any inspection of pure consciousness, a pure datum is simply revealed.

For example, if it were to be said that a phenomenological datum is a red patch, then that red patch would be a pure datum. If it were then said that that patch must be apprehended by a consciousness, then this would be an inference, not a phenomenological description. To say that every object is an object for some consciousness is an inference; it is not the result of any phenomenological inspection. In fact there is and can be no phenomenological awareness of "every object". "Every object" is a theoretical construction. There can only be the individual object before one. There can be no awareness of "every object". Every phenomenological awareness is of a unique, non-repeatable, pure consciousness.

To say that there is no such thing as an empty consciousness is also to make a claim outside of the realm of pure phenomenological description. All that is truly possessed as a result of a phenomenological act of inspection is a pure datum of consciousness. That datum cannot be divided up into subject and object. In this way of looking at things, there is no structure to consciousness. Or, to put it another way, there is only datum; there is no consciousness. Or, there is only consciousness (which is datum). But, there can never be consciousness *and* an object. All that there is is red. All that there is is blue. All that there is is sweet. All that there is is this noise. If it is postulated that such data must exist in or for a consciousness, this is an inference and does not exist as a phenomenological datum. Neither is there a raw sensory manifold or a congeries of phenomena. A raw sensory manifold is purely a theoretical construction. A congeries of phenomena is also a purely theoretical construction. There is no blooming, buzzing confusion. The concept of a blooming, buzzing confusion is not sufficiently phenomenological. There is only one sense datum at a time.

Notes

1. An especially clear and comprehensive discussion of the different types of solutions proposed to solve the mind-body problem can be found in Mario Bunge, *The Mind-Body Problem, A Psychobiological Approach*, Oxford: Pergamon Press, 1980, notably in Chapter 1. In this book a particularly able defense of emergent materialism is expounded and those who find this solution appealing are directed to this source which is rich in its history of the problem as well as in its cataloguing of the subtle differences between the diverse forms of solutions possible.

2. John R. Searle, 'The Mystery of Consciousness', *The New York Review of Books*, Volume XLII, Number 17, November 2, 1995, p. 60. Bunge's solution appears more persuasive when he argues that '... "mind-body interactions" can be accounted for, at least in principle, in terms of interactions among neural systems. My typing this sentence can be explained as a result of the action of certain ideation processes in my cortex on the motor center ... the so-called mind-body interactions are interactions among neural systems ... there is neither "upward causation"... nor "downward causation"...' *Op. cit.*, p. 15. While Bunge's "horizontal" interactive thesis seems extremely helpful, it is not clear that it explains how "ideation processes" can be "in" one's cortex, but this may be a problem of the linguistic form of the description rather than a difficulty inherent in Bunge's explanation. The mind-body problem seems very resistant to the most intelligent attempts to resolve it. How can such behavior as typing be the result of "ideation processes"? While this certainly appears to be an undeniable fact, how it is possible remains a mystery. Bunge's thesis is clearly and elegantly propounded, and his horizontal interactive thesis may provide an answer to certain problems which Searle does not address, but the greatest value of his work is in showing how and why what he refers to as 'the so-called *mind-body problem*' is '... one of the oldest, most intriguing, and most difficult of all the problems belonging in the intersection of science and philosophy ...' *Op. cit.*, p. xiii. For an extended treatment of the problem and related issues, one may be referred to Mario Bunge and Rubén Ardilla, *Philosophy of Psychology*, New York and Berlin: Springer-Verlag, 1987.

3. *Ibid.*, p. 64. To be fair to Searle, he does at times employ the word 'explain' instead of 'cause' as in '... all of our conscious experiences are *explained* by the behavior of neurons ...' p. 62 (emphasis his). But the use of explanation language is not in itself an explanation and constitutes a *petitio*. How do the behavior of neurons explain consciousness? This is a conundrum, not an answer.

4. *Ibid.*, p. 64.

5. *Critique of Pure Reason*, A99-102, A118-120, (However, in contrast, note A89-91), B130, B151-2. The temporal nature of a process whether one labels this 'empirical' or 'transcendental' would seem to create paradoxes

for the idea of synthesis despite arguments advanced by Waxman in Wayne Waxman, 'Time and Space in Kant', *Graduate Faculty Philosophical Journal*, Vol. 19, No. 1, 1966, pp. 43-66.

6. *Cf.*, In Kant's first *Critique*, he argues that '... we deny to time all claim to absolute reality; that is to say, we deny that it belongs to things absolutely, as their condition or property, independently of any reference to the form of our sensible intuition ...' (B52). Again, he argues that, 'It [time] is nothing but the form of our inner intuition. If we take away from our inner intuition the peculiar condition of our sensibility, the concept of time likewise vanishes; it does not inhere in the objects, but merely in the subject which intuits them' (B54). In his note to this statement, Kant adds, 'Time is not, therefore, something in itself, nor is it an objective determination inherent in things.'

7. For further discussion of how understanding must transcend individual language systems, *Cf.*, Robert E. Allinson, 'An Overview of the Chinese Mind,' in Robert E. Allinson (ed.), *Understanding the Chinese Mind: The Philosophical Roots*, New York: Oxford University Press, 2000, Tenth impression.

8. In Paul Lorenzen's John Locke lectures given in Oxford in 1967-8, he remarks that, 'The student needs to learn that the phrases "A" and 'A" do not refer to the linguistic acts of agreeing or disagreeing to a proposed plan A. *Cf.*, Paul Lorenzen, *Normative Logic And Ethics*, Mannheim/Zurich: *Bibliographisches Institut*, 1969, p. 77. The present author was privileged to attend Lorenzen's graduate seminar on the foundations of arithmetic in which Lorenzen (accompanied to every class by his spouse) offered a practical foundation for arithmetic that traced the origin of arithmetic to primitive acts of counting with sticks.

9. Similarly, in the case of Descartes, it is only after Descartes discovers the necessity of consciousness (or the *cogito* in his terms) that he formulates his criterion of clarity and distinctness. It is not that he starts out with his criterion of clarity and distinctness and then, armed with such a criterion, discovers the truth of the *cogito*. In the terms of this present work, every philosophical truth takes place in pure consciousness and it is only from the existence of philosophical truth that the existence of pure consciousness is known. Pure consciousness is discovered in transcendental reflection upon universal and necessary truth. Pure consciousness is not a psychological state to be experienced via the strategy of emptying one's mind of all objects.

Allegro moderato ma deciso
Quite lively and with decision

7 The Logic in Phenomenology

The logic in phenomenology must not be confused with the logic of phenomenology. The logic of phenomenology would presumably be the set of deductive reasons why it is rationally convincing that one should adopt a phenomenological perspective. The logic of phenomenology may be, in the end, that of which a reader may be convinced, but this is not the subject of this chapter. This chapter concerns itself with the logic *in* phenomenology.

Phenomenological Truth

For the nature of phenomenological truth, one may take a clue from the two roots of the word, 'phenomenological'. The first root refers to phenomena. This is, in the meaning utilized by this present, respective work, what appears to consciousness. With regard to the special usage of the phrase 'phenomenological truth' that is characteristic of this present work, phenomenological truth refers to the nature of the quality or the characteristics of what appears to or in consciousness. This is the domain of philosophic truth claims of the first order. Philosophy, as pure phenomenology, has no claim to make regarding what exists or does not exist outside of consciousness. Pure phenomenology is not idealism, as idealism adds the further claim (which requires access to a non-phenomenological realm to which existence is then denied) that all that there exists is consciousness, or that nothing exists outside of consciousness.

The second root, 'logical' refers to *how* philosophical claims are known to be true or the status of philosophical truth claims. In the context of 'phenomenology', 'logical' does not refer to either the structure of language, or the structure of concepts, or the sequence of arguments. Even 'logical' truths must be known to be true phenomenologically. The 'logical' in 'phenomenological' is the phenomenological validity status of what appears to consciousness. It is with this sense of the 'logical' that this chapter and indeed a large part of this entire work are concerned.

Phenomenological validity status has to do with both the universality and the inevitability of the phenomenologically discovered truths. Phenomenologically discovered truths are discovered to be true *as* universal and inevitable truths in phenomenological, introspective consciousness. Needless to say, this universality and inevitability of phenomenologically discovered truths is not simply psychological certainty. For this reason, the word 'certainty' is to be used carefully. The "phenomena" are *cognoscenda* which are seen to be universally and inevitably true. This is not because they are deductively true in virtue of following from some other premise. They are true because they cannot be otherwise. This is not because of any connection between terms or concepts; it is because of undeniable phenomenological facts, such as the undeniable fact of consciousness itself.

The fact of consciousness is not an empirical fact, because, unlike empirical facts, it cannot be otherwise than it is. It is not that there must be consciousness or that consciousness must exist. The existence of consciousness is a matter of contingent fact. But consciousness is discovered phenomenologically as a necessary datum. There is an immediate knowledge or an immediate awareness of the fact that consciousness exists. This very cognitive event of recognition carries with it an inevitability and universality, which is neither psychological nor logical in the deductive sense. It is logical in the sense that its truth-value is that part of the phenomenological cognition that is universal and necessary. In the present usage, the logical part of the phenomenological cognition describes the 'can never be otherwiseness' quality of phenomenological truths.

Neither are phenomenological truths transcendental conditions in the Kantian sense. A phenomenological truth is not transcendentally true in the sense that it is true because it is the condition for other or all other truths. If, by coincidence, it were the case that a phenomenological truth were to constitute a transcendental condition in the Kantian sense, this would be irrelevant to its *phenomenological* truth-value. For the phenomenologist, it does not matter whether or not a phenomenological truth were to be a transcendental condition, it must nonetheless be known to be true in a phenomenological sense on its own grounds. To put the matter briefly, it must be known to be true phenomenologically or else it simply falls outside the realm of truth claims made by the phenomenologist. It is transcendental, in the sense that this word is sometimes employed here, merely in that it can only be known to be true in an act of transcendental introspection.

All that is meant by the phrase 'transcendental introspection' is that in an act of transcendental introspection, empirical conditions are irrelevant to the universality and inevitability of the truth properties of the data being reflected upon. For example, it is empirically necessary (for human animals) to possess a brain in order to possess thoughts, but this empirical condition is not relevant to whether or not the putative truth discoveries made by that brain are or are not valid ones. These are two separate issues. It is not that the issue of needing or possessing a brain or not is an unimportant one. It is only that the status of possessing a brain is not sufficient to the solution of further problems such as whether a particular discovery made by that brain is a valid one or not.

Phenomenological truth candidates are simply and totally true (or false) as undeniable (or deniable) *cognitive facts*. They are self-certifying or self-falsifying. It is a separate question as to whether a metaphysics is necessary to provide the condition of the possibility that phenomenological truths possess the certifiability that they do. While it may be quite right to say that it is impossible to carry out either the epistemological inquiry or the metaphysical inquiry independently of each other, it nonetheless remains true that the epistemological side of the inquiry is self-constituted in the sense that the truths that are known inside the phenomenological standpoint stand on their own as truths apart from the issue of how or why they can exist as truths in the first place. Metaphysical conditions are explanations for the existence of phenomenological truths but they are not substitutes for the independent validation of phenomenological truths. From the standpoint of the order of discovery of truth, phenomenological truths must exist first. From the standpoint of the order of explanation, it is difficult if not impossible to avoid positing metaphysical truths in order to offer a complete explanation for how the epistemological truths can exist in the first place. Metaphysical truths, which are posited as explanations, are second order truths; such truths are not first order phenomenological truths.

Phenomenological truths cannot, strictly speaking, be "claims" of any kind. The claim of intentionality, which has been addressed above, is that a consciousness always must be a consciousness of an object. This is a claim because it claims to be true of the structure of consciousness, *not the fact (or event) of consciousness*. It possesses the quality of being a stipulative claim of the sort, 'one cannot have a consciousness without an object'. But how is such a claim justified? It would appear either to be an assumption without any evidence to support it, a pure stipulation which there is no obligation to follow, or a definition of consciousness which has no phenomenological grounds; i.e., is not grounded in an act of phenomenological inspection.

One can construct an argument of the syllogistic form 'Barbara' to prove that any act of consciousness is intentional. The major premise of such an argument is: every consciousness must be a consciousness "of" something (that 'something' is to be labeled an 'object'). The minor premise is: the subject knower has a consciousness. The conclusion is: therefore, the consciousness of the subject knower must be of an object. But, this is to use an argument form as legislation. There is no reason for the conclusion to follow unless the major premise is justified. In fact, the locus of determination of whether there is any foundation for this claim or not is during the act of consciousness itself (the minor premise stage). The scope of phenomenology proper is limited to the domain of the facts of consciousness (phenomenological data), and does not include either the premises or the conclusions of deductive arguments. The major premise and the conclusion of a deductive argument are both asserted outside of the domain of the phenomenological consciousness.

The "structure of consciousness" is never a phenomenological object. Whatever is meant by this abstract phrase, it would not appear to refer to a phenomenological datum of any sort, but would appear to refer to some theoretical entity or logical construction. Whatever existential claims are made about that which exists outside of consciousness are invalid from the phenomenological standpoint.

Phenomenology is also not ontology. It is of no immediate significance whether phenomenological truths have being or not. The entire question of being or existence falls outside the domain of phenomenological truth. Phenomenology can only refer to the inevitable and universal "facts" that appear to consciousness. Whether or not these "facts" have being is of concern only to the ontologist. The concept of a phenomenological ontology is a *contradictio in adjecto*. While the term "fact" may appear to be misleading, since by this term one is not thereby referred to what exists in the world, or what exists in accordance with criteria of science, there is nonetheless justification for the use of this term, because, in addition to carrying the meaning of 'presentation' or 'appearance' to which phenomenological *cognoscenda* naturally must conform, the word 'fact' carries the meaning of that which is not constructed, but is undeniably there for consciousness, as something which consciousness simply discovers or finds to be there. While 'appearance' could have this meaning, 'appearance' also seems to carry the notion of something which is visual (which a fact of consciousness need not be since a fact of consciousness may equally be a musical sound or a scent), and also carries the connotation of something which perhaps is not the case (that which is, after all, just an appearance). As a result, despite the problems that attend associating the term 'fact' with the phenomenological world, the term 'fact' is to be preferred to 'appearance' or even to the term 'phenomenon'. While the terms 'datum' or '*cognoscendum*' are also descriptive of the realm of intention of the phenomenologist, 'fact' will sometimes also be used in order to emphasize not simply something which is there for consciousness, but something which cannot help but be found in consciousness. A phenomenological fact is something which is not made up or which could or could not be an object of introspection, but rather something that is an undeniable feature of conscious awareness.

The logic that is embraced in phenomenology is the logic of cognitive validity. Somehow, this dimension of the concern and scope of philosophical inquiry and certification has remained undiscovered (explicitly) hitherto although it has very nearly been approached in the works of Edmund Husserl. It is of course the basis for why historically discovered philosophical truths have been and are true. But up until now, it has not been recognized as the *source* of these selfsame historically discovered philosophical truths.

This is why, in the end, despite the magnificence of Kant, his truth claims, have, by and large, fallen on deaf ears. As has oft been raised in this work, how did Kant *know* that there are two stems or sources (in Kant's sense) of knowledge to which he makes reference in his Introduction to his first *Critique*? (B29). If a third source of knowledge is involved or required, then that source of knowledge must be justified in some sense or at least acknowledged in a full sense. If it were to be acknowledged as a genuine and in fact a necessary form of knowledge that yields truth, then it should occupy the same level of importance for Kant as his argument from transcendental conditions.

Kant without his transcendental deductions would be a very different Kant. Hegel was not satisfied with Kant's "discovered but not explained or categorized truths" simply being transcendental *conditions* for what is known (though Kant in his first *Critique* does not seem to justify the truth claim that there are two sources of knowledge in this way or any other way).

If all philosophical truths were to be no more than truth conditions, this would degrade philosophy to a journeyman order type of knowledge in which philosophical truths would not be known in themselves to be true, but could only be assumed to be true, if other forms of knowledge were first possible. If other forms of knowledge were not well justified, then the conditions for those types of knowledge would become otiose, irrelevant and in fact arouse suspicion if argued to be the basis of any universal philosophical claims in the first place. This has been in fact the fate of much of the history of Western philosophy.

It is not so much that it is wrong that philosophical truths are or could be the basis for other sorts of truths; it is only that this should not be their only accreditation or source of truth value. In engineering language, philosophical truth claims that were based only on being conditions for other truth claims would lack redundancy (which, in ordinary language, according to Ockham, would be a philosophical virtue).

In an even simpler analogy, if one were building a foundation for a house, and the only support for the foundation were that the rest of the house would only be able to stand if this foundation were to exist, this would not be support enough. The foundation must be capable of standing on its own. Kant's transcendental deduction of his categories possesses no first order source of validation. Unfortunately, many of Hegel's truth claims made within his system stand or fall in terms of whether they genuinely (for Hegel) lead the way to the Absolute. As argued earlier, while Hegel did wish that truth claims would provide their truth conditions out of themselves, he does not seem to have provided compelling examples in every case.[1]

In the end, transcendental conditions become metaphysical axioms in the manner of axioms in mathematics. They retain the status of assumptions, regardless of whether or not one *must* presuppose these truths to be true if the rest of the philosophical system demands it. Transcendental conditions still lack the quality of being known to be true in and of themselves. If the argument from transcendental conditions is employed after phenomenological truths have been independently established, then one's metaphysics is not simply dependent upon an argument from transcendental conditions. However, in the absence of independently known phenomenological truths, transcendental conditions remain on the level of assumptions. That is why they were unsatisfying to the philosophical demands of Hegel. Hegel's categories may indeed seem more colourful than what he termed Kant's 'bloodless ballet of categories'. (Hegel was too generous to Kant. Kant's categories form a bloodless still picture, not a ballet.)

Despite the grand title of his work, *The Phenomenology of Mind*, Hegel did not seem to produce a phenomenology in the sense of this present work, but produced rather a dazzling array of sometimes richly metaphoric "deductions" among abstract concepts which formed a kind of system, the readily discernible touchstone of phenomenological truth of which was limited to select examples such as his surpassingly fine descriptions of the master-slave relationship, the relationship between stoicism, scepticism and the contrite consciousness, and the nature of the relationship that exists between the disciplines of art, religion and philosophy. The only phenomenologists there have been whose work is highly relevant to this present work were Husserl, who was a self-conscious phenomenologist and Kant who was, in certain significant aspects of his work, a phenomenologist, *malgré lui*.[2]

How to possess truths without making any assumptions at all is the task which Plato set for philosophy and which remains for succeeding philosophers to complete. Plato's practise, unfortunately, did not keep pace with his brilliant description of the nature of philosophical knowledge as outlined in *Republic VI*. He, too, sometimes, fell victim to the trap of the argument from transcendental conditions; e.g., what one would have to assume (as Forms) to know anything at all. Philosophers must be able to describe the nature of philosophical truth as truth that is discovered without making any assumptions as in Plato's famous description of the dialectic in *Republic VI*. To phenomenologize Plato, one must be able to describe the truths that are constituted by the phenomenological facts of consciousness which are revealed in concrete and precise moments of knowledge. In knowing such facts no assumptions whatsoever are made which are relevant to the truth value of the "facts" which are known. This is the proper sphere of philosophical inquiry and the reference point for the application of philosophical terms such as 'logic' and 'truth'. In *sensu stricto* only the fact or the presence and the qualities of the primary data of consciousness possess truth value or truth properties. Propositional truth is derivative from these basic truths. Truth in a manner of speaking, belongs to the phenomena in a broad sense, and not to propositions. While it is true that propositions or statements about the existence or the characteristics of the pure objects of consciousness and the characteristics of the relations among the pure objects of consciousness possess truth value, such truth value is a property of the *noemata* and not of the propositions. If the truth value belonged to the propositions, the truth would be limited to linguistic truth. The truth is also not restricted to a true relationship between a statement and a thing. For the type of truth referred to here is not the correspondence between a statement and an empirical fact but a property which is a necessary fact that belongs to the pure objects of consciousness and their relations. Statements about the pure objects of consciousness or their relations are true but their truth value derives from the constitutive truth of the *noema* not from the truth contained in the statements or the fact that the truth of the statements corresponds to a *noematic* truth since such a correspondence would be derivative. The truth contained in the statements derives from the truth that is described by the statements and is not a property that belongs to the statements. Hence, it is not proper to refer to this kind of truth as propositional truth except in a secondary sense. Phenomena proper thus, are what are known to be true, and only phenomena can be known to be true. This is the 'logic' in 'phenomenology'.

Notes

1. '... truth, to deserve the name, must authenticate its own truth ...' *Logic*, William Wallace (trans.), pp. 155, 285.
2. Kant himself did employ the term 'phenomenology' but it appears as if he meant it in a sense different from that given in this present, respective work. For one thing, for Kant, apart from certain passages in his epistemological writings (his writings on ethics are excepted here), it is in keeping with his majority thesis that one cannot know something as it exists in itself that one cannot experience consciousness directly. An intriguing work which inquires into Kant's relation to phenomenology is Ernst Wolfgang Orth's article, 'Can "Phenomenology" in Kant and Lambert be connected with Husserlian Phenomenology?', included in Thomas M. Seebohm and Joseph J. Kockelmans (eds.), *Kant and Phenomenology*, Washington, D.C.: Center for Advanced Research in Phenomenology and University Press of America, 1984. The sense of phenomenology which is meant in the attribution of the label to Kant in this present, respective work is that in his analysis of space and time, Kant was analyzing pure

objects, that is, objects which were not empirical objects, and thus, was doing phenomenology in this contest without being aware of the fact.

8 The Forgotten Fourth

While to suddenly enter into a discussion of Plato's *Seventh Epistle* might appear to be a digression, it is seemly both to finish with Plato and with one of Plato's favourite literary strategies. It is also fitting to end a discussion of knowledge with the writing of Plato's that contains his inspiring description of the transmission of knowledge that transcends the limits of language. Glenn Morrow refers to the *Seventh Epistle* as '... one of the most impressive of all his [Plato's] written compositions'.[1] Hans-Georg Gadamer refers to the notorious epistemological section that is the subject of this chapter as 'four precious pages'.[2] What makes this composition one of Plato's most impressive written works? Why are these four pages precious? And is there a relevance to deriving value for philosophy today from Plato's suggestions in this passage?

Much of these four pages are caught up with examining what Gadamer refers to as the 'ridiculously simple' example of the knowledge of a circle. What Plato is attempting in this short compass is to illustrate that in knowing a circle, one is already in possession of the knowledge of the Form of a circle and thus even in such an elementary case of knowledge, there is knowledge of the Forms. In the *Seventh Epistle*, Plato is not only arguing for the existence of the Forms, he is stating that knowledge of the Forms is possible. The process by which one achieves the knowledge of the Form of a circle, that is, understands what a circle is, is the same process through which one arrives at all knowledge of Forms.

Before proceeding, it is important to take note of the scholarly position with regard to the claim of the *Seventh Epistle* being a legitimate part of the Platonic *corpus*. According to the great Plato scholar, A. E. Taylor, writing in 1926, there is no longer any question as to the authenticity of the *Seventh Epistle*, Taylor points out that tradition accepted the *Seventh Epistle* as authentic from ancient times up until the fifteenth century.[3] Glenn Morrow puts forth a detailed, lengthy and cogent account of the grounds for the authenticity of the *Seventh Epistle*. In addition to pointing to the body of opinion of twentieth century scholars that differs from the nineteenth century scholars who held that the *Seventh Epistle* was not authentic (nor, according to them, were the *Parmenides, Sophist, Cratylus*, and *Philebus*), Morrow adduces copious and compelling historical, philological and stylistic arguments for the authenticity of the *Seventh Epistle*. For example, Morrow cites the cases of Cicero and Plutarch who regard the *Seventh Epistle* as genuine. He also remarks upon the general unanimity of the present body of opinion on the most decisive criterion, that of style.[4] To his list of arguments, one might add the argument that the long, digressive passage in which the theory of knowledge appears is an authentic mark of the literary devices of Plato. F. M. Cornford's judgement as to the authenticity of the *Seventh Epistle* is more cautious as when he refers to the *Seventh Epistle* in a footnote, he begins by saying, 'If *Epistle VII*, 342A ff. be accepted as genuine ...'[5] While Kenneth Sayre puts forth arguments to demonstrate that the *Seventh Epistle* is genuine and accepts the *Seventh Epistle* as genuine, and provides arguments to show why the arguments of those who reject *Seventh Epistle* are inferior to the arguments of those who accept it, in an interesting remark, he comments that, 'The fact that recent scholarship tends strongly to favor the authenticity of the Seventh Letter, needless to say, does not by itself put the issue to rest'.[6] Hans-Georg Gadamer refers to the authenticity of the *Seventh Epistle* being "contested"and the epistemological passage "called into question recently", but does not indicate by whom.[7] Gadamer nevertheless considers it worthwhile to write thirty pages about it. In any case, a proper understanding of the epistemological contents of the *Seventh Epistle* serves to illuminate other dialogues of Plato's, and also serves as a springboard of ideas that take one beyond the question of mere Platonic scholarship.

What then is Plato's account of knowledge that has stirred so much controversy and yet now is considered to form part of the authentic Platonic *corpus*? In the lengthy epistemological digression, Plato analyses the act of knowledge into five parts, all of which he considers to be necessary for knowledge to take place.[8] The five elements are: the name, the definition, the image, the resultant knowledge itself and the proper object of knowledge, the Form.[9] Knowledge itself is not strictly speaking a component since it is the resultant of the interaction of the other parts, but it is a separate *analysandum*.

What is of special interest for present purposes, is not the Fifth which is the part of Plato's doctrine that has received the most attention, but the Fourth. Since Anglo-American philosophy has been preoccupied with the analysis of logic and language and has been sceptical for the greater part of the twentieth century with respect to the question of whether universal or permanent knowledge is possible, in these respects, the background of the twentieth century and the beginning of the twenty-first century is not so dissimilar to that of Plato's own time. Plato's philosophical antagonists were the Sophists, who were especially well known for the relativistic theories of ethics that they taught. The Sophists captivated the youth of time via their skillful use of language, their logical and linguistic tricks and the power of their rhetoric. Philosophy today finds itself in the same plight as did philosophy in the time of Plato.

If Plato's five elements are examined from the standpoint of contemporary linguistically oriented epistemology, there is no question concerning the first three of Plato's elements. In fact, for the most part, it would appear as if the contemporary linguistic approach to the description of what is necessary for knowledge would stop with the Second, namely, the definition. In a broad sense, according to contemporary epistemology, once the definition of the *cognoscendum* is posited, the meaning of the *cognoscendum* is understood. There would be no necessary "knowledge" beyond this, and certainly no Form to know. The only possible reference for the consideration of "knowledge", or, the Fourth, might be for cognitive psychology. Since philosophy has presumably no interest in the actual physiological processes that occur, (Locke's, *An Essay Concerning Human Understanding* appears as an exception in this regard), this element of what Plato is describing presumably could be relegated to the province of the cognitive psychologist. The Fifth, needless to say, would be purely a product of Plato's fancy and would possess even less of a basis for a thoroughgoing consideration.

It is critical for the purposes of philosophical rectification, and in Chinese terms, for the philosophical rectification of names, (*cheng ming*) to draw present attention to the 'Fourth'.[10] In so doing, it should at once be pointed out that by the 'Fourth', one is not referring to the aspect of physiological processes or psychological processes, and it is not to be believed that Plato had any such intention. By the 'Fourth' Plato had in mind the final cognitive experience which he calls 'knowledge'. It may be that it is the current sceptical predilection that is the reason why this dimension of Plato's epistemology receives so little attention. Perhaps this is the influence of logical positivism. Perhaps it is the fear of being forced to subscribe to Plato's world of 'Forms', which has created an unwillingness to take Plato seriously today.

In the epistemological passage under question, Plato carefully examines the misleadingly simplistic appearing example of a circle. Plato was fond of examples from geometry and it is reported that above the doors of his Academy it was written, 'Let No One Enter Here Who Does Not Know Geometry'. The point of this was that Plato realized that if one could grasp how one knew geometrical truths, one could better understand how one could grasp philosophical ones. Plato's seemingly trivial example of how one comprehends what a circle is is an illustration in a microcosm of how one achieves knowledge of any philosophical truth. It is not then knowledge of a 'circle' that is under consideration; it is knowledge itself.

How does Plato attempt to show that knowledge is possible, which is not reducible to semantics or conventional definitions? Plato argues that 'names' cannot be sufficient for knowledge since a name can be altered. In the example taken of the circle, the name 'circle' can be used for 'square' and vice-versa. The realities considered, however, would remain unchanged. Therefore, the name by which something is called is not sufficient to explain knowledge.

The empirical image is also not sufficient to account for knowledge. In the case of a circle, for example, a small circle and a large circle are equally circles. Hence, no one image is adequate to satisfy the idea of a circle. In addition, as is well known, no circle is truly circular and thus no empirical circle fulfils the definition of a circle. The circle on the blackboard can be erased, but this erasure does not result in the disappearance of the circle.

It should be pondered why Plato did not consider the Second, or, definition, an adequate account for knowledge, since it would appear to most linguistic philosophers, that, if one knew the definition of whatever were under discussion, then one would have adequate knowledge, that is sufficient for one's purposes, of whatever one wanted to know. The reason that for Plato, a definition of a circle is not enough to account for knowledge of a circle is that for Plato, the words in a definition can change, so that one definition is not verbally or linguistically identical with another. In Book I of Euclid's *Elements*, a circle is defined as 'a plane figure contained by one line such that all the straight lines falling upon it from one point among those lying within the figure are equal to one another'. A circle can also be defined as 'a figure in which a locus of points on its circumference is equidistant from a fixed center point'. A circle can be defined as 'the figure in which everywhere on the periphery is equidistant from the center'. A circle can be defined as 'the figure whose extremities are everywhere equally distant from its center'. The point is even more obvious when it is considered that the same definition can be put into different languages. Current linguistic philosophers could then say that what is being understood in different languages was a common meaning of the definition. All that would be necessary would be to understand the meaning behind the definition. When this point is considered, one might well wonder why Plato did not apparently consider 'meaning' as one of the elements in an act of knowledge. This is because, for Plato, what is being referred to by the definition was the true Form or the 'Fifth'. This was what took the place of the 'meaning' element of today's linguistic philosophers.

For Plato, the meaning of the circle could not be an idea in someone's mind. It is unfortunate but understandable that Plato is often wrongly referred to as an idealist. For Plato, the circle must possess a permanent status that provides unity to thought and is the object of all definitions. In that event, knowledge of the definition, of what in Aristotelian language is the formula that states the essence, is insufficient. It must be known that this is the definition of a circle and for that the definition cannot be simply verbally self-referential. It is not the definition of the 'word' circle. Plato has already disposed of that possibility. It is not the definition of the image circle. For which image can satisfy the definition? Any circle that one draws on a blackboard or whiteboard or prints with the assistance of a computer's word processing program will perforce consist of points on the outside of the circumference which are not at the same distance from the center as a point taken from the inside of the circumference. The definition cannot be of a 'concept' of a circle since any concept of a circle depends upon someone's thinking of it. But what is known when a circle is known is not dependent upon any particular person's concept of a circle. Concepts come and go even within the same thinker's cogitations. But what one knows when one knows a circle does not disappear from existence from time to time.[11]

For Plato, to acquire knowledge of the circle required a process of cogitation that continually thought about the different elements until it became clear that the knowledge of a circle could not be reduced to one of its elements. To know properly that the definition is but a string of words that is only signifying a circle one must at the same time know that words are not sufficient for knowledge and definitions are but made up of words. When one understands the meaning of a circle, one understands something that is eternal and available to everyone. The act of knowing the circle is not so simple as being able to recite its definition. It is the understanding that there is something that can be so defined. This knowledge as Plato proceeds to say cannot be put into words. But it is suggested by the words that one uses. When one understands the meaning of a circle one understands something, which is not reducible to a name, a linguistic definition, or an image. One's understanding includes, for example, that a circle is not an empirical image. And this understanding is part of the understanding of the circle. The definition by itself does not serve to render up this meaning. To understand the meaning of a circle, one already understands more than what is given in the definition.

For Plato, the circle is what makes it possible that there can be a definition of circle in the first place. In truth, it is not possible to understand a "definition" of a circle; such a description of an act of knowledge is incomplete: it is parasitic upon always understanding more than the definition can provide on its own.

It is impossible to discuss the Fourth, the knowledge of a circle, apart from the Fifth. At the moment of the apprehension of the 'meaning' or Form, with the assistance of name, definition, and image, knowledge can take place. And, by this reference to 'knowledge', Plato did not mean a psychological event. Plato could have added a Sixth, namely the necessary occurrence of a certain brain process, but this would have led to an infinite series of posits or at least a very long list which would have included a living body, a body with a functional brain, and so on. For philosophical purposes, there is no need to mention all of these necessary conditions for knowledge as Plato is taking these conditions for granted, and is discussing only what is of relevance for the act of reflective understanding, once a functional and functioning brain (and body supporting that brain and so on) are assumed. Thus, there is no need for Plato to consider physiology at this point, and his category of the 'Fourth' cannot be a simple reference to a brain process.

Indeed, if Plato's reference to the 'Fourth' were to the realm favoured by cognitive psychology, it would not be very plausible why Plato would consider Forms and definitions to be crucial to the stimulation of a brain process, since such a process could presumably be stimulated by less reflective thought, such as the appetites which

Plato realizes do exist or in today's world, by direct stimulation of the brain by electrodes.

Plato must have considered that the Fourth represented a very important realm of consideration indeed, second only in his view, to the importance of the Fifth. While there has been a great deal of discussion of Plato's Fifth (the Form), there has been comparatively little discussion of his Fourth. It could even be argued that the Fourth is the most important "element" although it is not strictly speaking a component but the actual moment of knowing which is the sum-total of all the other elements.

The Fifth serves as only one component of four which constitute the Fourth and it is the Fourth (which is the resultant of the interaction of all five elements) that Plato is analysing. That the Fourth is actually knowledge of the Fifth is incidental in this regard since it is the Fourth which is the ultimate *analysandum*. In any case, it is with the knowledge of the Fifth that the philosopher is concerned, not with the Fifth itself.

In the present chapter, the Fourth stands for the act of understanding which incorporates and in some measure even transcends the object of understanding, and is at once the ultimate *analysandum* and the ultimate objective of the philosopher. *The Fourth consists of the union of meaning, and the consciousness or understanding of that meaning that is the knowledge of the Eidos.* A definition by itself is not adequate to knowledge of the *Eidos*, as has been suggested above, since a definition is only a string of words that signifies a meaning. But meaning has no 'meaning' by itself any more than beauty exists in the oil painting on the wall of the museum, apart from its experience in the mind of the subject appreciator. *The 'meaning' must be apprehended by the philosopher, and it is the very apprehension of the meaning that constitutes the knowledge experience for the philosopher.* The apprehension referred to above is not the psychological event, as this is of only minor and secondary philosophical interest. The apprehension is the moment of understanding or insight, which is the only locus of philosophical truth.[12]

Whether or not truth exists apart from this is a matter of the Fifth. It is only if the subject knower were to be granted the philosophical capacity for possessing knowledge of the *Eidos* that the notion of philosophical truth can be understood. The 'Fourth', then, which Plato thought of as the act of knowledge, is the precise moment when name, definition, image, and meaning/Form are assimilated and transmogrified such that an understanding of truth is the result. When what is true is understood, an experience has been undergone which transcends the words, the image, the definition, and even the meaning or true object of understanding. Knowledge is possible in and only in that moment in which the four other aspects are mere players in the overall performance of the dramatic moment of knowledge, or the Fourth. This overall performance is what is understood in that instantaneous cognition, which is that moment of philosophical insight, to which, for Plato, all philosophers aspire as the ultimate goal of philosophical endeavor.

For Plato, all of the components are necessary, but what results is not reducible to any of its component parts. The Fourth, properly speaking, is not an ontologically separate part: it is the result of the marriage of the parts. It is however, a part in the sense that it can be logically analyzed as a separate part from the other aspects. In another way, it may be said that all of the "parts" are only logical abstractions from that momentary act of knowledge, and do not really possess separate existence on their own. In this sense, even knowledge is an abstracted part. However, it is with this abstracted part that the philosopher must take the greatest concern as it is this part which has to do with the experiencing of that which is true. It may not be empirically or epistemologically divisible from its other components, except in that moment of transcendental reflection, but it may be logically isolated and analyzed for its unique epistemological value and for its very existence as an *analysandum*.

In another sense, all of the elements of which Plato is speaking are ontic impostors. No part is really knowable by itself. Each part is itself already a combination of all five elements. Strictly speaking, from an epistemological standpoint, there are never any parts existing by themselves; e.g., in order to possess an image, one must assume the presence and the interaction of all of the other elements. No element ever exists as an ontologically independent element with regard to the occurrence of the knowledge event.

In the *Seventh Epistle*, Plato is engaged in the self-described impossible task of attempting to put what cannot be put into words into words. This chapter consists of more words attempting to explain why Plato said that what he meant could not be put into words. Another way of putting what has been said above is that it is through the agency of language, definitions, empirical images and meanings that one is able achieve that philosophical understanding to which the name 'truth' is given. Just as the proper object of the art appreciator may be the feeling of 'beauty', one can say that the proper object of the philosopher is the experience that is at the same time the understanding of 'truth'. It is *through* and not *by* language, definitions, images and meanings that the philosopher comes to the truth that she or he understands, that transcends all of the other elements as something separate from all of these, that makes up the cognitive experience to which the philosopher aspires, just as the art appreciator through the experience of colours and shapes can arrive at the experience of beauty which is the *sine qua non* of the appreciator.[13] In Peter Shaffer's play, *Amadeus*, Salieri, when staring at Mozart's original score of the opening of the Twenty-ninth Symphony in A Major, exclaims, 'I was staring through the cage of those meticulous ink strokes at an Absolute Beauty'.[14] There is no reason why philosophy should not have its own intrinsic subject matter as well.

Whilst Plato was lavishing so much attention on the Fifth, he had bequeathed subsequent philosophers, the Fourth. In the virtual exclusive obsession Platonic scholars including the profoundly historically misleading example of Aristotle have had with Plato's Fifth (or his Ideas or Forms), both the Fourth and the importance of the Fourth and its unique appearance and its unique role in the world of the philosopher have been neglected.[15] By concentrating on the Fifth as Plato's main contribution to philosophy, Plato has been remembered as the creator of the theory of Forms.

For Gadamer, the Fourth is not so ultimate. He points out that any act of knowledge is ephemeral and thus knowledge suffers from weaknesses as an instrument.[16] Plato does at times even use the words 'right opinion' instead of knowledge when referring to the Fourth. Even Plato nods. These lapses of Plato's do not seem to cohere with the elevated descriptions of knowledge that he himself renders in other places. It must be recalled that some of Plato's loftiest dialectic concerns itself with the possibility of the knowledge of the Forms and not solely or even primarily with proving their status to be at the top of the dialectical hierarchy, as in *Republic VI* and in *Symposium* and of course in the *Seventh Epistle*. And, whether or not it is a Form which is known (in the sense that either Plato meant or was taken to mean by Form), Plato's account of knowledge merits special attention, nevertheless. The account of knowledge that is relevant here may not be the same as the account that Plato renders in *Theatetus* in which he seems to be concerned with showing the differences between opinion and knowledge and with explaining the nature of perception. The account of knowledge more relevant here is that account in which he is attempting to point to the unique kind of knowledge which is possessed

by the philosopher and the process by which the philosopher comes to
understanding (in the vocabulary of the present work and not in the
Kantian sense). This sense of understanding is the same as what is
meant by philosophical *knowledge.*[17] It is this account of Plato's and
this concern of Plato's that is described in the *Seventh Epistle* as the
core and the goal of the practise of the discipline of philosophy:

> There is no writing of mine about these matters, nor will
> there ever be one. For this knowledge is not something that
> can be put into words like other sciences; but after long-
> continued intercourse between teacher and pupil, in joint
> pursuit of the subject, suddenly like light flashing forth when
> a fire is kindled, it is born in the soul and straightway
> nourishes itself.[18]

Because of or just as in Western philosophers' two and one
half millennia's distraction with Plato's Fifth, Western philosophers
have come to be regarded and classified in terms of the theories they
have invented or the systems they have constructed rather than in terms
of the truths which they have discovered or the end-experiences of the
quest for wisdom which they have described. In the same fashion, one
can look at the entire collection of works Paganini or Scarlatti or
Beethoven has created and consider these to be the products of
Beethoven, Paganini or Scarlatti. But, one's proper appreciation of any
of these composers cannot (save in memory) be based on an
appreciation of all of their works. Beethoven's greatness is experienced
and appreciated precisely in and only in the moment of enjoying one of
his great compositions. Or, to be more precise, it is in a special moment
of the resolution of many musical themes, which have perhaps been
heard for the thirtieth time over in just so many years, that the very
greatest appreciation is stirred in the musical imagination. Such a level
of musical appreciation may even be restored in memory by the
production of a single bar of music such as a familiar bar of one of
Paganini's caprices or as in the famous opening bar of Beethoven's
Fifth.[19] It is not so much the composer's prodigious output that is the
source of a hearer's appreciation (that may inspire admiration for her or
his productivity, but it is not the source of musical delight), but it is
those moments when in experiencing her or his music, that one is able
to experience the same profound depths and heights and resolutions as
she or he did in composing it that is the origin of the listener's aesthetic
satisfaction. What makes Beethoven great is that he has been able to
conduct his musical audience to the same great heights of the

experience of musical grandeur and ecstasy that he himself was capable of experiencing. This is, in Platonic terms, the experience of the Form of Beauty. At the moment of the pure experience of Beethoven's Fifth, is one really attending to the sound of the notes?

In the same way, with Plato, or with Hegel or with any of the great philosophers, while they may be justly admired for the systems that they have created or for their enormous productivity, philosophical wonder and that unique philosophical experience, the experience of truth, is awakened only in the actual moment of reflecting upon, or reading certain passages in their works, or in the discussions of them with colleagues, teachers or students. Too much concentration on the Fifth, which, symbolically here can represent the doctrine or the dogma of a philosopher, has led students of philosophy to lose sight of the unique joys and the overarching status of the Fourth. For, while many may·disagree with the total systems of different philosophers, these same dissenters can still experience and enjoy the truth of certain of the special insights of the great philosophers. One need not be a Hegelian, for example, to savour and to marvel at such statements as 'Nothing great is accomplished without passion' or 'The owl of Minerva flies only at twilight'.

If the criteria of philosophical importance or truth were the systems as a whole of different philosophers, there would be no philosophical truth as all of these systems contain numerous and frequently self-invalidating flaws. Apart from distinguished exceptions such as the Oxford mathematician Roger Penrose, few today subscribe to the real existence of Plato's Forms. Hegel's Absolute Spirit would probably find even fewer adherents. If such a subscription were to be the measure of philosophical truth, it would be a serious disincentive to the reading of these philosophers from the past. Or, if the doctrines and the systems of philosophers, and not their insights were to be taken as the main motive for reading their works, the history of philosophy would become a course in the history of error not to speak of folly.

What still remains true today is that in reading these great works from the past, one can partake of certain moments of shared understanding wherein one can glimpse the selfsame truths which were seen by these past philosophers just as the past philosophers saw them, the entire experience of which is made possible just because of the fact that the past philosophers did see them. It is in these experienced moments of truth that the real content and value of philosophy lives. As one reenacts the certainty of the Cartesian reflective consciousness, one becomes aware of the nature of philosophical truth. One task of the philosopher today is to become more and more finely aware of the nature of philosophical truth so that philosophical truth can be distinguished sharply and appreciated separately from philosophical systems. In so doing, philosophical truths from the past can be appropriated and maintained, whether in their past form or reconstituted into present phenomenological descriptions, and preparations can be made to usher into existence new philosophical truths based upon a correct understanding of the nature of philosophical truth.

If, as some kind of historical empirical scientists, students of philosophy regard philosophical systems as a whole, the systems of past philosophers will naturally be rejected as all of them are filled with falsehoods, conjecture and contradictions. On the other hand, if students of philosophy are encouraged to experience and rediscover great moments of philosophical insight, a better understanding of the purpose of philosophical inquiry and a greater admiration for the work of past philosophers can be gained. At the same time, a new path can be paved and a substantial direction can be posited for the discovery of new philosophical truths, which will be the task of all philosophers of the future.

Notes

1. *Plato's Epistles*, Glenn R. Morrow (trans.), New York: Bobbs-Merrill Co., 1962, p. 55.
2. Hans-Georg Gadamer, 'Dialectic and Sophism in Plato's Seventh Letter', in *Dialogue and Dialectic: Eight Hermeneutical Studies in Plato*, P. Christopher Smith (trans.), New Haven: Yale University Press, 1980, p. 96.
3. A.E. Taylor, *Plato, The Man and His Work*, London: Metheun, 1926, pp. 11-16.
4. *Plato's Epistles*, Glenn R. Morrow (trans.), New York: Bobbs-Merrill Co., 1962, pp. 3-21; 45, 60-80, *et passim*.
5. F. M. Cornford, *Plato's Theory of Knowledge*, New York: Bobbs-Merrill Co., 1957, p. 9, n. 1.
6. Kenneth Sayre, *Plato's Literary Garden*, Notre Dame and London: University of Notre Dame Press, 1995, pp. xviii-xxiii.
7. 'Dialectic and Sophism in Plato's Seventh Letter,' in *Dialogue and Dialectic: Eight Hermeneutical Studies in Plato*, P. Christopher Smith, (trans.), New Haven: Yale University Press, 1980, p. 96. Gadamer does himself state that he "presumes that the *Seventh Epistle* is authentic" in another essay in the same volume. *Cf.*, *'Amicus Plato Magis Amica Veritas,'* p. 200.
8. *Seventh Epistle*, 341-345.

9. Whilst the words 'Form' or 'Idea' *(Eidos)* do not appear in the passage analyzed, the concept is implied by the 'Fifth'. That it is not directly utilized (nor is the term 'dialectic') might be an argument that Plato was moving away from the emphasis on this dimension of his theory. One must keep in mind that this is a work of the later Plato and may not be completely consistent with the theory of Ideas expounded in Plato's earlier maturity.

10. *Cf., Hsün-Tzu,* Book XXII, 3. 'Should a King arise, he would certainly follow the ancient terms and reform the new terms. Then he could not but investigate the reason for having terms, together with the means through which similarities and differences are found, and the fundamental principles in applying terms to things.' In this chapter, an attempt is made to restore the term 'knowledge' to its ancient (Platonic) and true meaning.

11. Sir Roger Penrose, the Oxford mathematician, considers that mathematical ideas have an existence of their own in the sense of the Platonic mathematical world. *Cf., Shadows of the Mind, A Search for the Missing Science of Consciousness*, Oxford: Oxford University Press, 1994, pp. 65; 428, 429. (For the purposes of this chapter, there is no need to distinguish between the existence of a separate realm of ideas for mathematical ideas and other ideas).

12. It is best to avoid the use of the term 'intuition' both because what is understood or known is something rational, though it is non-empirical, and not something mystical and because what is known is not known via some form of extrasensory perception.

13. It is of course difficult to describe the relationship between language and knowledge. The use of the word 'through' cannot imply 'by means of'. The use of the word 'through' perhaps carries with it the meaning of a window through which one looks. Part of the difficulty, of course, arises from the fact that theoretically abstracted data are being compared. With regard to the view of art that is being ascribed to Plato in this passage, one must bear Plato's view of art in mind that he presents in *Symposium* rather than the view he takes, for different purposes in the *Republic*. In *Symposium*, it must be remembered, it is stated in Diotema's speech that the experience of the Beautiful in itself is what makes life worth living. It could be argued that an appreciation of *avant-garde* art is not based upon an appreciation of beauty and further that the art products or music products of certain cultures do not necessarily strike those from other cultures as beautiful. In answer to such arguments, one may say that with respect to certain products of *avant-garde* art it may well be that new criteria such as humour may be more relevant to the appreciation of the art than beauty. The argument as developed above would then have to be applied *mutatis mutandi* to the experience of comic delight, for example, rather than beauty. With respect to those from different cultures, it may certainly require the cultivation and the acquisition of a particular taste before the artistic products of one culture can be appreciated by an audience comprised of those from another

culture. This process of cultivation is, however, merely a condition for the possibility of appreciating a different manifestation of what can be experienced as beautiful.

14. Peter Shaffer, *Amadeus*, Act One, Scene XII, Salieri's salon.

15. One must be grateful for the misunderstandings of philosophers. If Aristotle had not misunderstood Plato, there would have been no philosophy of Aristotle. In the words of Niels Bohr, when referring to Pauli, 'he misunderstood me very well'.

16. As a result, Gadamer considers that the '... so-called theory of knowledge in the Seventh Letter refers to the community which exists among people speaking to one another.' *Cf.*, *Dialogue and Dialectic: Eight Hermeneutical Studies in Plato*, P. Christopher Smith (trans.), New Haven: Yale University Press, 1980, p. 113. But Gadamer's "community of speech" would also suffer from the same weakness of ephemerality that Gadamer considers Plato to indirectly ascribe to knowledge.

17. It would be cumbersome to employ terminology such as *episteme* and *noesis* (the latter term, which Cornford, in his translation of *Republic VI*, translates as intelligence, or, rational intuition). The interesting choice of the phrase 'rational intuition' is probably too mystical sounding and mind boggling for a contemporary, intellectual audience which, ironically enough, is strongly rationalist in temperament and taste whilst insistently empiricist in its preoccupations. (The irony of the double mindedness of the contemporary intellectual is not a self-conscious one). Plato himself does not employ a fixed terminology as is evidenced by this letter which is another reason on behalf of its authenticity. Perhaps one of the reasons for his use of several words to convey the same idea is a combination of his dialectical strategy, to move the mind ever upwards and his conviction that one must not identify knowledge with the knowledge of words. It is also the case that when Plato is attempting to describe realities that transcend the phenomena, rather than electing to employ a technical vocabulary, he chooses, for the most part, to employ everyday language. As a result, vocabulary must perforce be used inconsistently since the language of common use, when utilized to describe the non-phenomenal, must take on a different sense. Thus, for example, in *Sophist*, *doxa* is used to mean 'judgement' and not opinion because opinion would have a different class of objects from those of knowledge of the Forms and their relations. *Cf.*, Cornford's discussion in *Plato's Theory of Knowledge*, New York: Bobbs-Merrill Co., p. 318. (Kant, who attempts to introduce a more technical vocabulary, while more fixed than Plato in the use of his terminology was also inconsistent. Heidegger represents the case of a philosopher who elected to employ a special technical vocabulary and even employed neologisms. The price of technical precision and univocity is a lack of general accessibility). *Episteme* (usually translated as knowledge and wherefrom the term 'epistemology' is derived) is the term most commonly used by Plato. The only difficulty, it seems to the present author, in using it

without occasionally also using allied terms such as 'understanding' or 'insight' is that the term 'knowledge' in today's world is frequently associated with scientific knowledge which is not what Plato meant by knowledge since according to *Republic VI*, what is considered 'scientific knowledge' today would not be considered knowledge at all by Plato, but would rather fall under what he called *pistis*, or the higher form of opinion or *doxa*. The Plato of the *Theatetus* does seem to attempt to look for knowledge in the world of appearances although he does not find it, but one wonders why he was looking for it there in the first place. If one excepted the problem that today's science was of phenomena (in the conventional sense of the term), one could conjecture that the scientific knowledge of today might be classified as true belief together with an account by Plato. For Plato true belief was different from knowledge since a jury could hold the correct opinion about who had committed a crime without actually knowing that their opinion was correct. This might in very rough terms be the equivalent of what scientists today might mean when it is said that something is known to be statistically true with a high degree of probability. For Plato, on the other hand, knowledge is of what is real and is infallible. It seems that, insofar as Plato's doctrine can be put into words at all, the words which best render Plato's meaning today are 'understanding' and 'knowledge'. Despite occasional lapses into the teaching that knowledge is an instrument, the core of the doctrine taught here is that it is knowledge, or the Fourth, which is the ultimate objective and concern of the philosopher, and of course, the knowledge with which the philosopher is concerned is knowledge of the Fifth.

18. *Seventh Epistle*, 341 C, Glenn Morrow (trans.).

19. The capacity to bring an entire musical work to mind with the hearing of a single bar is not dissimilar to the capacity of the memory to reconstruct an entire experience on the basis of a single sensory element such as Proust's famous account of memory springing from a taste of madeleine and/or tea (Proust is not altogether precise, though it appears to be due to a bit of both): 'And suddenly the memory returns ... The taste was that of the little crumb of madeleine which on Sunday mornings at Combray (because on those mornings I did not go out before church time), when I went to say good day to her in her bedroom, my aunt Leonie used to give me, dipping it first in her own cup of real or lime-flower tea ... And once I had recognized the taste ... the whole of Combray and of its surroundings, taking on their proper shapes and growing solid, sprang into being, town and gardens alike, from my cup of tea.' *Cf.*, Marcel Proust, *Du côté de chez Swann*, in *A la Recherche du temps perdu*, vol. 1 (Paris: Gallimard, 1954, C..K. Moncrieff (trans.), *Swann's Way, Remembrance of Things Past*, vol. 1, NewYork: Random House, 1934, p. 36.

Bibliography

Adamson, Robert and Henderson, A.G., *On the Philosophy of Kant and A Sketch of Kant's Life and Works*, London: Routledge/Thoemmes Press, 1993 (a reprint of the 1879 and 1854 edition).

Alexander, H.G. (ed.), *The Leibniz-Clarke Correspondence*, New York: Philosophical Library, 1956.

Allinson, Robert E., 'Anselm's One Argument', *Philosophical Inquiry, An International Quarterly*, Vol. 15, No. 1-2, Winter-Spring, 1993.

Allinson, Robert E., *CHUANG-TZU For Spiritual Transformation: An Analysis of the Inner Chapters*, Albany: State University of New York Press, 1989, 1996, Fifth Impression.

Allinson, Robert E., 'Moral Values and the Chinese Sage in the *Tao De Ching*', (concluding chapter), *Morals and Society in Asian Philosophy*, Brian Carr (ed.), London: Curzon Press, 1996.

Allinson, Robert E. (ed.), *Understanding the Chinese Mind: The Philosophical Roots*, New York: Oxford University Press, 1989, 2000, Tenth Impression.

Bachelard, Suzanne, *A Study of Husserl's Formal and Transcendental Logic*, Evanston: Northwestern University Press, 1968.

Baynes, Kenneth, Bohman, James and McCarthy, Thomas (eds.), *After Philosophy, End or Transformation*, Cambridge, Massachusetts and London, England: The MIT Press, 1987.

Beck, Lewis White, *Essays on Kant and Hume*, New Haven and London: Yale University Press, 1978.

Bennett, Jonathan, *Kant's Analytic*, Cambridge: Cambridge University Press, 1966.

Bernstein, Richard, J., *Philosophical Profiles*, Cambridge: Polity Press, 1986.

Bertens, Hans, *The Idea of the Postmodern, A History*, London: Routledge, 1995.

Binkley, Timothy, *Wittgenstein's Language*, The Hague: Martinus Nijhoff, 1973.

Bradley, F.H., *Appearance and Reality*, Oxford: Oxford University Press, 1930, Ninth Impression.

Bunge, Mario (ed.), *Problems in the Foundations of Physics*, Berlin: Springer-Verlag, 1971.

Bunge, Mario and Ardilla, Rubén, *Philosophy of Psychology*, New York and Berlin: Springer-Verlag, 1987.

Cahoone, Lawrence, *From Modernism to Postmodernism*, Oxford: Blackwell Publishers, 1996.

Calder, Nigel, *Einstein's Universe*, New York: Viking Press, 1979.

Collingwood, R.G., *An Essay on Metaphysics*, Oxford: Oxford University Press, 1948.

Collingwood, R.G., *The New Leviathan*, Oxford: Oxford University Press, 1958.

Collingwood, R.G., *The Principles of Art*, London, Oxford and New York: Oxford University Press, 1969.

Collingwood, R.G., *The Idea of History*, London, Oxford and New York: Oxford University Press, 1970.

Cornford, F.M., *Plato's Theory of Knowledge*, New York: Bobbs-Merrill Co., 1957.

Deutsch, David, 'Quantum Mechanics Near Closed Timelike Lines', *Physical Review D*, Vol. 44, No. 10, November 15, 1991.

Deutsch, David and Lockwood, Michael, 'The Quantum Physics of Time Travel', *Scientific American*, March, 1994.

Dicker, Georges, *Descartes, An Analytical and Historical Introduction*, New York: Oxford University Press, 1993.

Doney, Willis (ed.), *DESCARTES, A Collection of Critical Essays*, Garden City, New York: Doubleday and Co., 1967.

Dummett, Michael, *The Logical Basis of Metaphysics*, Cambridge, Massachusetts: Harvard University Press, 1991.

Feyerabend, Paul K., *Science in a Free Society*, London: New Left Books, 1979.

Fish, Stanley, *Professional Correctness*, Oxford: Clarendon Press, 1995.

Flood, R. and Lockwood, M. (eds.) *The Nature of Time*, Oxford: Basil Blackwell, 1986.

Frankl, Viktor, E., *Man's Search For Meaning: an introduction to logotherapy*, New York: Pocket Books, 1972.

Frege, Gottlob, *The Foundations of Arithmetic*, J.L. Austin (trans.), Evanston: Northwestern University Press, 1980.

Fromm, Erich, *The Anatomy of Human Destructiveness*, New York: Holt, Rinehart and Winston, 1973.

Gadamer, Hans-Georg, *Dialogue and Dialectic: Eight Hermeneutical Studies in Plato*, P. Christopher Smith (trans.), New Haven: Yale University Press, 1980.

Gardner, Howard, *Frames of Mind, The Theory of Multiple Intelligences*, New York: Basic Books, 1983.

Gay, Peter, *Freud, Jews and Other Germans, Masters and Victims in Modernist Culture*, New York: Oxford University Press, 1978.

Gram, Moltke, S., *Kant: Disputed Questions*, Chicago: Quadrangle Books, 1967.

Gribben, John, *In Search of the Edge of Time*, London: Black Swan Books, 1992.

Habermas, Jürgen, 'Work and Weltanschauung: The Heidegger controversy from a German perspective', *Critical Inquiry* 15, Winter, 1989.

Hacker, P.M.S., *Wittgenstein's Place in Twentieth-century Analytic Philosophy*, Oxford: Blackwell, 1996.

Hahn, Lewis E., *Enhancing Cultural Interflow Between East and West*, Taipei: Promotion of China Modernization Foundation, in press.

Hahn, Lewis E. (ed.), *The Philosophy of Charles Hartshorne*, The Library of Living Philosophers, Volume XX, La Salle, IL: Open Court, 1991.

Haldane, Elizabeth S. and Ross G.R.T., *The Philosophical Works of Descartes*, Vol. 1, Cambridge: Cambridge University Press, 1967.

Hartshorne, Charles, *Creative Synthesis and Philosophical Method*, La Salle, IL: Open Court, 1970.

Hawking, Stephen, *A Brief History of Time*, New York: Bantam Books, 1989.

Hawking, Stephen, *Black Holes and Baby Universes and Other Essays*, New York: Bantam Books, 1994.

Hawking, Stephen, and Penrose, Roger, *The Nature of Space and Time*, Princeton: Princeton University Press, 1996.

Hawking, Stephen and Penrose, Roger, 'The Nature of Space and Time', *Scientific American*, July, 1996.

Hegel, G.W.F., *The Encyclopaedia of the Philosophical Sciences*, William Wallace (trans.), Oxford: The Clarendon Press, 1892.

Hegel, G.W.F., *Phänomenologie des Geistes*, Hamburg: Felix Meiner Verlag, 1952.

Hegel, G.W.F., *The Phenomenology of Mind*, J.B. Baillie (trans.), New York and Evanston: The Academy Library, 1967.

Hintikka, Jaakko, '*Cogito, Ergo Sum*: Inference or Performance?', *The Philosophical Review*, Vol. 71, 1961.

Husserl, Edmund, *Ideas, General Introduction to Pure Phenomenology*, W.R. Boyce Gibson (trans.), New York: Macmillan Publishing Co. Inc., 1962.

Husserl, Edmund, *The Paris Lectures*, Peter Koestenbaum (trans.), The Hague: Martinus Nijhoff, 1970.

Jones, W.T., *A History of Western Philosophy*, New York: Harcourt, Brace and Co., 1952.

Kant, Immanuel, *Kritik der reinen Vernunft*, Hamburg: Felix Meiner Verlag, 1956.

Kant, Immanuel, *Critique of Pure Reason*, Norman Kemp Smith (trans.), New York, St. Martin's Press, 1965.

Kant, Immanuel, *Anthropology from a Pragmatic Point of View*, Mary J. Gregor (trans.), The Hague: Nijhoff, 1974.

Kramer, Elmar J. (ed.), *Interpreting Arnauld*, Toronto: University of Toronto Press, 1966.

Lewis, David, 'The Paradoxes of Time Travel', *American Philosophical Quarterly*, April, 1976, Vol. 13, No. 2.

Linden, Eugene, *Apes, Men and Language*, New York: Penguin Books, 1974.

Lorenzen, Paul, *Normative Logic and Ethics*, Mannheim/Zurich: Bibliographisches Institut, 1969.

Mohanty, J.N., 'Kant and Husserl', *Husserl Studies*, Vol. 13, No. 1, 1996.

Montagu, Ashley, *Touching: The human significance of skin*, New York: Harper and Row, 1986.

Mure, G.R.G., *An Introduction to Hegel*, Oxford: Clarendon Press, 1959.

Nagel, Thomas, *The View from Nowhere*, New York: Oxford University Press, 1986.

Nerlich, Graham, *What spacetime explains, Metaphysical essays on space and time*, Cambridge: Cambridge University Press, 1994.

Nietzsche, Friedrich, *Beyond Good and Evil*, Walter Kaufman (trans.), New York: Random House, 1966.

Parker, Taylor, Sue, and Gibson, Kathleen Rita, *"Language" and intelligence in monkeys and apes, Comparative developmental perspectives*, Cambridge: Cambridge University Press, 1990.

Penrose, Roger, *The Emperor's New Mind*, New York: Oxford University Press, 1989, 1990.

Penrose, Roger, Shimony, Abner, Cartwright, Nancy and Hawking, Stephen, *The Large, The Small and The Human Mind*, Cambridge: Cambridge University Press, 1999.

Plato, *Plato's Epistles*, Glenn R. Morrow (trans.), New York: The Bobbs-Merrill Co., 1962.

Poidervin Robin Le and MacBeath, Murray (eds.), *The Philosophy of Time*, Oxford University Press, 1993.

Proust, Marcel, *Du côté de chez Swann*, in *A la Recherche du temps perdu*, Vol. 1, Paris: Gallimard, 1954, C.K. Moncrieff (trans.), *Swann's Way, Remembrance of Things Past*, Vol. 1, New York: Random House, 1934.

Resnikoff, H.L. and Wells, R.O., Jr., *Mathematics and Civilization*, New York: Holt, Rinehart and Winston Inc. 1974.

Rorty, Richard, *Philosophy and the Mirror of Nature*, Oxford: Basil Blackwell, 1983.

Rorty, Richard, *Contingency, Irony, and Solidarity*, New York: Cambridge University Press, 1989.

Rorty, Richard, *Essays On Heidegger And Others*, *Philosophical Papers*, Volume 2, New York: Cambridge University Press, 1991.

Rorty, Richard, *Anti-Essentialism in General: The Number Seventeen as a Model for Reality* (First Romanell Lecture), 1992.

Rorty, Richard (ed.), *The Linguistic Turn*, Chicago: The University of Chicago Press, Second Edition, 1992.

Sankara and Gaudapada, *The Mandukyoupanisad with Gaudapada's Karika and Sankara's Commentary*, Swami Nikhilananda (trans.), Mysore: Sharada Press, 1968.

Sartre, Jean-Paul, *Being and Nothingness, A Phenomenological Essay on Ontology*, Hazel E. Barnes (trans.), New York: Washington Square Press, 1966.

Sayre, Kenneth, *Plato's Literary Garden*, Notre Dame and London: University of Notre Dame Press, 1995.

Schilpp, Paul Arthur and Hahn, Lewis Edwin (eds.), *Albert Einstein, Philosopher-Scientist*, Library of Living Philosophers, Vol. VII, La Salle, Illinois, Fifth Printing, 1991.

Searle, John R., 'The Mystery of Consciousness', *The New York Review of Books*, Vol. XLII, Number 17, 1995.

Sebeok, Thomas A. and Sebeok, Jean-Umiker, *Speaking of Apes, A Critical Anthology of Two-Way Communication with Man*, New York and London: Plenum Press, 1980.

Seebohm, Thomas M., and Kockelmans, Joseph J. (eds.), *Kant and Phenomenology*, Washington, D.C.: Center for Advanced Research in Phenomenology and University Press of America, 1984.

Shaffer, Peter, *Amadeus*, London: Andre Deutsch Ltd., 1980.

Sidgwick, Henry, *Outlines of the History of Ethics*, Boston: Beacon Press, 1960.

Sklar, Lawrence, *Philosophy of Physics*, New York: Oxford University Press, 1992.

Urmson, J.O., *Philosophical Analysis, Its development between the two world wars*, London: Oxford University Press, 1971.

Waal, Frans, De, *Good natured, The Origins of Right and Wrong in Humans and Other Animals*, Cambridge: Harvard University Press, 1996.

Walsh, W.H., *Metaphysics*, London: Hutchinson University Library, 1963.

Weiskrantz, L. (ed.), *Thought Without Language*, Oxford: Clarendon Press, 1988.

Weiss, Frederick G., *HEGEL, The Essential Writings*, New York: Harper and Row, 1974.

Williams, Bernard, *DESCARTES, THE PROJECT OF PURE ENQUIRY*, Harmondsworth and New York: Penguin Books, 1986.

Wittgenstein, Ludwig, *Philosophical Investigations*, G.E.M. Anscombe and R. Rhees (eds.), G.E.M. Anscombe (trans.), Oxford: Blackwell, 1958.

Wittgenstein, Ludwig, *Tractatus Logico-Philosophicus*, D.F. Pears and B.F. McGuinness (trans.), London: Routledge and Kegan Paul, 1961.

Wittgenstein, Ludwig, *The Blue and Brown Books*, New York: Harper and Row, 1965.

Wittgenstein, Ludwig, *Culture and Value*, Chicago: The University of Chicago Press, 1980.

Index

For Product Safety Concerns and Information please contact our EU
representative GPSR@taylorandfrancis.com Taylor & Francis Verlag GmbH,
Kaufingerstraße 24, 80331 München, Germany

Printed and bound by CPI Group (UK) Ltd, Croydon, CR0 4YY

08/06/2025

01896999-0009